Hateful Contraries

Hateful Contraries

STUDIES IN LITERATURE AND CRITICISM

By W. K. WIMSATT
With an Essay on English Meter
Written in Collaboration with
Monroe C. Beardsley

KENTUCKY PAPERBACKS
UNIVERSITY OF KENTUCKY PRESS
Lexington, 1966

Copyright © 1965 by the University of Kentucky Press
Printed in the United States of America by the
University of Kentucky Printing Division
Library of Congress Catalog Card
No. 65-11823

F. W. H.
HUMANITATE
INSIGNI
DOCTORI ET DUCTORI
D. D. D.
W. K. W.

ACKNOWLEDGMENT

THE ESSAYS in criticism and critical history which compose this book were published (all but one), in their original versions, over a period of about twelve years, from 1950 to 1962.

The first essay in the collection, "Horses of Wrath: Recent Critical Lessons," has been rewritten from parts of the following three: "Criticism Today: A Report from America," in *Essays in Criticism*, VI (January, 1956); "Poetic Tension: A Summary," in the *New Scholasticism*, XXXII (January, 1958); and "Horses of Wrath: Recent Critical Lessons," in *Essays in Criticism*, XII (January, 1962). Parts of "Criticism Today" have been adapted in my Epilogue to *Literary Criticism, A Short History*, written with Cleanth Brooks (New York: Alfred A. Knopf, 1957). And parts of the original "Horses of Wrath" are used in the Introduction to the present volume.

"Aristotle and Oedipus or Else" is revised from a lecture delivered first for the Program of Directed Studies in Yale College, 1958, and thereafter on a number of other occasions. It has not been published before. A considerable degree of compression in this essay is due in part to the fact that it parallels two of my chapters in *Literary Criticism, A Short History*, written too soon for me to take into account Professor Else's radical reinterpretations of Aristotle's *Poetics*.

Acknowledgment

"The Criticism of Comedy" is very slightly adapted from the Introduction to *English Stage Comedy, English Institute Essays, 1954* (New York: Columbia University Press, 1955). The other essays have appeared in the following places: "Two Meanings of Symbolism: A Grammatical Exercise" in *Renascence*, VIII (Autumn, 1955); "The Concept of Meter: An Exercise in Abstraction" in *PMLA*, LXXIV (December, 1959); "The Augustan Mode in English Poetry" in *ELH, A Journal of English Literary History*, XX (March, 1953); "The Fact Imagined: James Boswell" in the *Yale Review*, XLIX (Autumn, 1959); "Eliot's Comedy: *The Cocktail Party*" in the *Sewanee Review*, LVIII (October, 1950); "*Prufrock* and *Maud*: From Plot to Symbol" in *Yale French Studies*, No. 9 (Spring, 1952); "What to Say About a Poem" in *Reports and Speeches of the Eighth Yale Conference on the Teaching of English, April 13 and 14, 1962*, Office of Teacher Training, Yale University, 1962.

"The Concept of Meter," written with Monroe C. Beardsley, provoked two replies, one from Professor Joseph W. Hendren and one from Professor Elias Schwartz. These may be consulted, together with the comments which the editor gave the original authors the privilege of adding, in *PMLA*, LXXVI (June, 1961) and LXXVII (December, 1962).

Parts of the essay on James Boswell have been repeated in my Introduction to *Boswell for the Defence 1769-1774*, edited with F. A. Pottle (New York: McGraw Hill Book Co., 1959; London: Heinemann, 1960).

"What to Say About a Poem" has been republished, along with the remarks of seven other scholar-critics and the "responses" of the author, as a *CEA Chap Book, What*

Acknowledgment

to *Say About a Poem,* edited by Donald A. Sears and distributed as a Supplement to the *CEA Critic,* XXVI (December, 1963).

I wish to thank the several editors for their courtesy in extending permission for the republication of these materials.

Drafts of several of the essays were read before learned meetings. Some were written specifically for the occasions. I am grateful to all the audiences and all the chairmen. In addition to the Program of Directed Studies in Yale College, 1958, already mentioned, let me name English Section II, The Modern Language Association of America, Boston, 1952; the Annual Symposium of the Catholic Renascence Society, Philadelphia, 1954, and Milwaukee, 1955; the Conference on Methods in Philosophy and the Sciences at the New School for Social Research, New York, 1957; the Conference on Style, Indiana University, 1958; the Annual Meeting of the Lecturers in English, St. John's College, Cambridge, 1961; and the Yale Conference on the Teaching of English, 1962.

As always, I owe a great deal, in one way or another, to many friends—and especially to Monroe Beardsley, who renewed an earlier collaboration in writing one of these essays with me, and without whose help an essay on meter would not have been written; to Cleanth Brooks, who over a period of seven years collaborated with me in writing *Literary Criticism, A Short History,* the close relation of which to parts of the present book I have indicated above; and to F. A. Pottle, who collaborated with me in editing *Boswell for the Defence* and to whose instruction, both early and late, I owe nearly all that I know about Boswell.

Acknowledgment

Richard Foster was kind enough to read the original essays at a time when I first thought of collecting them; his carefully considered suggestions have played a large part in their revision and rearrangement.

Silliman College W. K. W.
Yale University
4 August 1964

CONTENTS

Acknowledgment	*page* vii
Introduction	xiii

ONE
Horses of Wrath: Recent Critical Lessons	3

TWO
Two Meanings of Symbolism: A Grammatical Exercise	51
Aristotle and Oedipus or Else	72
The Criticism of Comedy	90
The Concept of Meter: An Exercise in Abstraction	108

THREE
The Augustan Mode in English Poetry	149
The Fact Imagined: James Boswell	165
Eliot's Comedy: *The Cocktail Party*	184
Prufrock and *Maud:* From Plot to Symbol	201

FOUR
What to Say about a Poem	215
Notes	245
Index	255

Notes for the Title of This Book

>   I in none of these
> Find place or refuge; and the more I see
> Pleasures about me, so much more I feel
> Torment within me, as from the hateful siege
> Of contraries. . . .
>   .   .   .   .
> For only in destroying I find ease
> To my relentless thoughts.
>   —John Milton, *Paradise Lost*, IX. 118-130,
>   Satan in Paradise

> Without Contraries is no progression.
>   —William Blake, *The Marriage of Heaven and Hell*

> I wish I could say Tom was any better. . . . I am obliged to write and plunge myself into abstract images to ease myself of his countenance, his voice, and feebleness—so that I live now in a continual fever. It must be poisonous to life, although I feel well. Imagine "the hateful siege of contraries."
>   —John Keats to Charles Wentworth Dilke,
>   21 September 1818

INTRODUCTION

MY EXPOSITION begins by quoting a British critic in an American quarterly for the winter of 1953. Not that his essay is a weak or unimpressive instance of the sort of contention that I wish to illustrate. On the contrary it is the most thoughtful instance of its genre that I know—not only expressing discontent with a certain externally identifiable school of criticism but naming the grounds of the feeling in considered theoretical terms. John Holloway's essay "The Critical Intimidation," in the *Hudson Review*, voiced a double complaint: namely, that American criticism in the tradition of Richards and Eliot was trying too hard to operate in a "scheme of things where science was the norm," and that in some way connected with this fault the same school of criticism had gone too far in the pursuit of the ironic principle. He thought it could not be right to liberate poetry from the restricted range of "picturesque lyricism," only to shackle it again to another restricted range, that of "paradox, ambiguity, and ironic contrast." He thought that certain American critics had made too easy a gift to science of the art of prose; they wanted to make poetry too separate a thing, whereas poetry is really just a refinement of a certain "straight-forward" kind of non-scientific or impressionistic "truth" which is shared by "ordinary" prose on many occasions.[1]

Introduction

Mr. Holloway, I think correctly enough, saw a close connection between the cognitive critical enterprise in America and the classic principle of reconciled opposites. But to pursue first the simpler part of the argument: so far as his essay expressed a deep misgiving about excess of cognitive effort—of thinking in criticism—he was far from being alone in his attitude at that date. In America, for example, we had Leslie Fiedler's "Credo" in the *Kenyon Review* symposium of 1950—"Toward an Amateur Criticism." This was one of the earliest announcements of a sort of emancipation from criticism, a New Amateurism, a "passionate commitment to not having any commitment," which was celebrated recurrently in articles and reviews in America during the 1950's. In England all along, the same views found ready expression. The traditional stance of the appreciators, the "art of praise," known so well to Gosse, Saintsbury, Raleigh, Quiller-Couch, and Garrod, was not to be easily abandoned. Professor Sutherland, for instance, in his Inaugural Lecture Delivered at University College, London, in 1952—*The English Critic*—began with an allusion to "gargantuan American anthologies whose sheer weight must make the college boy in Indiana and Minnesota, his satchel in his hand, creep more unwillingly to school than ever before. . . ." And he proceeded to describe the English critical tradition as "urbane," "cheerful," "addressed to the common reader," aimed at communicating enjoyment, biographical, often "rambling and discursive," "amateur" rather than "professional," "impressionistic" rather than "scientific." As a parting shot at American criticism, Professor Sutherland quoted with approval Mr. Fiedler's proclamation of 1950.

Introduction

During the later years of the decade the campaign in America was carried somewhat vociferously into the newspapers—for example, into the New York *Times Book Review*. Thus: February 15, 1959, the novelist Saul Bellow's front article "Deep Readers of the World, Beware." ("The Search for Symbols . . . Misses All the Fun and Fact of the Story.") Or December 13 of the same year, the poet Karl Shapiro's equally conspicuous "What's the Matter with Poetry?" ("A 'diseased art'"—"for this he blames a bloc of 'critic-poets' entrenched in the universities.") Or May 15, 1960, from a writer on the other side of the Atlantic, David Daiches: "A Critical Look at Our Criticism," a protest against critical clichés—somewhat undercut by his admission that "every age has its own clichés, and that sometimes clichés are not clichés, or at least not bad clichés."(*When* they are bad, when not, would have been a new-critical question which Mr. Daiches avoided.) During these years and for a good many years earlier the same vein of thinking, or anti-thinking, might be conveniently sampled almost any week in the *Times Book Review* on the page entitled "Speaking of Books," written by J. Donald Adams. And the counterpart of it all in a British publication could be supplied from the *Times Literary Supplement*—in almost any number. The following from December 2, 1960, is a good enough example:

In England, as in America, we are faced every day with the miserable prospect of more and more criticism which has less and less interest for the general reader or connexion with contemporary literature. Pedantry's latest disguise is that of many-sided urbanity, and the kind of people who a generation or two ago would have been out of harm's way collating editions of *Tottel's*

Introduction

Miscellany are today making a nuisance of themselves with owlish reflections about Paradox, Tension, and Ambiguity, not to mention ponderous ruminations over Wit and Irony.

With these words of an anonymous belletrist I conclude my series of illustrations, but the passage calls for one special remark before being left. It is untypical of the school of anticriticism in one respect, for the author has gone strangely out of his way to make enemies. With his scorn for sober learning (collating *Tottel's Miscellany*) he is bidding for the alienation of at least one large party of his most natural allies, the old-guard resistance to criticism in America.

II

IT IS PERHAPS not possible that criticism should give these sentiments of the scholars and appreciators the lie direct, or even the countercheck quarrelsome. Certainly honor does not require it. Perhaps some concessions, stopping short of the abject, might be part of a tentative retort.

I think the critical theorist ought to be ready to say that he has nothing really against the exercise of amateurism in literary discussion—the celebration of poetry as a record of some kind of "total revelation" or "vague but full report." He ought to be ready even to grant that there are times when this kind of talk may be the most appropriate thing—in a classroom perhaps, or on the front page of the New York *Times Book Review*, in the *Saturday Review*, or in the *Times Literary Supplement*. The only reservation the theorist need have about such critical impressionism, or expressionism, is that, after all, it does not carry us very far in our

Introduction

cogitation about the nature and value of literature. It is not a very mature form of cognitive discourse. And the critic will hold that cogitation about the nature of literature is a worthwhile activity of intellect. And if its real relation to critical judgment and the habit of poetic appreciation is understood, it should inform and tone the mind for the better exercise of the hours of amateurism. It should improve the "man of taste" and "the public critic."

The notion of poetry as a simple kind of fullness of experience or vivid sensation, or the very quality of experience, was after all not unfamiliar to the critics who thirty years ago were "new" in America. It was one of the escapes from theoretical criticism against which they were most explicitly reacting—whether in the British tradition of the scholarly appreciators, or in rhapsodic expressions of the self, like that of Anatole France, or in the bright acrobatics of latter-day art-for-art's-sake, the *Smart Set* or the *American Mercury*, or whether finally in the scientifically fortified version of sensationalist poetics which was the most impressive in that era, the "literary mind" of the psychologist Max Eastman. Some of the recent objectors to criticism are like very late comers to a conversation who have not taken the trouble to find out what the beginning, or even the middle, was about.

But then, I think the critic ought to be ready to say that there is often enough some justification for the complaint against pedantry in criticism—even if, too, there is often very little understanding behind the complaint. For there are both pedantic and unpedantic ways of conceiving and living with any critical principle at all. And often enough, in proportion to the theoretic success of a principle, the

Introduction

pedantic and wooden applications, rather than the habit of living or thinking with it, follow. I fear it is just the irritated realization that his own seminal essays of the 1920's had helped to produce a formal school, a generation, or two generations, of classroom practitioners and trade journal critics—a sense of being followed and acclaimed by a legion of disciplined epigonists—which led Mr. Eliot in some later utterances, and notably in the Minneapolis speech of 1956, to attempt a partial repudiation of his own earlier views. (And that of course accounts for the merely academic sound, the flabbiness, the somewhat weary belletrism of these recantations.) It is possible—this has been amply and unhappily demonstrated—to use conceptions like "paradox" and "ambiguity" as simple keys to be inserted into poems, or as tags to be tied to parts of poems. But then, the critic must surely be allowed to add, that is possible with any set of critical conceptions at all, any principles. The crop of pedantries that has followed in our time on the acceptance of the ironic principle has been no more absurd than, for instance, the use of romantic touchstones—the greatness of the author's soul betrayed in a line, the honest feeling, and vivid imagery, and all that, which became so automatic and so tedious during a much longer period of time.

The principle of ironic opposition is nowadays flourished in its boldest distortions, not by practical critics hardening a pedantic routine, but by fiery didactics, the younger brethren of Prometheus and Orc. In sections II and III of the first essay in this book I have attempted to distinguish what I consider an inevitable and proper literary interest in the contraries from certain extreme gestures of the current Prometheans, certain loud, wild neighings of the "horses of

Introduction

instruction." I illustrate the same theme at other places in the book and return to it emphatically in the last section of the last essay.

The movement of the New Amateurism in American criticism ran a course of about ten years. Its ideas are still heard, but I believe not so loudly or so exultantly.[2] The reason for this is not that there is no longer any audience for the ideas, or that the main targets of the attack, the critics "entrenched in the universities," are not still entrenched, or that there is not even a measure of truth in the accusations of the amateurs. The reason is simply that, having had their say, these anticritical voices no longer have anything to say. That is the nature of anticriticism. Or, so far as it is not merely an assault but pauses to "defend" itself, it does so with weapons other than its own "ignorance."[3] Anticriticism is the end of something or aims to be. It proclaims a defeat. And maybe there has been a measure of defeat. Criticism has never, in this age or any other, triumphantly demonstrated its propositions and swept the board. But the effort to be critical, that is, to add to our enthusiasm for literature a measure of reflection about the experience and thus to justify it to ourselves and even to improve it, seems no more likely than literature itself to be permanently quelled.

One

HORSES OF WRATH:
RECENT CRITICAL LESSONS

It is not easy to trace the steps by which we have arrived at a situation in literary criticism, or the steps by which critics in the past arrived at any one of their situations. At whatever moment in the past we elect, or chance, to begin our narrative, a good many things have to be taken for granted. Let me begin the unambitious story which I intend, or let me make a hasty departure into it, with German romanticism at about the time of Schiller, the Schlegels, and Schelling. This was a criticism, or a theory about poetry and about general reality, which occupied the most elevated intellectual ground of that day and probably the most elevated that any literary criticism within Western history has ever occupied. This was the time of the reaction, first strongly asserted by Kant, against analytic scepticism—the time of the visionary reshaping when thinking became creation, and philosophy hence became poetry or, in some versions, poetics or aesthetics. Poetics, history, folklore, and comparative religion came together; Friedrich Schlegel and Schelling rediscovered and explored the authority of myth. After the hard, flat era of the eighteenth century, poetry along with metaphysics was revindicated as an exuberant vital utterance, an expression of transcendent interest and worth.

It has always been difficult, however, to make poetry the

whole of higher knowledge, the whole of moral, religious, and political authority. The romantic theory was in effect a highly ambiguous and double claim—a claim both for poetic freedom and for poetic responsibility. It was thus the cloud-capped starting point for certain quite opposite lines of poetic theory that come down through the nineteenth century toward our own day. One of these, moving from Kantian disinterest, formality, and beauty, through French academic aesthetics and then early symbolist and Parnassian poetics, was what we look back on as art-for-art's-sake—the end-of-the-century gilded celebration of autonomous poetic power. At the level of general aesthetics and linguistics, the philosophy of Benedetto Croce is the voraciously systematic expression of this view.[1] Not so far removed from art-for-art's-sake as we might like to think, and in some phases part of it, was the movement, technically so much more subtle and more interesting to us, which came out of romantic "imagination" and "symbol" and became *symbolisme*. This seems to have come not so much from the German philosophers directly as through Coleridge and Poe (and probably Heine) to Baudelaire, and thence to the era of Mallarmé and Wagner. Here was a much more subtle "music" of "ideas" than the neoclassic theory of painting the passions had conceived—and a new quasi-spiritual reaction against the philosophy of science.

But those kinds of theory, both pure art and symbolism, were directly at odds with three main kinds of theory that developed the opposite accent of the romantic heritage—not the accent on autonomous privilege but that on moral and social power and evolutionary responsibility. Here were three kinds of didacticism: one, the earliest and most fully

Horses of Wrath

romantic, we may call the rhapsodic, the bardic, the prophetic, which is brandished for instance in the *Defense of Poetry* by Shelley or the *Heroes and Hero Worship* of Carlyle; a second, the most nearly allied to a proper literary interest, the classical humanism, severity, and loftiness, both German and French in origin, which is fully expressed in English by Matthew Arnold; a third, owing much to Hegelian dialectic, getting under way more slowly but more modern and more resolute, the Franco-Russian complex of ideas under the heads of the real, the natural, the social or the sociological. This last was the most didactic and the most confidently evolutionary of all. Tolstoy is the greatest literary artist who gave himself to this kind of theory. The vigorous retractation of a whole literary career which he wrote in his old age shows the social and equalitarian conscience at its closest to a genuine literary concern. Tolstoy on what is true and telling in literature, on what is effete, jaded, hedonistic, and merely aristocratic, hits hard, and we may have to take him into account in a way in which we do not have to take into account Zola on the novel as an experiment in a social-science laboratory or Marxist critics on literature as a blueprint of the new order.

But in order to manage this little history, let me begin to pull it in now toward ourselves, toward the English language, and toward America in the past forty years—and even toward the academic. (In academic criticism you see less genius than in some other kinds, but more deliberacy, self-consciousness, program, literalism, and repetition. When a critical conception arrives at academic status, it is a public fact, an established part of history.)

Looking around the American critical scene during the

Hateful Contraries

first decades of our century, you notice for one thing the flashy tailends of the art-for-art's-sake tradition, the cosmopolitanism of the *Smart Set* and the *American Mercury* writers. You notice also the continuation of Arnoldian humanism in the long influence of P. E. More and Irving Babbitt, and the approximate end of that humanism in the twin detonations of the anthologies for and against it in 1930. You can see, too, the socio-real tradition, under the names of naturalism and Responsibilities of the Novelist, and the uglier name of Muck-raking, and also the coming of age of honest America, a matter of smoke and steel, the prairie schooner, and slabs of the sunburnt West. And then the most acutely didactic accent, the Marxist criticism of the 1930's—rampaging until it became obvious to the literary intelligences connected with it that this kind of thing would never do. International events, from the Finnish war on (whether relevantly or not), played their part here.

Turning now to some issues other than that most directly drawn between freedom and didacticism, you can find, during the years between the wars, plenty of psychologism, and most obviously the Freudian kind, in the shape of motivations for novels and poems pulled from the unconscious, and literary biographies rewritten into case histories and ordeals. Plunging for tragic and comic motives into depth psychology and anthropology goes back through Freud to Nietzschean rhapsody and repose and Hegelian conflict of ethical substance. And then there is the quieter kind of affectivism, the equipoise, the beautiful harmony of impulses, promoted by Richards and his colleagues in the twenties, which slips back through the exquisitely refined hedonism of Santayana to the affectivism connected with utilitarian

Horses of Wrath

ethics during the nineteenth century. J. S. Mill's two essays on poetry, for instance, show how this eighteenth-century heritage might get into criticism; they echo the way it had already done so in Wordsworth and Coleridge.

But by and large, the literary discussion of the nineteenth century, unlike that of the eighteenth, had not been notable for any systematic affectivism. And when this romantic and aesthetic plea reappeared with Richards in the 1920's, it had so much to say about the mere incipience of impulses and their equipoise that it was a new witness for something like a classical disinterest or detachment. With all its up-to-date paraphernalia of verbal analysis, Richardsian aesthetics was readily available or at least convertible for purposes of cognitive literary talk, and for that reason Richards became a venerable name in the schools and among analysts and grammarians, persons who recognized their business to be not the fanning nor the feeding and watering of emotions but the explication of the sources of emotion in the uses of language.

All this connected of course readily enough with "neoclassicism." I have been delaying only through purposes of climax and emphasis, not through absentmindedness, to say that looking around the critical landscape of that now remote period, one notices too the conspicuous figures of Pound and Eliot, deriving attitudes from the philosopher T. E. Hulme, from the precise grammatical statements of Gourmont, and from the whole tide of the French symbolist and musically ironic poetics. (With Pound there is the thing called "imagism" too, and at least a flourish of something supposed or pretended to be due to the fact of Chinese ideographic writing. But that can hardly be important.)

Hateful Contraries

Impersonality, craftsmanship, objectivity, hardness and clarity of a kind, a union of emotion with verbal object, a norm of inclusiveness and reconciliation and hence a close interdependence of drama, irony, ambiguity, and metaphor, or the near equivalence of these four—such ideas made up the new system as it worked its way into practical criticism about 1935 or 1940. And, however far short it fell of being able to convince old-line literary historians or to demonstrate beyond appeal that this or that poem meant this much or that much or was excellent or not, the arrival of this kind of criticism was a good thing and meant a new technical and objective interest in poetry.

II

BUT CRITICAL IDEAS, somewhat like poetry itself, do not stand still very long. The past twenty-five years on the English-speaking critical front have seen several new, or newish, large critical claims making headway.

The most academic, the most professional, the most scholarly of these has perhaps been the kind of graduate-school study which seeks to substitute for the poem, not the author, as in former decades, but precisely and deliberately the audience for which the author may in any sense be proved to have written the poem. If we look back to the mid-eighteenth-century, at the first clear start of the modern historical method, in such documents as Thomas Warton's *Observations on the Faerie Queene of Spenser*, Bishop Hurd's *Letters on Chivalry and Romance*, or even Johnson's *Preface* to Shakespeare, we can see that the incipient historicism of these authors, their sympathy for the Gothic or the Elizabethan, hesitates somewhat between a plea for tolerance of antique authors, despite the barbarous ages in which they wrote, and a plea for appreciation of the inspirational opportunities afforded by those very ages. But the decisive concept for the time was personal "genius"; that is, criticism was on the side of Shakespeare in spite of his Elizabethan handicaps. In the nineteenth century there was nationalism, folklorism, and cultural determinism—the race, milieu, and moment of Taine's *History*. But literary studies, especially in England, tended to marshal such interests rather squarely behind the author. That is, they were important because they showed the mind of the author, what made him write the way he did. Sainte-Beuve's profession of intense interest in the author's boyhood, his brothers and sisters, his parents and his grandparents, is an extreme yet typical instance of such Shandeyan depth in criticism. Despite the cultural massiveness of Courthope's *History of English Poetry*, it is mainly right to say that English and American literary research (following good continental models) continued until fairly recent years to be a pursuit of the author, his whole history, both internal and external, and his habitat. It requires perhaps only a tilt of the mirror to turn the habitat into the author's audience. And the audience had of course all along received attention. It was clearly one name for the socio-real focus. But to shift the accent of value in academic research (the accent on both the value of poetry itself and the value of research into poetic history) was yet another step, and that has been a fairly recent one—and perhaps only halting. Until recently it had been the normal aim of academic research to be able to announce: "And thus we prove what the author was trying to say," "thus we prove his learning and his accuracy," "thus we prove his sincerity," or "thus we prove his deep feeling." But a new mode, prominent during the later 1940's and the 1950's, seemed to entertain the aim of announcing: "And thus we prove that the author's poem was addressed to the audience of his day, or to the real audience, or to the audience that mattered," "thus he knew what he was doing, and thus he was a good author." This was not just a rumor out of the realms of higher conversation but an actually discernible phenomenon. Numerous articles in journals and books from university presses had titles referring to *Shakespeare's Audience*, to the Restoration courtier, to *The Theatrical Audience in the Time of Garrick*, to the rise of a reading public, to the number of Victorian persons who bought Macaulay's *History of England* or Tennyson's *Maud*. A thoughtful account of the theoretical implications of this trend appeared in F. W. Bateson's book of 1950, *English Poetry: A Critical Introduction*. The essential function of poetry is "the expression in language of the sense of social solidarity." And Bateson believed, "on the evidence of the poetry," that "at any one period" there was "only one social group in England that was functioning healthily." If we modern readers want to understand a poem of the past, "we need to be able to identify ourselves as far as possible with its original readers, the poet's contemporaries, whose ideal response to the poem in fact constitutes its meaning."

A violent clash between such views and those of the school of close analysis would seem not to have been strictly necessary. The musings of at least one analyst, William Empson, had all along been likely to fray out into

Horses of Wrath

the loose ends of what this or that person in the seventeenth century may have been thinking, and his book of 1951, *The Structure of Complex Words*, in such chapters as that on the salon standard of wit in Pope's day, showed a very refined social orientation. On the other hand, one was also likely to encounter a certain simpler kind of social contextualism, an open-air view of poetry such as that expounded by the Marxist critic Edwin Berry Burgum in his article on "The Cult of the Complex in Poetry" in the issue of *Science and Society* for the winter of 1951. The notion here is that we put the words of a poem not so much together and against one another as naked and alone or in very small clumps against the special yet open context of their cultural origin. The word *earth* in a passage of Aeschylus is itself, and especially for the Greeks, a complex value, and the word *Zeus* another and antithetic value. "The simplest idea becomes complex when related to human experience." Thus a kind of evaluative atomism results from facing the audience. Or, a somewhat different emphasis in historical study might produce a kind of evaluative diffusion. Roy Harvey Pearce's "Historicism Once More" in the *Kenyon Review* (Autumn, 1958), makes a plea for a new radical relativism and at the same time for something so innocent as merely a greater concreteness or existential fullness of sympathy for the various moments of the historic past, "the authentic existence of the other."

In a poem there is outline, texture, form; and there is something happening . . . something *still* happening. . . . As it still happens, it brings, inseparably, the life of its culture with it. If we accept the form, we accept the life. If we accept the life, we accept the culture. This is historical understanding and historical knowledge.

Hateful Contraries

We have come, therefore, to the deep end of historical criticism.[2]

To put the import of this kind of historicism briefly: The old "New Critics" were now accused of being not scientific enough because in their fear of history they would not face the facts. But it turned out also that they were being too scientific, in that their categories did not pay enough respect to the inviolable concreteness of history, the authentic existence. A sort of counterpart to Mr. Pearce on the other side of the Atlantic was, I should say, Miss Helen Gardner in her two series of lectures (London, 1953; Durham, 1956) —where she seemed to wish to register a kind of plain reader's protest against criticism, a plea for the warm and life-like fullness of an author or work and thus for the enlargement of our own imaginative life, and for something which she called "style" in literature (but which, strangely enough, she supposed to be quite different from "form")[3] —all this of course in opposition to the modern excess of both symbolism and analysis in critical reading.

There is an obvious affinity between this kind of historicism and the New Amateurism which I have described in my Introduction. At the same time, Miss Gardner participated in the more usual complaint of the literary historian against modern critics—that the critic, through insufficient recourse to the dictionary, was unaware of the author's literal and primary meaning. Consult, for instance, Miss Rosamond Tuve, or the late C. S. Lewis in his *Studies in Words*. In this version of the complaint, the historian stands forward as a very severe purist, a champion of, and believer in, a very refined degree of abstractionism, of word-splitting, of air-tight univocal meanings. It is difficult really to

Horses of Wrath

reconcile these two kinds of historicism, though they march fairly close together.

III

THE ACTUAL bad conscience which developed during the 1950's in some critics with regard to nice analysis was expressed not only in direct misgivings about analysis, or pleas for open contextual reading, but also partly in the form of proclamations about the need of doing justice to the overall structures of stories and dramas, their motives, plots, actions, tragic rhythms, their deeper, wider, and more bulky symbolism, their bigger meaning—in short, all that part and aspect of them which might be too massive and too important to be penetrated by verbal criticism. This kind of conscience had had a summary and in some respects quite impressive exposition a little more than a hundred years earlier in Matthew Arnold's Preface to his *Poems* of 1853, where he repented of the inaction or suicidally limited action of *Empedocles,* appealed to the great serious actions of the Greek tragedies, and thought Shakespeare enjoyed such rhetorical virtuosity that he had been a bad influence on romantic poets, notably on Keats. Keats, like a modern critic before the bar in Chicago, was too much interested in words and images.[4] These ideas of Arnold's were part of his ambitious humanistic and moralistic program for literature, which, as we have said, was one branch of postromantic didacticism. Later on there had been a different criticism concerning prose fiction, not that of Zola, but that of Flaubert, James, and Ford, and this, I think, was not so far from the spirit of symbolist poetics. It does not appear that Henry James was much afraid of being caught in the mesh of words or of piddling away his effort on the texture or surface of things. If a woman put her hand on a table and looked at him in a certain way, that was for James, or for one of his characters, an event. And the event interlocked with every other event in the world. The artist tried to conjure or pretend some kind of circle around it. It is not in these great theorists of prose fiction that you find scruples against dallying with the details of the medium. But you do, as I have suggested above, find it again more recently, and not only in high academic fortified places built on supposedly neo-Aristotelian principles, but faring forth in more momentous campaigns under the standard of myth and the ritual origins. Here metaphor is action, and big action. For the first time since Dryden and Le Bossu the literary gist is supposed to be big enough and solid enough so that you would think it could be rendered essentially from one language to another. The rhythm of the tragic idea—the going out in quest, the confrontation and passion, the discovery or education—is the big thing. One book that invests this theory with a very shrewd kind of persuasion, a most earnest drag, is Francis Fergusson's *Idea of a Theatre*. The action of the one little man, the Aristotelian protagonist, here becomes a community action or a "psychic motif." The real protagonist turns out to be the chorus—as presumably it does in some actual non-Aristotelian drama of today.

But we have now named a thing which must be distinguished as another and no doubt the most important among recent critical trends. Surely the hugest cloudy symbol, the most threatening, of our last twenty-five years in literary criticism is the principle of criticism by myth and

Horses of Wrath

ritual origin. It is true that this new mythopoeic interest is not always associated with any strong mistrust of rhetorical inspection. Rather the opposite. Expression and symbolism make a ready enough alliance with myth and ritual. This is in the nature of things. For all four are theories of the creative imagination, the fiat of the human spirit as deity or as participating in deity. Herder and Schelling and Cassirer (with Susanne Langer) join Lévy-Bruhl and Frazer and the other Cambridge classical anthropologists (Harrison, Murray, Cornford) in the secularization of the spirit according to the philosophy of myth or of symbolic form. Philip Wheelwright's *Burning Fountain*, one important book of the 1950's in the mythic mode, was a magnificent synopsis of relations between a special semantics on the one hand and on the other ritual anthropology interpreted by the darkness visible of depth psychology. The semantics states the difference between a scientifically bare "steno-language" and the "plurisignations," the trans-logical "depth-language," common to poetry, myth, religion, and metaphysics. The anthropology dwells on hereditary and "preconsciously rooted" symbols—symbols of the "threshold," the world view of primitive man, the death and rebirth of the vegetation god. (The *Fire Sermon* of Buddha, the *Oresteia* of Aeschylus, the *Four Quartets* of Eliot may be cited to define the infrared range of illustration.) To a reader who had the new yearning for a grossly structural poetics, Wheelwright's book may well have looked like a deplorable recelebration of imagery and thematic "para-plots." And in its insistence on a special semantics for poetry and myth, it actually seemed to one reviewer (Meyer Abrams in the *Kenyon Review*) like a surrender to positivistic logic by allowing that logic to prescribe that the grounds of a debate about poetry should be analytic and linguistic.

But again, myth and ritual (as I have indicated we may read in Francis Fergusson's book) are patterns of action, and of large action. In that way they can have their easy enough connection with an antiverbal poetics. And they stress what is large and public about poetry, what can give it religious and social dignity and didactic claims. The validation for the new myth philosophy is thought to lie in the primitive racial unconscious, in the Jungian "archetypes" or "primordial images." Thus it eschews the risky appeal to objectivity, but plunges, in the vast reservoir of racial and prelogical unconsciousness, for a base that is intersubjective or at least collective. It arrives at the phase of prophetic, of total apocalyptic, vision. (All literature is a displaced or indirect mythology, and all literary works are parts or moments of one total apocalyptic work. Literature is made of other literature. The one great literary work or vision is the total of man's divinely human, created reality.) Along with the Greeks and the Indians (from whom Friedrich Schlegel also once drew inspiration) there is Milton, there is Blake, there is Melville, there is Yeats (supplying his own theoretical *Vision* of primary and antithetic cultures), there is Eliot, there is Joyce, and maybe there is Faulkner. It is now time to notice what both myth and gross poetic structure have in common with the recent academic orientation toward the poetic audience. The three new trends have in common a horizontal or folkways alignment (in contrast to the vertical and aristocratic alignment of the Eliot formalism). All three show to some degree the didactic and evangelizing interest which was prepared in the nineteenth-century socio-real tradition. Despite the fact that sociology does come out of the nineteenth century, the humanism and the literary theory in English and French during the century were mainly inspirational, individualistic, and heroic. It is the present century, as we all know, which is the century of the common man, the realization of the Revolt of the Masses. The literary trends I have named conceive men, whether common or elite, in large multiples, thinking and responding in classes. At the same time the romantic lyric focus in literary criticism has given way to a newly intense interest in, and reliance on, the largest and most readily mythologized forms of literature, epic, drama, and the prose novel.

Some of the ideas of the arch-mythopoeist of our time have been foreshadowed, in fact appropriated, in the preceding paragraph. Northrop Frye's *Fearful Symmetry* (1949) announced in the last chapter the Blakean inspiration of an apocalyptic construct which came to realization in his Four Essays entitled *Anatomy of Criticism* (1957). Earlier drafts and later applications are collected in his *Fables of Identity* (1963). The *Anatomy*, especially in its "Polemical Introduction," is written from an exceedingly keen awareness of the history of criticism and of the problems for criticism which we have just been surveying. It intends to escape from the main problem of criticism—that of literary evaluation—by the announcement of a very bold separation—that is, simply a separation of the act of "criticizing" literature from the act of valuing it.

This is something like what both Eliot and Richards at moments in their thought during the 1920's had touched upon, but it now appears with a surpassing starkness and

Hateful Contraries

insistence. I refrain from saying "with systematic insistence," because, although the whole volume is an astonishing invention, I believe that the confrontation of the concepts of value and criticism is never in fact squarely made, and not only that the Four Essays themselves are in fact heavily charged with value assertions and implications, but that the Polemical Introduction, where the main argument about value is carried on, is notable for a series of finely disguised contradictions in this respect.

This is an Introduction which manages to talk at one place about the "greatest classics," the "profound masterpieces" (those which best exhibit the primitive mythic formulas), and to distinguish these from "mediocre work," and yet in another place to say that historical criticism ought to develop towards a "total and indiscriminate acceptance," and that "on the ethical level . . . criticism has no business to react against things, but should show a steady advance toward undiscriminating catholicity." Mr. Frye recognizes that we *will* have our valuing of poetry, we must have it, and it does mean something. Yet it is all subjective and just a part of the history of taste and something which may be called "public criticism"—which has been carried on by Lamb, Hazlitt, Arnold, Sainte-Beuve. What we have never yet had and what we need is a scientific criticism, an objective conceptual system which (in a strictly purified *literary* way) will "establish an authority"—for the public critic and the man of taste—though at the same time it will not be concerned at all with good and bad in literature and, most surprising of all, must never get itself mixed up with the actual "experience" of literature.

Horses of Wrath

Like the beaver, which according to some sort of bestiary, and no doubt archetypal, tradition would, when pursued, bite off certain parts of its anatomy and throw them to the pursuers, this kind of theory makes a radical gesture of sterilizing itself of the usually troublesome value attachments. At the end of his Polemical Introduction, the author stands before us in the shining white garments, the rubber gloves, of the anatomist—the passionately neutral dissector.

Frye's book, as I have suggested, stands at the summit of mythopoeic criticism to date. It achieves some sort of maximum of hyper-Aristotelian, minutely subdivided conceptualization, rampant pigeonholing, an earnest proliferation, a superfoetation of archetypal phantoms, of heroes, myths, modes, cycles. And the values which it consistently promotes are all the "great" values of the archetypal patterns of human experience. There is a legitimate sense in which the book represents all that the resurgent amateurs and appreciators, the professed anticritics of the 1950's were protesting against. On the other hand, there is a sense in which it is the achievement of all that any amateur could dream. For, as one reviewer, again Meyer Abrams, in the *University of Toronto Quarterly*, has put it, the categories of Frye are not really scientific, but belong rather to imaginative metaphysics, the "monistic compulsion of the human spirit." Seeing these categories is like seeing the whole world to be full of Sir Thomas Browne's quincunxes, rather than like finding four-leaf clovers in a field. "Could even an initiate," asks Abrams, "predict, in advance of publication, that Frye would discover" a "displaced" form of the "dragon-killing myth in the cave episode in *Tom Sawyer*?"

Hateful Contraries

IV

ONE IMPORTANT THING to be noted about this moment in mythopoeic criticism is a certain kind of infidelity to its origins. In America it is strongly oriented toward the apocalyptic tradition in English poetry—Milton and Blake specifically—and nowhere more than in Frye, who first got considerable notice by his book on Blake the prophet, the title of which, *Fearful Symmetry*, looks in retrospect as if it should have been saved for the later *Anatomy*. The multiplication of entities in the *Anatomy*, the tables and levels of meaning, are in one sense a fair enough parallel to and extension of the Blakean prophetic universe. Yet they represent too a certain important contrast to the more largely molten, cloudy, and indefinite universe of Blake. What another critic has called the inherent or "built-in haziness" of myth criticism,[5] gives way in Frye's system to a supercomplication and crisscrossing of categories, like lines of many colors across an ordnance map, what one might call a certain built-in maziness of "new" myth criticism.

The energy which keeps the categories molten in Blake is of course the fire of the contraries. *The Marriage of Heaven and Hell* is in no danger of ever hardening into any permanently recognizable image. Frye, as I have indicated, inhabits the Blakean furnace comfortably enough; he knows all about that. Perhaps he would say it is simply to be taken for granted. And perhaps so. A generation of critics today, especially in America—the younger evangelists of Blake and of Yeats—is not likely to suffer from absentmindedness regarding the lovely colors of combustion, the fiery permanent discontent which may be generated by contemplating the gospel of contraries.

The idea of harmony *in spite of* conflict, or simple reconciliation of apparent or superficial conflict, is a staple Greek and Roman, Medieval and Renaissance, idea. The idea of harmony, or at least of some desirable wholeness or sanity or salvation, only *because of* or *through* some kind of strife of contraries may not at first sound much different, but the difference between these ideas is actually profound—the difference, for example, between Satan and Prometheus. Creative conflict is the heart of romantic poetics and in particular of Blake's poetics. It is perhaps a good enough heart of a poetics. At the same time, this doctrine lends itself peculiarly to a certain grand obscurity about the relation of poetics and poetry to the life of actuality. Blake himself is an excellent model for confusion among our present critics. His most brilliantly mysterious tabloid of the doctrine is his *Marriage of Heaven and Hell*.[6]

The Tygers of Wrath are Wiser than the Horses of Instruction

Perhaps they are—at least sometimes. But what feeds the wrath of the tigers? *The Marriage of Heaven and Hell* in one of its phases celebrates rebellious energy in its own right, making rebellion a creative and sufficient principle of reality and human action, but then, moving inevitably to a complementary phase, this philosophy turns out to be, just like any other rebellious philosophy, only a preface for the supplanting of orthodoxy.

The whole creation will . . . appear infinite and holy. . . . This will come to pass by an improvement of sensual enjoyment.

Hateful Contraries

A certain obscurity in Blake's philosophy—about the difference between his own mind and the whole universe, about the difference between what it is to understand and face the fires of strife and what it is to live for and rejoice only in them—may go far to account for the corruption of a certain amount of his poetry. To take the shortest kind of example available, I will advance the opinion that such lyrics as "The Ecchoing Green" and "London" are good poems, and one thing that makes them good is that they stay inside the real world—the village scene, the London scene. Such ideas of paradox and discord as these poems generate are not forced and elected but faced and delicately rendered out of the very materials of the poems. On the other hand I will make the assertion that such a poem as "My Pretty Rose Tree" is a weak little poem, and that the reason is that here the mythographer of contraries has altogether lost his footing in reality and has ascended into the stratum of whimsy. We may be able to discern some features of reality behind this garden fable, but they are the features of a comedy of manners, and they wear all too uncomfortably this solemn and arbitrary prettification.

Coleridge's passage on the reconciliation of opposites, which was quoted in 1918 by Alice Snyder in a monograph on that subject, and then by Eliot, and by Richards, and latterly has been quoted by almost everyone else, is perhaps too well known to need further mention here. But another English romantic poet who was much absorbed in "the hateful siege of contraries" was Keats.[7]

Though a quarrel in the Streets is a thing to be hated, the energies displayed in it are fine; the commonest Man shows a

Horses of Wrath

grace in his quarrel. . . . This is the very thing in which consists poetry.

Perhaps too easy, somewhat too simple. Perhaps not enough attention is paid to the opponent. Perhaps Keats did not live long enough to achieve a maximum theoretical realization of what is so delicately caught in the fabric of his great odes or what can be consulted as raw life experience, the anguish of choice, in so many of his letters.

Probably it was no one English romantic poet, but their greatest prophetic inheritor, W. B. Yeats, who knew, before the end, as deeply as any, all that was at stake—neither the easy solution of the witness of a street fight nor the equally easy celebration of the eternal Orc. Yeats knew the experience of prolonged frustration, he knew the poetry that could come of this; and he knew the felicity of Solomon and Sheba, he knew the dangers of this to the man as poet. Probably no man has kept up, eked out, teased along so successfully, through closing phases of a long career, the sense of uncertainty and noncommital, of ironic unrest. Out of this sprang the vital utterance of the aging poet.

> *The Soul.* Look on that fire, salvation walks within.
> *The Heart.* What theme had Homer but original sin?
>
> Homer is my example and his unchristened heart.
>
> I must lie down where all the ladders start,
> In the foul rag-and-bone shop of the heart.

Yeats I think may be said to have attained to something like a maximum technical knowledge of how the cultivation of the contraries is maintained.

Hateful Contraries

V

LET US ASK ourselves a blunt question: Is a theory of literature as tension of opposites a theory of literary autonomy? or a didactic theory? A charter of literary freedom? or a directive of moral choice? Richards the psychologist with his tenderly balanced scepticisms and his norm of "sincerity," Eliot with his "demon of doubt which is inseparable from the spirit of belief," and the New Critics, with their repeated major premises of "interest," "drama," and "metaphor" advancing often enough to an emphasis on "inclusiveness" and "maturity," have tended at moments unhappily toward the didactic.

Murray Krieger, in his book entitled *The New Apologists for Poetry* (1956), asked some difficult questions about the "self-containment" of the poetic "context" and its relation to the world of reality. Krieger has always made a strenuous effort, and perhaps more successfully than anybody else, to sharpen the dilemmas of critical dialectic to a feather edge. In the final chapter of a later book *The Tragic Vision* (1960), he persists in his earlier line of inquiry, carrying it this time to the level of what he calls "thematics"—the philosophic commitments of poetry. And thus:

It may, of course, seem at best silly and at worst heretically presumptuous for a critic to argue for an intolerable world view just to satisfy the needs of an aesthetic and a literary method. But . . . it is really a commonplace to say that every poet must, at least provisionally, be something of a Manichaean. This is but a way of our asking him not to stack the cards. . . . But if he does no more than this—if, that is, he submits his thesis to the hellfires of antithesis with no doubt of the issue and only to allow his

Horses of Wrath

thesis to be earned the hard way—he is in no more danger of heresy than is any profound version of Christianity that is willing to take into account all worldly imperfections without reducing the extent or the goodness of God's sway. . . . this position, however mature and qualified, cannot finally make literature more than "Platonic," bearing its propositional thesis.

This is making things about as difficult as they can be made for either a poet or a critic who wishes to retain, along with his aesthetic noncommitment, the feeling of a practical human being. And perhaps it will have to be conceded that within the pure literary perspective the claims of belief and action are difficult enough. But larger offstage questions do make a clamorous demand and will be heard from the wings.

The following collocation of materials has been arranged by me with the special design of provoking the Prometheans. Of course they will cry "unfair." It must be unfair. But if any Promethean will make the effort to explain why it is unfair, much, very much may be explained.

James Brown, 45 years old, of Devon, was sentenced to life in prison today for the strangling of a high school girl last October. . . . A confession read to the jury during the trial told how Brown became aroused as he watched the girl knitting during a committee meeting at the Devon County Grange last October 20. . . . Brown followed the girl in his car after the meeting. . . .
   —From a New England newspaper, during the spring of a
   recent year (names and dates adapted).

He who desires but acts not, breeds pestilence.
Sooner murder an infant in its cradle than nurse unacted desires.
   —William Blake again, *The Marriage of Heaven and Hell*.

Hateful Contraries

There are two alternatives to *nursing* an unacted desire. One is to suppress the desire; the other is to act it. I take it there can be no doubt as to which Blake thought he meant, if he had to mean either. The verbal achievement of this "Proverb of Hell" is that the starkness of a choice is covered in the ugly word *nurse*.

The Manichaean, the Dionysian, the Nietzschean note which creeps into so much criticism can be listened to much more thunderously (and perhaps more instructively) in certain chapters of Russian fiction.

> ... you must go and deny, without denial there's no criticism and what would a journal be without a column of criticism. Without criticism it would be nothing but one "hosannah." But nothing but hosannah is not enough for life, the hosannah must be tried in the crucible of doubt.... I ... simply ask for annihilation. No, live, I am told, for there'd be nothing without you. If everything in the universe were sensible, nothing would happen.... Suffering is life. Without suffering, what would be the pleasure of it? It would be transformed into an endless church service; it would be holy, but tedious.
>
> I know, of course, there's a secret in it, but they won't tell me the secret for anything, for then perhaps, seeing the meaning of it, I might bawl hosannah, and the indispensable minus would disappear at once, and good sense would reign supreme throughout the whole world. And that, of course, would mean the end of everything.

These words are spoken, of course, by the Devil—the alterego of Ivan Karamazov—the night before his brother's trial for murder, as Ivan lapses into a brain fever. Through pride, perversity, and ironic mistrust of self, he will sabotage his own testimony and thus bring about the notable "miscar-

Horses of Wrath

riage of justice" which is the grotesque climax of that terrible story.

Or let us listen to a more severely abstract idiom—that of a writer in the *Philosophical Review* for July, 1957. This writer devotes some pages to urging what might seem to a casual reader a rather bald matter, namely, that there is an important difference between "moral worth" and "moral credit."

We enjoin persons (including ourselves) not only to perform right acts but also to develop in themselves dispositions to perform right acts from good motives, to do those things which are morally worthy. But we do not enjoin anyone to perform morally creditable acts, for this would mean saying to him, "Perform morally worthy acts against unfavorable circumstances." If unfavorable circumstances are present, we shall hold up the ideal of performing morally worthy acts in *spite* of such odds, of course, and this is one of our most highly valued character ideals. But if morally creditable acts as such were directly commanded or enjoined, agents would be under an obligation to set up such odds for themselves in order that these might then be overcome. Many writers have commented on the moral absurdity of such an ideal.[8]

Self-administered doses of division—this enterprise may be respectable enough so long as it is neurotic. The more deliberate and coolly elected the anguish is, the sillier it seems. In the large world of reality around us, if the stakes are set high enough, we will not have much difficulty in coming to the conclusion that hesitation and bewilderment, endless debate and conflict, are not actually viable objects of human choice. In the intensely reflexive conflicts, the introspective depths, of literature it is perhaps less easy to see this. But it is not impossible. In the age of Johnson, Sir Joshua portrayed Garrick courted simultaneously by the Muses of Tragedy and Comedy: One side of his face in a comfortable gloom, the other lit by a queasy smile. "How happy could he be with either, were t'other dear charmer away." An illustration in Arthur Koestler's *Insight and Outlook* shows how in more recent days the same external effect is achieved by the selective application of galvanic charges to the muscles of the human jaw.

VI

BUT LET US back off and reapproach some of these problems at an easier pace. One part of the difficulty about the myth and ritual claims has all along been their solemnity—the deep cathartic function and the vast canonical subject matters, the cycles of death and rebirth, the contrasts of celestial and demonic, which they impute to or prescribe for the poetry of serious worth. These ideas may be called unhistorical. Like eighteenth-century Gothicists and Druidists, the myth critics want to push us back into some prelogical and hence preliterary supposed state of very somberly serious and mysterious mentality. And hence they are forgetting where they are in history and are overlooking at least two great types of lesson: the lesson of religion, especially that of the Hebrew and Christian religion—which is the true lesson of solemnity—and the lesson of accomplished poetry, in Homer, let us say, in Horace, in Dante, Shakespeare, Pope, which is surely a different kind of lesson. I will run the risk of seeming frivolous by saying that it is much less like a lesson of solemnity than a lesson of strife and fun. And to round out our pattern of competing principles, let me add a third modern lesson, that of abstract philosophy.

The ancient and pagan division of poetry into tragic and comic, while it is a division, is also an inclusion and a suggestion that the two things may be complementary. On the other hand, there is Plato, especially in the *Philebus* or, as the Cambridge translation of 1945 calls it, *Plato's Examination of Pleasure*, saying that the pure kind of pleasure arising, for instance, from the knowledge of geometric forms is better than the impure pleasures offered by comedy and tragedy which arise from pain and certain kinds of triumph over pain (as in life itself, which is at once tragic and comic). This kind of Platonism, the numerical and geometric, may be traced here and there down through the centuries, in Augustine and Boethius (where the orientation is musical), in eighteenth-century reasoners on order and harmony like Hutcheson, where the orientation may be again visual. During the early part of our own century the same thing, with frequent appeals to Plato's *Philebus*, has appeared in the aesthetics of "significant form." The ideas of Bell, Fry, and Wilenski, or of Jay Hambidge, on painting and sculpture have a clear enough resemblance to art-for-art's-sake in the phase of Whistler and Wilde, and this whole school of formalism (intent on the "significance" of the cube, the "significance" of the cylinder, as well as on the porcelain nicety of certain French verse forms) has contributed a shade of meaning to the term "formalist" when it has been used in a merely polemic way during the recent course of literary debate. Nevertheless, the school of significant form provides us with a legitimate and sufficiently sharp modern contrast both to literary taste and to critical analysis accord-

Hateful Contraries

ing to the principles of tension, drama, metaphor, paradox, irony, and wit. Another early modern solution to the problem was the opposite of the Platonic, and just as extreme. This was the eighteenth-century resolution by surrender to feelings—whether dismal or tender. The analysis of wit has been equally an opponent of that. Thus I find no difficulty in explaining to myself a liking for the American school of ironists and for what they have in common with the theory that prevailed in the time of Coleridge and the Germans.

Yet I am ready to admit also that the norm of irony gives me some difficulty in relating my thoughts about poetry to my thoughts about the rest of life. The reconciliation of opposites as it was meditated by Schelling and Coleridge had a largely metaphysical bearing. How to get subject and object together and yet explain their distinctness; how to unify inner and outer, general and particular, thought and emotion, art and nature, or a longer series of almost any such opposites one might name—this was the speculation that preoccupied these deeply introspective, transcendentally-minded men. An irony of a more darkly moral coloring, a sardonic self-transcendence, was known to Friedrich Schlegel and others. The twentieth-century American irony of poetic inclusiveness, looking back to conversational ironic symbolism, and finding a theoretical hint in quotations from Coleridge by Eliot and Richards, has had a strongly emotive and at times a moral accent. There is a direct concern with human affairs and human values here (human "interests"), good and evil, pleasure and pain, rather than precisely with the mysteries of knowledge and creation, the activity of that "synthetic and magical power" the imagination. It seems to me that the recent ironists have put a hard problem very compellingly.

Pain and destruction are the two great components of the problem. You can show that pleasure is only an elusive and phantasmal byproduct of things and qualities; it cannot be pursued in itself with any success; and you can subsume pleasure under the head of interest, which is the general affective counterpart of knowledge and objects. But pain is not like that; it can sometimes be avoided (that is, it does not *always* increase through flight, as pleasure diminishes through pursuit); and when it cannot be avoided we wish it could be. It is one of the most positive experiences we have. On the other hand, destruction is clearly negative, the termination of experience, being, and interest. But then the question here is: Why? There is a religious answer that speaks of patience and atonement. This answer is not at odds with poetry, but neither is it available to poetry as a formal solution to the poetic problem.

Let us say that we recognize the fact of material concreteness in human experience, and though matter itself be not evil (as in the Persian scheme), yet it does seem the plausible enough ground for some kind of dualism, division, tension, and conflict, the clash of desires, and evil and pain. Spirit and matter, supernatural and natural, good and evil, these tend to line up as parallel oppositions. Even so rarefied and geometric a material concept as that of symmetry has its danger for the concept of beauty in unity. How *could* symmetry be part of the definition of beauty? Think, says Plotinus, what that doctrine leads us to: "Only a compound can be beautiful, never anything devoid of parts" (I.vi.1).

Hateful Contraries

But parts and composition (and decomposition) seem to be inescapable in the human situation, and on the modern view, art, especially verbal art, confronts this fact. We say that art ought to have the concreteness of recognition and inclusion; it ought to have tension, balance, wholeness. Anybody can see that there could never be any drama or story, either comic or tragic, without evil. Nor for that matter (though this may not at first glance be so obvious) could there be any pastoral or idyllic retreat, any didactic or satiric warning, any lyric complaint—or any lyric rejoicing—so far are the springs of human rejoicing buried in the possibility, the threat, the memory of sorrow. About hallelujahs in Heaven we know next to nothing.

Of course we will say that we don't call evil itself, or division, or conflict, desirable things. We only call facing up to them, facing up to the human predicament, a desirable and mature state of soul and the right model and course of a mature poetic art. And I think there is some comfort in this answer—though again, with a certain accent, it may sound somewhat like telling a boy at a baseball game that the *contest* is not really important but only his *noticing* that there is a contest. The great works and the fine works of literature seem to need evil—just as much as the cheap ones, the adventure or detective stories. Evil is welcomed and absorbed into the structure of the story, the rhythm of the song. The literary spirit flourishes in evil and could not get along without it. And so, unless I am mistaken, we face here some kind of problem concerning *The Marriage of Heaven and Hell.*

If we take the relatively cautious course of saying that in

Horses of Wrath

poetry there has to be an ironic balance of impulses, rather than clear Fourth of July choices and celebrations, it will sound, and I fear with some reason, to a moralist like Yvor Winters as if we entertained only wavering beliefs and purposes, no moral commitments. And if we talk more boldly about evil being "reconciled" in poetry, we are going to sound to a commentator on T. S. Eliot like Marshall McLuhan, and I fear with some show of reason on his side, as if we were propitiating evil, giving some dark earth spirit its rightful place in the scheme of things. Mr. McLuhan will call us, along with Eliot, a generation of Manichaean dualists, split personalities, pagans trying to stand on tiptoe. At this point no doubt Faulkner's *Fable* ought to be interrogated. It appears that a critic ought to inquire whether in Faulkner's *Fable* reconciling good and evil has not taken the form of making God Himself something capacious enough and something ambiguous enough to *include* both good and evil and to make atonement for his *own* evil—as in the last reveries of the humanist philosopher Paul Elmer More.

So far as I am pushing any thesis in this part of my essay, I am trying to suggest that the inveterate desire of the literary theorist for some kind of substance, as opposed to either Platonic idea or Platonic semblance, is closely tied to, and may even be a cover for, a deeper desire that literary art should embrace something which we cannot very well imagine human substance as being free from, the fact of evil, both as suffering and as destruction. This kind of embrace may very well be a thing that is more necessary to verbal art than to any other. I think there may well be certain truly Platonic forms of fine art—notably drawing and carving,

Hateful Contraries

arts which Plato himself was apparently concerned to purify in the geometric direction. But verbal art can scarcely be interesting in that way.

And I have been touching on the idea that if verbal art has to take up the mixed matter of good and evil, its most likely way of success, and its peculiar way, is a mixed way. And that means not simply a complicated correspondence, a method of alternation, now sad, now happy, but the oblique glance, the vertical unification of the metaphoric smile. To pursue the ironic and tensional theories in the way most likely to avoid the Manichaean heresy will require a certain caution in the use of the solemn and tragic emphasis. Dark feelings, painful feelings, dismal feelings, even tender feelings move readily toward the worship of evil. And they have the further disadvantage that they run readily into pure feeling itself, its indulgence and the theory of that, as in the eighteenth century. There was a girl in Mrs. Thrale's set at Streatham who could weep so prettily that she was sometimes called upon to give a parlor demonstration. It is true that pure laughter too has its limitations. It may be idiotic. But bright feelings and the smile go with metaphor and wit, and when playing on serious topics, wit generates a certain mimicry of substance which is poetry. There was another member of the Streatham set who in a *Preface* to Shakespeare noticed that "Shakespeare has united the powers of exciting laughter and sorrow not only in one mind, but in one composition." By this line of suggestion and by quoting further authorities of this tenor we might arrive at a theory that sounded too much like the homely formula "grin and bear it," or perhaps like a prescription for *The Most Lamentable Comedy and Most Cruel Death of Pyramus and*

Horses of Wrath

Thisbe. But the theory also could be made to sound more like a phrase in Aristotle's *Poetics*—the four words *anōdunon kai ou phthartikon*—not painful and not destructive, a description which Aristotle meant for the comic object as distinguished from the hideously suffering tragic object. But the phrase, even in Aristotle's system, can easily be lifted so as to operate not only at the level of poetic object but at that of poetic utterance, poetry itself, and then it will refer not only to comedy but to tragedy too.

VII

THUS I ARRIVE at a concluding part of my effort, the exposition of critical alternatives. And here, since I am an invincible Ramist and visualist in these matters, maintaining that as theorists we can make no progress unless in the direction of clarity (even though a certain deep obscurity and mystery be intrinsic to our materials), I resort to the use of a diagram. This, however, is so simple that it almost does not have to be drawn. It represents two oppositions and their point of intersection, and hence it has five positions or places, representing what I conceive to be five main or even ultimate types of literary theory. Suppose we have number I, the theory or class of theories which may roughly be called "genetic"—that is, the theories that assert: "Poetry is, or expresses, a genuine experience of the author." Put this, let us say, at the top of the diagram. And suppose then number II, the "affective" theories: those that assert: "Poetry is what moves or pleases, or is relevant to the interests of, a certain audience." And put this at the bottom of the diagram. And suppose then number III, what we may call the "contentual"

Hateful Contraries

poetic theory or group of theories. They can also be called the "didactic." They are all the theories that assert that poetry is a statement of some kind of true message—religious, moral, social, historical, scientific. Put these on one side of the diagram, let us say the left. And then opposite them, on the right, put number IV, a group of theories which we may call (with perhaps a certain customary inaccuracy regarding Aristotelian hylomorphism) the "formal" theories—or else the "technical" or the "stylistic." These are all the theories that assert that poetry consists in technique, style, texture, structure, or form: that poetry is "beautiful language," or "effective language."

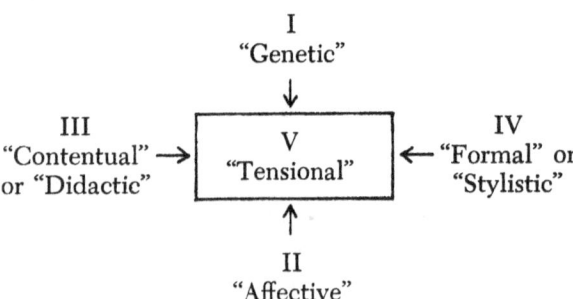

And then, finally, in the center, about equidistant from each of the other four (And for emphasis let us draw a box around the area), put number V, a type of theory which may be called for the moment simply the "tensional," and which I describe roughly as a theory which asserts that "Poetry is the expression of a relation between subject and object: dramatic, metaphoric, involving complexity of values. Poetry is more than beautiful language, and less than (or at least different from) religious, moral, and social truth."

Horses of Wrath

I have not tried to include here every possible specific theory of poetry or of art—every theory that has a name and a place in the history of theories. Certain readers will be likely enough to note the absence of the theory of art as play (to name a few examples nearly at random), the theory of vivid sensory realization, the theory of empathy, or the contrary theory of aesthetic distance, or the most specific recent theory, that of poetry as myth. My opinion is that all other theories than the five I have presented either reduce to one of these five or else are rather easily put aside as not fitting the facts. Numbers I, II, III, and IV are extreme or pure theories—each I believe asserting some truth about poetry—and all perhaps being points of reference for the more complicated theory, Number V—though all four will not be equally conspicuous or equally available in the discussion of every particular poem. Let us observe that Numbers I and II form the axis set up both by the intensive historical method in literary studies and by affectivism of both the Freudian and the Richardsian types. On the other hand, Numbers III and IV form the axis of pure, classical cognitive study. That is, despite the difference between the didactic and the formal, these two kinds of theory have in common that they look to something conceived as outside both specific author and specific audience—some referential truth on the one hand, or on the other some verbal character.

Numbers I and II are theories which lean more or less heavily toward subjectivism and relativism. In my opinion they are not really theories of poetry, but theories of its origins and results. However, these theories may actually pose difficult problems for cognitive theory, and they may well represent (or distort) dimensions which (as we shall see) the cognitive theorist cannot get along without.

As for theories of type III, the cognitive but simply contentual, I remark: Nowadays nobody holds seriously and overtly for poetry as a vehicle of historical and scientific truth. (Strabo's view that Homer is valuable because he teaches the geography of the Mediterranean region may be mentioned as a classical instance of such a view.) But nowadays many persons do take quite seriously the view that poetry conveys religious, moral, or social truth. During the Renaissance, moralism or didacticism in poetic theory meant a certain kind of thing: namely, that poetry was to recommend, adorn, or otherwise enforce or assist a doctrine; doctrine, however, was determined by other than poetic norms (by philosophy and revelation). The same thing holds for a great deal of modern sociological and realistic theory, and notably for the Marxist kind. But in romantic and postromantic theory other than the social, the didactic virtue of poetry is conceived, on the contrary, as autonomous. That is, poetry itself creates moral and religious norms; it takes the place of philosophy and religion (as in the justly celebrated prophecy of Matthew Arnold). Or, all so-called revelation has always been really poetry.

On the other hand, theory of type IV, the stylistic or formal, corresponds to at least one of the subclasses of what was known during the nineteenth century as art for art's sake. Nowadays there seem to be very few students of poetry who will overtly and completely confess to this theory. We almost all want somehow to be deeper than that. The accusation that somebody *else* is in fact a mere "formalist" is, however, heard not infrequently. Sometimes

Horses of Wrath

that somebody else is a critic of the dramatic and tensional school (a practitioner of theory V in my diagram). Sometimes he is a neo-Aristotelian, one of those who talk most emphatically about the poem as an "object," a whole object, an Aristotelian *synolon*. As the purpose of my essay is more expository than polemic, I am not much interested in arguing here that the label "formalist" is affixed with more justice to either one of these schools, though I do not try either to disguise even for a moment my inclination toward position V in my diagram.

What in fact does anybody have against "form," "style," "structure," "beauty"? Nothing—of course. Let us summarize a few things which everyone knows. Certain arts of visual design, abstract and arabesque, and perhaps certain kinds of music, strongly invite being described in a purely formal way. But poetry is an art of words. And words have meanings. And characteristically, in its greatest instances, poetry has dealt with all the most intense, the hottest, human experiences and problems: with love and hate, sex, war, murder, youth and age, sickness and death, scepticism and faith—with religion. There is a certain sense in which religion is the only theme of important poetry. To tell your audience in the classroom or critical journal that despite all this warmth and depth of content, the only thing that matters, the defining character, is something called "form," or "structure," or "beauty of language"—this will be a fairly cold device, a kind of sellout, a maneuver almost cynical. Structure of meaning, texture of meaning (form, style, technique) are of course actually parts of meaning—important factors in constituting the whole meaning. This is bound to be so—except on the supposition that "meaning"

Hateful Contraries

includes only something severely abstract and doctrinal or something practical. You cannot structure a supposed given meaning now one way, now another way, without affecting the actual whole meaning.

But then set against that kind of truth an opposite kind:— the truth, namely, that it has always been diffcult, wildly paradoxical, self-defeating to try to affirm a complete union or identity of poetic and moral or religious (social or political) values. Such affirmations almost necessarily tend to be either rigorously moralistic, and hence exclusive of great batches of the world's recognized literature, or else so exceedingly flexible, latitudinarian, and inclusive, as to be quite ambiguous from any definite moral or religious (or political) point of view.

Thus sketching briefly, perhaps even assuming, some of the main reasons against the simple cognitive theories of both types III and IV, the didactic and the formal, I arrive at the observation that the tension between these two types of theory has in fact tended, throughout literary history, to keep either one from ever clearly triumphing. At the same time, Number V, the tensional theory also is a very difficult thing to maintain. And thus most cognitive theories do in fact tend to be reducible to one of the extremes, the simply didactic or the simply formal.

VIII

LET ME NOW attempt to add some reasons or perhaps only to develop those already implied, in favor of the more complicated and central kind of cognitive theory, the tensional. This is a theory which says that a unification or resolution of theories III and IV, the contentual and formal, will operate not flat and straight along a line of abstractly purified cognitive theory, but with a kind of parenthetical bulge or reach, both up and down. This unification will conceive something of both a speaker and an audience in a verbal transaction—though not strictly *the* speaker, or author, of the poem, and not strictly *the* historically determinable audience for whom he may have uttered the poem most directly. The theory tries to use a certain kind of claim coming in from the direction of I and II (speaker and audience) to exert a pull upon III and IV (doctrine and form), and thus both to complicate the two claims of message and form and to implicate them with each other—to turn the means and end of the ordinary pragmatic, rhetorical relation in language into the parts and whole of the dramatic and aesthetic relation. Different persons, different interests, different feelings, different values, different rhetoric, different metaphor. Metaphor is the holding together of oppositions. The logical impurity of metaphor is a ready slant, a twist, of abstract idea toward the inclinations of speaker or audience or of both.

One way to put the dramatic thesis would be to say: All poetry (even, for instance, a deeply meditative lyric, or a didactic verse essay) has something of that element of tension or struggle which we easily enough think of as necessary to a novel or a stage drama. And through this tension poetry gives a fresh vision of reality, a fullness, completeness, concreteness of experience. It will be an experience that includes pain as well as pleasure, evil and ugliness as well as beauty and good, an experience where tragic and comic can be discriminated but where they show a complementary and an easily mixed relationship.

One technical difficulty with the theory will sometimes

be that of locating the *dramatis personae,* the speaker and the audience—especially the audience. The speaker may not be so obvious as Browning's inmate of a Spanish Cloister or the melancholy *poeta ignotus,* Il Pensoroso, of Gray's *Elegy,* or the blind bard of *Paradise Lost;* he may be almost fully universalized, like the gentlemanly ethical rationalizer of Pope's *Essay on Man.* Still we more or less readily accept the notion that some speaker, some *persona,* some mask, even though nearly transparent, some special voice, some tone, is there. We may often feel less sure that that tone entails the idea of any special audience. Poems addressed to a coy mistress, to Dr. Arbuthnot, to Death, to the West Wind, may be too special. It would be all too easy to multiply instances of meditative poetry where the reflective, the philosophic, the sensitive and superior speaker is talking, even though somewhat emotively, only to himself—or, what is much the same thing, to anybody at all or to anybody or everybody who is interested in listening. And that might be thought a *reductio ad absurdum* of the theory. But I think even that is not such a reduction. For if and when a poem is an address of the speaker to himself, the poem still by that very fact is different from science and metaphysics, which properly, I believe, are not addressed to anybody at all, but are simply and purely uttered. (On the other hand, practical discourses *are* addressed to somebody, but then they are practical—that is to say, informative or persuasory.) The most inclusive and incontrovertible formula for the dramatic aspect of the theory will be achieved in the statement that the self-consciousness of the poem, in any event, always unites both speaker and "mock-audience." The two parties to the drama are joined in the consciousness of the actual audience, the good reader. And thus reflection transcends and envelopes emotive response.

The term "thee" in stanza 24 of Gray's *Elegy* ("For thee, who, mindful of th' unhonor'd dead") refers to the same person as the "me" of stanza 1 ("And leaves the world to darkness and to me"), and this person is any sensitive, melancholy unknown poet, any "youth to fortune and to fame unknown," and hence again, by extension, any person at all who happens to be reading the poem. The addition to the poem of the last nine stanzas, including the epitaph, and the revision of four other stanzas, have on the one hand created a phantom research puzzle for literal detective minds and on the other have produced the critical opinion (to be sure, a minority opinion) that Gray spoiled his poem by a merely personal appendix to an initially marmoreal statement of something universal. But the truth, I believe, is that Gray remarkably fortified his poem by that addition and revision—completing the personal promise of the first stanza, giving depth and resonance to the "universal" by the dramatization of the "I" in its complementary and responding image, the "thou." He thus made his famous *Elegy*, the only successful serious poem he ever wrote, something like a special paradigm of the dramatic, reflexive act of saying and knowing which is basic to the whole poetic business.

But a second kind of difficulty for the dramatic and tensional theory—a dissatisfaction and a protest, and perhaps a more heavily weighted one—will relate to that danger of Manichaeism to which I have alluded in earlier sections of this essay. The question which the technical moralist or the poetic theorist with a moral and theological concern (Murray Krieger or his orthodox opposite, for instance) seems most likely to keep asking will run about as follows: Just how is it possible for the poet to give ample and fair play, not only to faith and control, but to the contagious opposites which prove and intensify those virtues—how possible, that is, without either adulterating a pure philosophy about these matters or creating at least moments of imagery which are a yielding and a seduction? The Knight of Temperance in the second book of Spenser's *Faerie Queene* breaks up the bower of the enchantress Acrasia, but the feat requires his first getting safely past a few stanzas of very superior pinup girl art. The requirement, moreover, is hardly accidental to the poetic needs of the passage. If these stanzas were not at least potentially seductive, it may well be questioned if they would constitute the necessary poetic features at that place in the plot. This example is conveniently allegorized for us by the poet himself into something like a type of what we are talking about. Much more natural and exciting examples might easily be multiplied. It may be said, with as much certitude as anything about literature can be said, that the poet does not write even a moderately good poem about sheer control or about sheer indifference—any more than about sheer sensate experience. Again, Milton does not achieve his *Paradise Lost* by making Satan a weak or unimpressive figure. It is a well-known scandal that critics have all along tended to read Milton as himself "of the Devil's party." The theologian may not find it directly edifying (though Mr. Empson may) that Hell in the poem is a more convincing place (a more interesting kind of poetry) than Heaven. Examples, either backward in time to Dante's *Commedia* or forward to Tennyson's *In Memoriam,* to the difference between Newman as a poet and Hopkins, or to

Horses of Wrath

Eliot's *Waste Land,* are too easily multiplied to make the experiment interesting. A serious poet seems always likely to be engaged either in some division or mixture of sympathy or in expressing some doubt about the actual prevalence of some value in a given part of the natural world. And when this doubt reaches total, or cosmic, and hence religious, proportions, it may readily enough slide into some doubt or hesitation about the actual rightness of the supposed value.

But again (and here an apparently slight difference may be the turning point in a large argument), the poetic conflict is one which may well be deeply fraught with theoretical ambiguity, doctrinal inscrutability. Eliot's *Waste Land* may have been during the 1920's, to persons of a settled religious thought and habit, a somewhat shocking poem. On the other hand, to persons of already sceptical, agnostic, or troubled temper, we may well suppose the same poem to have been a source of something like a dim religious light. Milton's portrait of Satan has that kind of dramatic solidity which makes its interpretation depend in part on the temper of the interpreter. It is true that a poet always has a perspective, and this perspective (correct or incorrect) is not a mere accident or addition to the dramatic conflict, but an intrinsic part, a condition, of any conflict at all. The confrontation of human motives is not like the mere contrary pull of bundles of hay to the donkey. Yet the perspective as such is not a doctrine, not a didactic stance, and on the other hand the perspective as such, or alone, is not what makes the poetic virtue. The perspective may even be wrong from the moralist's point of view, and the idea of poetic tension explains how it is possible nevertheless for the poem to have its own validity.

Hateful Contraries

Most likely we attempt to excuse the poem of full philosophic commitment by an appeal to dramatic realization (which is a kind of image). At the same time, most likely we also attempt to excuse the poem of full responsibility for vivid realization by an appeal to some more theoretical kind of knowledge. But this paradox is, I believe, no more than that.

The defender of poetry will say on the one hand that the poet does not in fact conduct his tensional discourse as a rival pair of peep shows—one of the flesh and one of Heavenly (or Utopian) light and grace. Nor does he conduct it as a school dispute, nor yet as any kind of philosophical melodrama—truth and falsity disguised as personages and fighting out their duel to one only canonical conclusion, the triumph of truth. The theater of poetic conflict is human substance itself, or, to enlarge this, "ethical substance," as Hegel put it. Not that the poet can deliberately or professedly move toward conflict itself as a goal. This is as much a self-defeat as any other direct move on a poetic goal. But the man speaking in the poem will move, toward whatever his goal is, honestly, with a sense of the obstructions and drags, the limitations, in a word, the wholeness of the experience. Poetry is not a direct mimesis of any pure kind of human value, either positive or negative. Rather, the literal drama of the mixed human experience is a kind of intensity and depth which is the opportunity for the poetic reality, the poetic objectification. The poetic dramatization is a special kind of vision, closely related to, and usually involving, the fullness and depth of the analogical or metaphoric vision—as Milton's or Dante's Hell and Heaven are elaborate reverse

Horses of Wrath

images of each other, as Joyce's Dublin is a dilapidated speculum of the Western tradition.

Neither the poem nor the poet himself (of course) need be in the position of saying that the virtues themselves, such as chastity, charity, courage, justice, or pure faith and perfect love of God (or whatever the given poet conceives as virtues) are not real goods, to be sought in real life as intensely as may be. Among the modern critics who, moving from poetry to life, talk about "earning" a genuine faith or view of life by knowing the opposites, there are none I suspect who really believe or would suggest that chastity is a virtue which is worthless without the experience of adultery, or charity and justice, without an experience in murder or in robbery. ("Woe unto the world because of offences, for it must needs be that offences come, but woe to that man by whom the offence cometh.") About faith and scepticism, as about Marxist and post-Marxist liberalism, the dialectic of our times may well leave us more in doubt. But to present the argument of the critic in its necessary and I believe correctly guarded form: He will say that the human condition is intrinsically a material and mixed condition, where faith and love of God and fellow man can scarcely occur except in a milieu that is full of the possibility of their opposites. And this possibility, however it is minimized and pushed to one side by the discipline of the saint, the austerity of the cell, the devotion of the ritual (or the laws of the party), is still a tensional element that is part of the moral quality of the experience. Religious philosophy recognizes this fact clearly enough in its account of faith as an act of the intellect, but directed by the will.

Hateful Contraries

Let us utter here the platitude that there is no moral quality in an assent to the Pythagorean theorem, or in either a doubt or a belief that Mars is habitable.

Let me conclude with a broader kind of observation but one which I believe has at the same time, compared to the mere poetics which I have been expounding, a special relevance to the exact place in history where we find ourselves. I think one might summarize the best poetic debates of the past thirty years in America with the observation that the theory of poetic tension is likely to be involved in difficulties with two main kinds of simplification: on the one hand, with the simplifications of hedonistic and utilitarian science and sociology, and on the other with the simplifications of theological and moral doctrine. For the fact is that, no matter how correct anyone may conceive a given doctrine to be, it is still an abstraction and a simplification. At the same time, the religious doctrines have a backing of depth and substantial mystery—whereas the naturalistic are in the end phenomenological, sensate, and flat. So the religious mind would seem, in the end, to be more hospitable to the tensional and metaphysical view of poetry than the naturalistic mind is able to be. And this is borne out in recent history. The metaphysical criticism which was "new" in the 1940's (working by the norms of wit, irony, metaphor, drama, tension) has had some of its strongest champions among poets and critics of the Anglican school and has enjoyed for the most part at least a friendly reception in Roman Catholic schools and journals. The same school of criticism has met with strong disapproval from Marxist and other socially oriented thought and in general from the naturalistic Saturday and Sunday popular press.

Two

TWO MEANINGS OF SYMBOLISM:
A GRAMMATICAL EXERCISE

The term "symbol" as it is used in modern times represents a large field of meanings, with two poles exerting complementary semantic energies through the whole. For one thing, there is symbol in the general sense of verbal sign (or any other deliberate human sign), the sign that is related to the world of things by an expressive act of the mind and which just in virtue of this act differs from signs in the merely symptomatic order of cause and effect (smoke, for instance, as a sign of fire). The symbol-sign represents things, or stands for them, or takes their place as an object of negotiation. Symbol conceived in this way, with a further stress on the creative power of the symbol-making human mind, is the key to several recent forms of idealistic thinking— philosophies arguing that the act of expression, and most properly the act of linguistic expression, is the primary reality, from which all else is scientific abstraction. Language "produces and posits" its own world of reality.[1] That formula would fit, I think, without great unfairness (if a few qualifications were kept in mind) the ideas of Croce, Cassirer, W. M. Urban, or Mrs. Langer. In certain statements by Cassirer, and in various more special theories of symbolism (in English, the literary theories of Eliot, Pound, or R. P. Blackmur, for instance), the claim stops short of full idealism. Symbols are assigned only a quasi-creative status;

Hateful Contraries

they are unique halfway points of control between man and his experience, stabilizers and carriers of experience, mediated presentations. These moderate notions are likely to be applied in a special way to the literary use of language[2] rather than to language in general, but in any case they tend to cast a light in the direction of language in general. This whole group of notions constitutes, if you like, some sort of analogy to the ancient doctrine of the Logos.

But in the second place, to turn back to more ordinary ways of thinking, there is "symbol" in the far more restricted sense of some special kind of thing or event in the world of reality—a flower or a flame if one happens to look at these in a certain way. And from this meaning there is also "symbol" in the sense of some special detail of a painting or some special word or group of words in a writing, a literary symbol in the full or proper sense, the words that refer to the flower or the flame.

It may be worthwhile dwelling for a few moments on the great variety of logic which such symbols are capable of showing. Sometimes they work in a fairly simple way from the specific to the general and from the concrete to the merely abstract. If a novelist describes a character riding in a Cadillac or wearing a big diamond pin, those objects will be identified by the critic as symbols of the character's affluence and power. (Such symbolism is the ordinary reliance and the ordinary limitation of the nineteenth-century propagandist method known either as realism or as naturalism.) But again, symbols may work along various associational lines, synecdochic and metonymic. They may also work along the horizontal lines of the logician's tree,[3] from concrete object to comparable concrete object, from

Two Meanings of Symbolism

species to species, as, for instance, do the numerous sexual symbols or the father symbols which are so interesting to psychologists. This is like metaphor, the difference lying in the fact that metaphor is an image called in for illumination of some object already in focus as part of a story or argument, whereas symbol is itself in focus as part of a story or argument, though in such a way as to show significance beyond itself. Characteristically, symbol *combines* both the vertical abstractive movement and the horizontal metaphoric. It works both from the individual toward the universal and from the object of less interest to the object of greater interest, from the artificial to the natural, from the outer to the inner, from the physical to the psychological, the spiritual, and the transcendent. The concrete symbolizing the abstract is not the same as the physical symbolizing the spiritual, but the two have a close relation, especially in neo-Platonic literature. They have in common a reference from the more tangible to the less tangible. Symbol can hardly work in directions opposite to these I have named. We do not speak of love symbolizing a flame, or of the maternal womb symbolizing a pottery vessel.[4]

Sometimes the order of images in a story follows or apparently follows the lines of representational necessity or probability, though at the same time a symbolic significance is managed. Then we have realism, though realism of a superior sort, the poetic sort. Sometimes the order openly prefers the norms of symbolic meaning to those of representation. Then we move off through various shades of romance, allegory, myth, and surrealism.

Thus I conclude my diagram of the special symbol or literary symbol proper.

Hateful Contraries

Let me now risk a preliminary and tentative statement that I do not believe the difference between the word-symbol in the poem and the thing-symbol outside the poem to be an important difference for literary criticism, at least not in the sense that one part of a critic's discourse can be directed to the word-symbol, another to the thing-symbol. The critic's effort must in this respect be all at one level. There are no flowers or flames or other things pasted into a poem as in a collage. The literary critic, like the poet, has to stop with the words. Or, to put the matter somewhat differently, the realm of thing-symbols can enter the poem only as that realm is mediated by words.

The difference between the two main meanings which I have been defining, the symbol as verbal expression in general and the symbol as special word naming a special thing, may in certain instances be so great that, as I have suggested, the term "symbol" seems to fall apart into two almost equivocally related uses. Nevertheless, the term does hang together and in a great deal of literary criticism manages to keep both meanings present without generating for most readers a sense of contradiction or cheating. The aim of this paper is to proceed, by a somewhat devious route, to show some relations between these two radical meanings of the term.

II

EVEN A CURSORY GLANCE at the history of symbolism will raise some difficult theoretical problems. It is not really my aim in this essay to take that glance. Yet I cannot continue without some reference to the fact that the origins of the

Two Meanings of Symbolism

symbolist tradition in patristic and medieval exegetic procedure bring us back to that difference between thing as special symbol and word as special symbol, a difference which does not seem to me important to the literary critic. The fact is, as we read for instance in Aquinas, that the Biblical exegetes were thinking directly about things, a universe of things, as special symbols. And a poet like Dante followed the exegetes, at least in his theorizing. That kind of thinking came down into fairly modern literary theory by the route of Renaissance nature philosophy and the doctrine of "signatures" or "correspondences" as entertained by visionaries like Boehme or Swedenborg. In mid-eighteenth-century England, the correspondences are illustrated for poetry by that curious figure Christopher Smart in his antiphonal commentary on the cosmos, *Jubilate Agno*, written in the madhouse. All through romantic literature, in the Germans from Herder on, among the English in Coleridge and Carlyle,[5] and among Americans notably in Emerson, we trace ideas of the "great alphabet of nature," "universal signs . . . diffused through nature," the "visual language of God." (These phrases are quoted from De Quincey, who was partly a sceptic in the matter, but they might be readily paralleled.)[6] It should be observed, however, that by this period, theories of imagination and of knowledge in general had been so far idealized, the outer objective world and the inner creative force of knowing had been so far unified, that these expressions no longer have quite the clean-cut meaning which once they might have had. The English idealist Bishop Berkeley at the beginning of the eighteenth century was a rhapsodic exponent of such symbolic doctrine. By the end of the nineteenth century and the beginning of the

Hateful Contraries

twentieth we have a situation such as Wallace Fowlie has recently reported to us, where Claudel, following both Aquinas and Mallarmé, combines the notion that the poet *names* each object in the universe and gives it its *rightful* place with the further notion that the world is constantly reborn for the poet and that each poet "bears in himself . . . a subjective maze of images" corresponding to the endless metaphorical richness of the world.[7]

The thesis—taken at its most hardheaded, that is in a medieval or early Renaissance, rather than a postromantic, form—means (or at least involves the concept) that individual things in the objective world and classes of things have more or less properly definable symbolic meanings or at least ranges of such meaning. For the purposes of the Scriptural exegete, it would appear to me (though I don't stake a great deal on this guess) that a simply traditional or revelatory fixation of symbolic meaning would be sufficient. That is, if the individual object Jerusalem appears in certain documents in such a way that it stands for the Christian society or for Heaven, or if the specific object or substance water appears in such a way as to symbolize death and rebirth, then those meanings will legitimately enough tend to attach to the same objects in later works written in the same tradition. From the literary point of view some complication may be thought to occur through the fact of prefiguration—the individual and historical correspondence of Old Testament persons and situations to those of the New Testament, a matter with which Scriptural exegetes are greatly concerned. But I am ready for the moment at least, to say that here is something that lies beyond or to one side of the question about poetic sym-

Two Meanings of Symbolism

bolism. For I suppose that we ought to keep our poetic discussion of Dante—or for that matter our poetic discussion of the Bible—at a level where what we are talking about may be appreciated either with or without involving our Christian belief. The poetic discussion has to get along without appealing to the prophetic, the historical, the supernatural. The poetic universal is of a different sort from the historic and Incarnational. It is true that Professor Auerbach in his *Mimesis* and in other essays has recently shown the relevance of Scriptural *figura* or typology to medieval poetics and poetry. Extraordinarily rich adaptations of the method run through *The Divine Comedy*. The conjunction of humble and exalted in the exegetic tradition (harlot and Church, scarlet thread and blood of Christ) does help to explain the medieval indifference to the classically separate decora of comedy and tragedy.[8] But I think it is the adaptation of the Scriptural method by the secular poet, the overlay and more abstract play of symbolic meaning, which mainly enters into the poetic problem. Dante's *Comedy* makes massive use of Scriptural materials. The poem is in some sense founded on history. We can, furthermore, talk about the solidity and realism of his narrative technique and can contrast it to the Platonic thinness of full allegory, the mere "allegory of poets" which he attempted in the *Convivio*.[9] But the *Comedy* is after all not real history; it is a fiction (a *bella menzogna*) and only as such is it an object of full poetic criticism.

III

To push our inquiry into the definition of symbolic meaning very far we have to turn from individual historical objects to natural classes of objects. The interpretation of such classes may no doubt be affected in traditional ways, but at the same time they put to us much more insistently than do individual objects the question, basic for the natural art of reading poetry, whether the world and its parts have symbolic meanings that are at all strictly determinate, whether the "book of nature" described by such authors as Saint Bonaventure in the thirteenth century and Drummond of Hawthornden in the early seventeenth, is written in one language, a scientifically specific language, or in the polysemous ambiguity of poetry itself. A quidditative and teleological view of the world invites, I suppose, some fairly restrictive theory of its symbolism. I have never read a full-dress defense of such a theory by a modern poetic theorist. The "archetypal" and apocalyptic myths of which critics nowadays so often speak are qualities of "the collective unconscious" rather than of the physical universe.[10] The blending of the old objective theory with shades of expressionism such as I have alluded to in Claudel would seem to be fairly normal even among neoscholastic writers—so long, that is, as they are looking at poetry rather than at interpretation of the Scriptures. As for secular criticism the thesis of a speaker at the meeting of the Modern Language Association in Detroit a few years ago seems to me perfectly sound—that the modern conception of fluid symbolism has much less in common than some may like to think with the fixed theories that appear in earlier times.[11]

The defense of something like fixed, or correct, or at least central areas of natural symbolic meaning will proceed today, I suppose, along a line that one might term "total contextualism." The defender would say that we have to try

Two Meanings of Symbolism

to see through the special and local contexts in which an object may be placed, so as to understand its place in the whole universe of space, time and spirit—so far as any of us may grasp that universe. He would say that a given class object or substance (like water) or a natural object of universal experience (like the sun) may have many momentary and local meanings, but that at the same time it will have some more basic meaning or range of meanings. The sun over the Sahara desert may mean to somebody thirst and death, but universally, even to that person, it has or has had the meaning of life. Water may kill a man who drowns, but more universally it is a necessity of life. This defender would speak, I suppose, of antithetic and complementary ranges or poles of meaning inherent in given objects, like life and death in water. And he would argue, presumably, that the poles are seen in the light of each other; especially the negative, by a kind of cosmic irony, in the light of the positive. And further, that all the marginal, momentary, vanishing, and more specially arranged meanings with which objects in given verbal contexts may be invested always enjoy a part or shade of their character and interest in virtue of the substrate of their deepest natural meanings, along with which or against which the slighter meanings are implicitly interpreted.* The "irony is always, and only, a trick of light on the late landscape."[12]

---

* "All guidance to the right sense of the human and variable myths," said Ruskin, "will probably depend on our first getting at the sense of the natural and invariable ones. The dead hieroglyph may have meant this or that—the living hieroglyph means always the same; but . . . it is just as much a hieroglyph as the other; nay, more—a 'sacred or reserved sculpture,' a thing with an inner language. The serpent crest of the king's crown, or of the god's, on the pillars of Egypt, is a mystery; but the serpent itself, gliding past the pillar's foot, is it less a mystery?" (*The Queen of the Air*, Lecture II.)

Hateful Contraries

I think the poetic theorist will have to confess a considerable respect for that argument, and it may be that the truth of it or of something like it is in the end all that can give the mind a grip or a starting point for a real evaluation of the myriad performances of poetic inspiration. At the same time, I think the poetic theorist will have to protest that such a general view of reality, such a confidence in an ultimately definable order and significance in things, does not provide a grammar of sufficient finesse for actually coping with the structure of poems. Keeping the universals too much in mind may even do something to obstruct the critic's experiments in reading. The universals are likely enough to run into tautologies. A tree is a widely used symbol of life —but only a live and flourishing tree. A dead or truncated tree is a symbol of death.

IV

CONFINEMENT to a general theory of correct symbolism would of course be felt even more acutely by the poet himself. Formulary or stereotyped symbolism as a creative technique is a contradiction. It has always tended to fizzle out into the quaint conceptions of bestiary, lapidary, emblem book, or the debased patristic style of the Euphuist. It is clearly better to be wrong with the Ramistically inclined Sidney than to be right with his opponent, the Euphuist Gosson. This is not to say that such writers as Dante, Chaucer, Shakespeare, or James Joyce, who have had a wide range of formulated and quasi-symbolist meanings at their command, have thereby suffered a handicap. The point is that they knew what to do with such knowledge. The twist, the turn, the transformation, the hidden metaphor, the illusory conventionalism, are their pervasive principles. The observation is valid not only for specially symbolic words and phrases but for all the genres, figures, and other conventions which learned inquiry into poems has always been so much concerned to identify. Literary scholars in recent years have no doubt been aided in their reading of Dante and other medieval poets by a knowledge of the famous four levels of interpretation; but I believe that so far as these scholars have tried to determine or limit, or in any way prescribe, their own readings of medieval poetry according to their knowledge of these schemes, they have done their reading a disservice.[13] I have in mind neither the plans of the medieval poet nor those of the medieval theorist but rather the actual accomplishment of the medieval poet in his shaping of the complex of words, symbols, and reality which are always the poet's medium. If we are going to criticize poetry at all, we have to take it insofar as it is something accomplished. What a dull poet Chaucer would be if he repeated half so literally and flatly as some modern commentators do all the gimcracks and formulas that in one way or another are assimilated into his poetry. How happy we ought to be that there is no law compelling us to remember the mazes of exegetical repertory through which recent scholarship has partly succeeded in compelling Piers the Plowman to plod his weary way. What a dreary business our reading of Dante would be if we really tried to take his *Comedy* as "allegory," if we really tried to follow at every step the directions for polysemous reading set forth in the letter (or supposed letter) to Can Grande.[14] How lucky we always are that we have the poet in his poems and *outside* of his own theoretical pronouncements and outside of any other contemporary (or classical) theories by which he may be supposed to be writing.

There is a passage in the *Quaestiones Quodlibetales* of Aquinas which, along with the usual scholastic distinction between secular literature and the Scriptures, is not, I believe, taken seriously enough by modern students of medieval poetic theory, and indeed it may seem forbidding. It perhaps appears an oppressively simple view of the whole nature of poetry. Aquinas says in effect that it is wrong to look in secular poetry for any allegorical, any tropological, any anagogical meanings. The only kind of meaning to be found in secular poetry is literal meaning. *In nulla scientia, humana industria inventa, proprie loquendo, potest inveniri nisi litteralis sensus; sed solum in ista Scriptura cujus Spiritus Sanctus est auctor, homo vero instrumentum.*[15] This, as I say, sounds bad for poetic theory, and it may be bad for a certain kind of retrospective critical intentionalism. But it seems to me to fit very well, or at least to be adaptable to, the needs of a correct modern theory. It is clear, for one thing, that by the term *literal* in this passage Aquinas cannot mean to rule out of poetry the range of natural metaphoric and analogical meanings which are actually there. (The places where he speaks of metaphor in poetry and compares it to metaphor in Scripture are often enough quoted nowadays.) "Literal" in this passage of the *Quodlibetales* is opposed quite strictly to the other three divinely intended levels, the allegorical, the tropological, and the anagogical. Human poetry might very well *refer* to these levels of meaning, or point to them, and in some way involve them. Dante and many other medieval poets would show that this could

Two Meanings of Symbolism

be done, and would easily theorize around any difficulties. But the human poet, not being at the divine level, could hardly speak down from it with a real message about divine meanings. The doctrine of Aquinas would seem to mean at least that we ought to avoid looking for intended messages in poetry; we ought to read it as accomplished or constructed symbolic art, an art where symbols have not a catalogued or correct meaning, but whatever meaning the poet is able to demonstrate dramatically in the very conjunction of symbols which constitutes his poem. The passage in the *Quodlibetales* may in fact leave a little to be desired if we try to take it as instruction for reading the secular poet at the appropriate "literal" level. Is the poet, even at this level, a message-intending authority? I should think not. Even there, Aquinas, if asked, would have had to say that the poet is not the same kind of authority as the writer of Scripture. *Proprie loquendo,* the poet doesn't have a message even at the literal level.

V

WHATEVER the metaphysics of the situation with which we are dealing, the attentive and conscientious reader of poetry must first of all be struck by the great variety and indefinability of the ranges of symbolic meaning that open in the poem before him. "My fair Starre (that shinde on me so bright)," writes Spenser in his funeral elegy *Daphnaida,* "Fell sodainly and faded under ground." Here I suppose we will say that a star symbolizes something like mutability, the uncertainty of fate, death and loss. "Dim as the Borrow'd beams of moon and stars To lonely, weary, wand'ring

Hateful Contraries

travelers Is Reason to the soul," says Dryden in his *Religio Laici*. Here it seems to me the stars symbolize the uncertainty or insufficiency of merely natural reason in religious inquiries. "Bright star, would I were steadfast as thou art. . . ." Here the well-known romantic symbol has a meaning nearly the opposite of Dryden's. "At the stars, Which are the brain of heaven, he" (Satan, in Meredith's sonnet) "look'd and sank. Around the ancient track march'd, rank on rank, The army of unalterable law." Something like the inscrutable and unalterable law of the universe might be the abstract name of the symbolic meaning here. "Lilac blooming perennial and drooping star in the west, And thought of him I love. O powerful western fallen star!" Here Whitman's meaning swings back quite close to that of Spenser in *Daphnaida*, yet the difference is important too. This is a "powerful fallen star," an assassinated democratic leader.

The symbols of the poet are objects in all their qualities and in all their kinds of relationship—resemblance and difference, contiguity and association in time and space, causal operation and reception of effects. Add to natural and primary objects (like stars) the whole range of human artifacts. Think of Aeneas crossing the Styx in Charon's ferry in the sixth book of the *Aeneid* (or Dante not using Charon's ferry in the third Canto of the *Inferno*) and Walt Whitman "Crossing Brooklyn Ferry" or Edna St. Vincent Millay:

> We were very tired, we were very merry—
> We had gone back and forth all night on the ferry;
> And you ate an apple and I ate a pear,
> From a dozen of each we had bought somewhere.[16]

Two Meanings of Symbolism

Lastly, it seems to me that if we will experiment with working, neither inward nor heavenward from the external symbol to its psychological or spiritual meaning, but outward from our own directly known inner experiences toward objective correlatives for them, we can see even more readily the difficulties that lie in the way of putting limits to symbolic meaning. There is a poem by Emily Dickinson which compares memory to a house with furniture in it:

> Remembrance has a rear and a front,—
> 'Tis something like a house;
> It has a garret also
> For refuge and the mouse.[17]

In Plato's *Theaetetus* memory is compared to an aviary full of various fluttering birds. Why couldn't I compare the memory to a menagerie full of prowling and menacing animals—the menagerie of our vices, as in Baudelaire's phrase? Or, if like Hamlet, I think of memory as the repository of a freshly received injunction, the image I invoke may be that of a writing tablet. If like Titus Andronicus I nurse my resolves even more fiercely, I write on a "leaf of brass" with a "gad of steel."[18] I look up *memory* in the index of Bartlett's *Familiar Quotations*, and I find that memory is green or has leaves, it clings, it has a grave, it is a light or a lamp or a morning star, it plays an old tune, it holds a "rooted sorrow," it is a "silent shore," it has caverns, it is a place where fantasies throng in, it is guilty of plagiarism, it is the "warder of the brain." But, you will retort, in each of these various instances memory is something different. We have different symbols, not for the same meaning, but for the different meanings. And, of course, I agree. But this

Hateful Contraries

only shows the abstractionism involved in any attempt to give fixed interpretations to either natural or artificial classes of symbols or to prescribe symbols for given defined meanings. The poet abstracts too in his own way, in his choices and juxtapositions, but he claims for his abstraction only the correctness of his momentary context.

VI

THESE EXAMPLES may not reveal anything profound. The existence of such instances, however, is the grammatical or technical ground for the expansive statements which we find everywhere in romantic theory: the cosmic speculation of A. W. Schlegel, for instance, that "everything signifies everything else, every part of the universe mirrors the whole."[19] Or that of Emerson:

The metamorphosis of Nature shows itself in nothing more than this, that there is no word in our language that cannot become typical to us of Nature by giving it emphasis. The world is a Dancer; it is a Rosary; it is a Torrent; it is a Boat; a Mist, a Spider's Snare; it is what you will; and the metaphor will hold, and it will give the imagination keen pleasure. Swifter than light the world converts itself into the thing you name, and all things find their right place under this new and capricious classification.[20]

The concrete symbols of which the universe itself is composed are external to poet and poem, substantive entities which have their own basic natures and orientation in the universe, and hence have some kind of objective claim on our interpretation of them. Yet the poet can use these symbols only in conjunction with one another and with his

Two Meanings of Symbolism

own interior experience, and he can lay hold of them only with words. And words, even the most usual and specific, those that name or may be supposed to name quiddities, do something to the things they lay hold of; they exert a pull and tear, a push and shaping power, an ordering and reordering energy which refuses to be limited by any description. In poetry we do not encounter things presented simply in their usual classifications, with some correct symbolic meaning attached. We have a world of things and meanings *shaped up* by words, ever variously. It is this fact which leads the critic to talk very little today about the natural meanings of symbols. Through this fact we arrive at the modern preoccupation with the verbal symbol itself, the complex of words presenting or creating its own reality, the poem as "objective correlative" of an interior meaning, a state of mind, which has no other expression.

The "tenor" and "vehicle" of the metaphorical situation tend to merge. These two modern terms have, in fact, arrived on the critical scene at a time when poetry itself has reached a stage in its development where it may be doubted whether the things the terms are supposed to stand for can any longer be separated. The knight on horseback tends to be absorbed into the landscape through which he rides. The plot is lost in its symbols. We have a phenomenal rather than a substantial symbolism.

VII

IN SHORT, I have started this paper by distinguishing two polar senses of the term *symbol*—symbol as specially conceived and significant concrete object, or as name of such object, and symbol as the creation or definition of reality in any expressive sign at all, and more especially in the verbal sign. I have tried to suggest how the resolute and discriminating analysis of symbol in the first sense will subjectively enrich the concept of symbol but will at the same time flatten it out so that it tends to become coterminous with all poetic expression, and conceivably with all verbal expression whatever. We move from the restricted notion of symbol as a special concrete object having an abstract significance, or a special physical object having a spiritual significance, to the general notion of verbal expression as an outer manifestation of the inner, the notion of the outer, if we like, as the disparate counterpart or metaphor of the inner. The grammatical exercise which I have attempted to perform strikes me as a miniature analogue or shorthand for the main development of modern philosophy from Galileo to Croce. The pattern may be more satisfactory for the theory of poetry than for the metaphysics of reality. I have seen it brilliantly suggested that the breakdown of respect for substantive quiddity which occurred in the late Renaissance was accompanied by a decline in the performance of poets.[21] But this has by no means been demonstrated. Something almost like the opposite seems to me the truth.

When a term tends to move in the way we have seen from one meaning to another, and when in certain contexts there is a further tendency for both meanings to appear, in a kind of telescoping or compression, we are likely to have something deeper than merely confused semantics to deal with. The two polar meanings of the term *symbol* which we have discussed may be considered the grammatical counterpart of

Two Meanings of Symbolism

a dualism or unresolved ambiguity that seems always to have been involved in idealist and in formalist aesthetics. In the *Enneads* of Plotinus we find a passage saying that every being has unity and form and beauty, even so simple a being as a piece of stone. But in another passage, in order to illuminate or define the very concept of form, Plotinus has recourse to the example of a sculptor conferring upon a piece of stone the shape of a carved image.[22] So in the neoidealism of Croce, an inverted form of neo-Platonism, we have the creative act of intuition-expression in its broad sense, which includes every act of concrete knowing (the knowing, for instance, of a small scrap of bronze), and we have the *same* intuition-expression in the merely quantitative difference which defines the act of knowing called Art with a capital A (the knowing of an elegant bronze figurine). So in some versions of neo-Thomist aesthetic, there is form and beauty in the general or transcendental sense, a character of everything and of all art work, and then there is some way in which works of fine art are specially turned back toward their genus or specially directed toward beauty. In the recent quasi-expressionist school of "symbolic form" we have symbols in general as the molders and creators of reality, and then we have the special class of "presentational" or aesthetic symbols which, in a clearer way than merely "discursive" or scientific symbols, illustrate this molding and positing power.[23] All these doublings, I think, betray weaknesses and difficulties in the systems that involve them. At the same time, as I have been suggesting too, such doublings may embody their own mystery and stand for their own truth which can scarcely be put in a more univocal way.

Hateful Contraries

The two meanings of the term symbol and their parallels which I have cited, if we would relate them more clearly to a realistic and dualistic account of experience, may be said to center in the fact that all our verbal knowledge is to some extent also bound to be a knowledge of things. (This is the converse of the symbolic-form doctrine that all our knowledge of things is a knowledge of words or other symbols.) Add to this the notion that there may be instances where thing knowledge and word knowledge are in a peculiar way brought together and intensified. I offer a final parallel in the word *understand*. "Understanding poetry" is a phrase which has recently made a notable appearance in the literature of teaching poetry in America. But *understand* in such a phrase would seem to have more than one simple meaning. We understand a word, in a foreign language, let us say, if we know the thing it refers to. But to understand the thing itself may be a different matter, the degree of difference depending on the nature of the thing. Many types of verbal discourse do not involve a high degree of thing understanding. Certain things—an automobile, for instance, and the driving of it or the mechanics of it—may be understood without any very distinguished use of words. Poetry, I suggest, is a type of discourse where a certain kind of thing knowledge is intimately dependent on word knowledge, and compressed into it. The words are saturated with thing knowledge. This is equivalent to saying that poetry is a type of discourse where symbol in the *special* sense pervades the whole structure and invites the theory of symbol in the *general* sense. This has always been true of poetry, though it has remained for what is called in modern

Two Meanings of Symbolism

times "symbolist poetry" to show it in a special way. And this fact—the difference between Dante and Claudel, Tennyson and T. S. Eliot in symbolic usage, and yet their community as symbolists—is the last version which I shall offer of the ambiguity which has been my theme.

ARISTOTLE AND OEDIPUS
OR ELSE

PROFESSOR Gerald F. Else's translation and commentary in depth, *Aristotle's Poetics: The Argument* (Cambridge, Mass., 1957), has met with unanimous acclaim from the reviewers for his learning and the shrewdness of his reasoning. Just as unanimously these classical scholars have described the several "fundamental reinterpretations" which he has attempted as more imaginative and bold than acceptable or convincing, "more likely to provoke thought than to change minds." His ingenuity has seemed exaggerated, "drastic," "daring," "startling," "bizarre," "a disaster . . . like a bad dream."[1] The reasons urged against him have been sober and for the most part minutely philological. And as Else's peculiar strength does lie in close semantic and grammatical analysis, no doubt the pinpoint ripostes of which he is the target are in a measure justified. Only one reviewer, Thomas Gould, in *Gnomon*, December, 1962, has urged that a greater interest in the metaphysical vision which frames Aristotle's scrappy remarks on poetry might have guided Else's philological penetration to happier results. Gould observes, in what amounts to a pregnant short essay on the opposition between Aristotle and the father image of his teacher Plato, that Aristotle's philosophy of concretely emergent formal causes was a systematic revision of Plato's separatist and diagrammatic view of the forms, and that Aristotle's defense

Aristotle and Oedipus

of the truth and goodness of artistic (or humanly imposed) forms was a consistent part of that revision. This is instructive and relevant, even if scarcely novel. I do not see how a literary critic could ever have conceived the problem in any other terms. Accepting gratefully the large measures of philological intelligence placed at the general reader's disposal by Else and by his reviewers, and not venturing specifically to contend against Else with his own weapons, I would nevertheless venture a short essay of inquiry into perspectives. The ulterior intent of the following respectful dispute with Else is to raise some questions about the relation of a critic's general human and literary perspective to the slant of his grammatical inquiry. Or, about what the amateur or general student of criticism is entitled to say when he is confronted by the historical and philological specialist on a foray of reinterpretation. What rights if any does the general literary student have? It would appear that specialist reinterpretation of a critical document can change, or threaten to change, our basic views about the document. If this document is important enough, specialist reinterpretation can hence threaten to change our views about a literary and critical tradition—and hence, to some extent, about the nature of criticism itself, and of literature. This is a serious matter.

Two conspicuously novel parts of Else's "argument" which I select for examination are that concerning the venerable topic of tragic *katharsis* and closely tied up with that (especially as Else manages things), another concerning the *hamartia* (tragic error) and in a subsidiary way the *anagnōrisis* (recognition or discovery).

II

THE *katharsis* in Aristotle's definition of tragedy has been from early times taken as an affective clause—concerning the aim and result of tragedy in the emotions of the audience. This is indeed plausible: because (as Gould in his review of Else has remarked) Plato delivered a two-pronged attack on poetry: (1) cognitive—poetry, he said, tells lies; and (2) affective—poetry (in part because it does tell lies) feeds and waters the passions. And Aristotle seems to have made a symmetrical retort to that attack: (1) poetry in some way gets at a high and universal kind of truth; (2) in some way, though it does arouse passions of pity and fear, tragic poetry does not arouse them harmfully but in fact produces a relief from them. The whole debate of the scholars through the centuries, therefore, has been concerned not with any question whether or not by *katharsis* Aristotle meant an effect produced in the spectators' souls, but with the question what kind of effect he meant. Despite the compromises which the history of the debate has produced, there are basically two possibilities: (1) Hippocratean, medical, purgative, *katharsis* as simply a discharge of bad emotions or bad emotive potential; and (2) the more refined version which we may call the religious or lustratory —*katharsis* as purification. On this latter view the passions themselves are improved or sublimed. Pity and fear are raised to something unselfish, a kind of cosmic awe in the face of suffering. This is a modern, a Butcherian view, a Renaissance view, perhaps also neo-Platonic. So far as it is a theory of what Aristotle actually meant, it seems to have

Aristotle and Oedipus

nothing in particular to support it. Truth, as Plato had said in the *Phaedo,* is a kind of *katharsis* of all such disturbing emotions as the pleasurable and the fearful (*alethes . . . katharsis tis tōn toioutōn pantōn* [*hedonōn kai phobōn*]). Aristotle's phrase in Chapter VI of the *Poetics, tēn tōn toioutōn pathēmatōn katharsin,* sounds much like one of those polemic allusions to Plato which Gould believes are very important for understanding what he means about poetry. As Gould, once more, has very well observed, Aristotle's opinion about the benefits worked by poetry will be part of his general opinion about the benefits worked by human arts—more specifically, I should say, by the educative arts. Book VIII of the *Politics* deals with education. And Chapter 7 of that book maintains that the art of music should be studied for the sake of several benefits, and one of these is purgation—the purgation of religious frenzy, which some persons experience as a result of hearing sacred melodies. "Like experiences" avail for pity and fear and other emotions. "The word purgation we use at present without explanation, but when hereafter we speak of poetry, we will treat the subject with more precision. . . ." It is worth our while to recollect that not only did the term *mousike* embrace both instrumental music and verbal poetry (as in Plato's unfriendly discussion, *Republic* II and III), but instrumental music (despite Aristotle's severe intellectualism in the approach to poetry) was actually a part of the dramatic experience which he was discussing in the *Poetics.*

S. H. Butcher's delicate development of the lustratory version of *katharsis* may well be what most of us could wish Aristotle had said. It may do much more than other versions of *katharsis* to promote a union of our minds with the play. The more plausible purgative reading of Aristotle inclines more or less inevitably toward the physiological. It is difficult to make anything of such a theory for critical purposes. As numerous theorists—Goethe, for instance, and F. L. Lucas—have pointed out, this kind of theory is something like an apologia for dancing with the argument that it is healthful exercise. This kind of theory may come down to recommending the drama as a preparation for a good night's sleep. The extreme or clinical version of the theory is nowadays (or was yesterday), I believe, known as *Psycho-Socio-Hypnodrama*.[2]

It is easy therefore to understand and to sympathize with Gerald Else's drive to discover that Aristotle said something different. On the other hand, it may well be that Aristotle was not the perfect critic. He may simply have wished to be more Rotarian and more psychiatric about the benefits of poetry than we should like a pure literary critic to be. And the attempt to mend his idea of *katharsis* may (as we shall see) entail displacements in other and more valuable parts of his theory. My own view is that it is impossible for literary theory to make anything of *any* affective version of *katharsis*, but that the theory itself is a harmless enough psychiatric appendage to Aristotle's actual literary theory. We can take it or leave it. And to leave it just as it stands, even in the lowest pragmatic tradition, will be better than, in the interest of redeeming it, to twist a syllable of Aristotle's actual description of how tragic dramas were, or ought to be, constructed.

Aristotle and Oedipus
III

IT SEEMS that there was a certain ancient, primitive, religious and moral (partly superstitious) Greek conviction (about killing)—a taboo, a fear—which survived as part of Athenian law. And this was to the effect that the very worst kind of killing was that which happened within the family. This was blood guilt. One might kill a thief or a rapist, or kill an enemy in war, or a fellow citizen in self-defense—or, for almost any reason, a slave. And that was all right. Or at the worst, one suffered no extreme punishment or attaint. But to kill one's father or brother was a profoundly different thing. The guilty person was polluted—subject to the ultimate punishments. He might, however, be legally (or ritually) cleansed or purged. The principle of equity came in Athenian law to be invoked against that of pollution— under certain circumstances—for example, very likely under that of some kind of ignorance on the part of the killer. This concept of religious and legal purgation is precipitated in the dramatic images of Athenian tragedy—in the *Oresteia*, for instance, and—Else thinks (though clearly I should think not in the same way)—in *Oedipus the King*. The chief document which Else draws upon for this part of his argument is the *Laws* of Plato, Book IX. And I should say that so far as the argument is a historical, cultural, and *external* one, it is convincing, ample, and interesting.

The *external*, however, is invoked, as always, for the sake of its bearing upon the *internal*. Else's argument concerning *katharsis* bears hard upon several words in the *Poetics*. The crucial one, sufficient I believe for the present examination, is the word *pathēmatōn* in the classic definition of tragedy which we have already quoted in part from Chapter VI. Tragedy is a *mimēsis* of a large and serious action, through pity and fear working out a purgation of . . . something—*pathēmatōn (di' eleou kai phobou perainousa tēn tōn toioutōn pathēmatōn katharsin)*. The word—we have been saying—has traditionally been taken in the sense of *emotions*—the *katharsis* of suchlike emotions, the spectator's emotions. How is any other meaning conceivable? In this way—perhaps. This Greek word, *pathēma* in the nominative singular, is synonymous with its cognate *pathos*, and that word appears and is defined in a different sense in an important later chapter of the *Poetics*. Chapter XI: "The *pathos* is a destructive or painful incident" *(pathos de esti praxis phthartikē ē odunēra)*. In the same vein, Chapter XIV: "The tragic incidents take place within the context of family relationships" *(en tais philiais eggenētai ta pathē)*. Else, who makes a specialty of detecting Aristotle's morning-after additions to his own text (see the *Index Supplementorum*), decides that the cathartic clause in the definition of Chapter VI is just such an afterthought, tucked in after the meaning of the *pathos* had been established in the later chapters. (It is an embarrassment for anybody's theory that the tragic *katharsis* is not mentioned anywhere else in the *Poetics*.)

Despite the fact that he himself makes such a sustained appeal to the *Laws* of Plato in the anthropological part of his argument, Else lays great emphasis on the principle of *internal* criticism—the interpretation of the *Poetics* by close study of the text itself. At the same time, in a display of one of his most engaging virtues, he admits and underscores (p. 441) the fact that there is that passage in Aristotle's *Politics* (VIII. 7, which I have quoted above) telling heavily

Aristotle and Oedipus

in favor of the traditional identification of the *pathēmata* with the spectator's emotions (or "feelings"). It is an oddity perhaps also deserving of mention that on pp. 434-36 of Else's book both *pathēmata* and *pathē* appear in quotations from the *Eudemian Ethics,* and both here mean "feelings."

IV

THE TRAGIC ACT, we know, takes place as a result, or under the circumstances, of a certain *hamartia.* (Chapter XIII: ". . . suffering downfall not through evil or vice, but through a certain error [or fault], through a big error [or fault]"— *mēte dia kakian kai mochthērian metaballōn eis tēn dustuchian alla di' hamartian tina . . . di' hamartian megalēn.*) Two main kinds of emphasis in the interpretation seem possible. To simplify each one to its extreme: on the one hand, the view of *hamartia* as some kind of mistake, error, or blunder, an involuntary fault, scarcely, if at all, guilty or deserving of punishment—an appropriate mechanism of the drama of fate or inscrutable destiny. And on the other hand, the view of *hamartia* as a deliberate and morally culpable crime (a *sin,* as in the New Testament Greek). Something like this is a requirement for the neoclassic theory of poetic justice in the tragic outcome. (Among modern scholars who have advanced the view, one might notice Lane Cooper of Cornell and his pupils in the volume *Aristotelian Papers.* Antigone, for instance, is guilty of stubbornness and despair. Imagine another kind of character, imagine Ulysses, faced with the same dilemmas—in the cave, for instance.)

Gerald Else's view of *hamartia* is by no means so unusual

as his view of *katharsis*. He adopts a fairly simple, straight version of the first extreme—*hamartia* as ignorant mistake. This is, of course, entailed by his theory of *katharsis* as purgation of a crime by mistake.

We are now in a position to attempt a summary statement of Else's view of the *hamartia* and the *katharsis*. In five stages:

1. The protagonist performs his deed (a killing in the family).
2. He finds out only later whom he has killed.
3. He is stricken with remorse and shows appropriate signs of this (e.g., he puts out his eyes).
4. This remorse convinces the audience of the protagonist's innocence. They recognize or discover his innocence. He is purged of his guilt in the judgment of the audience. Like the "judges at the Delphinion or in Plato's state," they reach the reasonable conclusion that he is *katharos*, free from pollution.
5. As a result, the audience experiences pity (Fear is not mentioned). This pity produces, or is, the pleasure proper to tragedy (the *oikeia hēdonē* of Chapters XIV and XXIII in the *Poetics*).

The play still produces an "emotional end-effect." No escape from that. But that effect is now "pity" and "pleasure." *Katharsis*, on the other hand, has been removed from the effect and is relocated as a "feature of the structure" of the play, a central mechanism—technical, legal and religious, a ritual, a specifically Hellenic element of the dramatic content. It seems worth saying firmly that Else is not simply insisting on something like a cognitive counter-

Aristotle and Oedipus

part to an emotive effect of *katharsis*, an "objective correlative," "scenes of pity and fear," as some have laid the emphasis.

V

WE HAVE SEEN *katharsis* and *hamartia* according to Else, and *katharsis* according to the classic commentary of the Oxford Hegelian S. H. Butcher (1895; 4th edition revised 1907). It remains for us to consider what is by far the most difficult of the four main ideas that enter into the comparison I am making. What of *hamartia* according to Butcher? Here is a view of *hamartia* which seems to me superior, in subtlety and relevance, to all others with which I am familiar, but one which is seldom if ever noticed in recent discussions.

This view is made possible by the fact that the Greek conception (or one important Greek conception) of faults and guilt was not, on the one hand: (1) just what we find in Europe during the Christian era—a conception of free will or choice, and hence either merit or guilt. Nor, is it on the other hand: (2) the simple opposite of that: a Socratic ethic, the conception that all evil comes through ignorance—that knowledge is virtue.

The main evidence (outside of the Greek plays) for any interpretation at all of Aristotelian *hamartia* is to be found, I think, in certain passages of his *Nicomachean Ethics*. Else, it is true, objects to the kind of invocation of the *Ethics* (especially a passage in V. 8) which I am now going to make—on the grounds that the rather complicated distinctions drawn here by Aristotle apply only to the Athenian

Hateful Contraries

legal situation (the five courts set up by Draco and Solon to judge crimes according to degrees of responsibility). But this argument (especially in view of Else's generous use of Plato's *Laws* and in view of his own invocation of the *Ethics* in a way to which I will refer a little below) seems to me to beg the question.

In *Ethics* V. 8 Aristotle is discussing the topic of *blabē*—an injury inflicted by one person upon another. And he distinguishes four degrees of responsibility. The lowest is mere accident—as *we* might say, "contrary to reasonable expectation," a piece of bad luck, an *atuchēma*. Next there is the kind of accident which happens, as *we* might say, through "culpable negligence," a manslaughter; Aristotle calls it a *hamartēma* (The term refers to the physical deed resulting from a mental mistake, *hamartia*). Thirdly, there is the deed which is voluntary but not deliberate, a "second-degree murder" (done in passion), a simple injustice, as Aristotle calls it, an *adikēma;* but in his phrasing, persons who commit such a deed are *hamartanontes* (committing a *hamartēma*). And finally, there is the fully deliberate act, with "malice aforethought," first-degree murder, an injustice to which is added a vicious intent, *mochthēria*. From other passages in the *Ethics*, one of which (III. 2) Else would disallow on the ground that the usage is merely "colloquial,"[3] it seems that Aristotle will sometimes associate the term *hamartia* even with *mochthēria*.[4]

It seemed to Butcher, and I must say it seems to me, that these passages in the *Ethics* at the very least suggest a dubious and wavering relation between the term *hamartia*, along with its cognates, and the ideas of volition and responsibility. Some kind of kinship between these passages

Aristotle and Oedipus

and Aristotelian dramatic criticism is vividly suggested in the examples of *hamartia* which they adduce.

> . . . those injuries done in ignorance are mistakes *(hamartēmata)* when the person acted on, the act, the instrument, or the end that will be attained is other than the agent supposed. . . . The person may be the striker's father, and the striker may know that it is a man or one of the persons present, but not know that it is his father. (V. 8)

> Again one might think one's son was an enemy, as Merope did. (III. 1)[5]

True, there is a passage in *Ethics* III. 1 (heavily invoked by Else) where Aristotle remarks that from ignorance on the part of one who injures another person spring pain and repentance and hence also pity and pardon. Still it is a terrible thing even to be in a position to need such *repentance* and such pardon. And there may always be some doubt, some wonder.

The fact is, as Butcher noticed but as nobody nowadays seems to wish to notice, that Aristotle looked on good and bad luck as indexes of moral character. "Chance *(tuchē)* and what results from chance are appropriate to agents that are capable of good fortune *(eutuchia)* and of moral action generally. Therefore necessarily chance is in the sphere of moral actions . . . good fortune is thought to be the same, or nearly the same, as happiness, and happiness to be a kind of moral action, since it is well-doing" (*Physics* II. 6). "One must assume that accidents and strokes of good fortune are due to moral purpose; for if a number of similar examples can be adduced, they will be thought to be signs of virtue and moral purpose" (*Rhetoric* I. 9). In *Rhetoric*

Hateful Contraries

I. 5 one of the examples of bad luck *(dustuchia)* is that an arrow is shot and hits the wrong man (The etymological meaning of *hamartia,* we may remember, is a missing of the mark with bow and arrow.)

It would seem that we are dealing with a very ancient thought, a persistent human attitude. Indeed, "a man . . . cannot but be evil if he be overtaken by hopeless calamity; . . . any man is good in good fortune and bad in bad . . . they are best who are loved by the gods."[6] *Fortes Fortuna adjuvat.* "When I hear a Man," says Joseph Addison, "complain of his being unfortunate in all his undertakings, I shrewdly suspect him for a very weak Man in his Affairs. In conformity with this way of thinking, Cardinal *Richelieu* used to say, that Unfortunate and Imprudent were but two Words for the same Thing" (*Spectator* no. 293). The modern version of these ideas is part of the psychology of the unconscious. Freud's little book *The Psychopathology of Everyday Life* is a rich anthology of anecdotes about unconsciously deliberate slips, cultivated bad luck, accident-prone persons.

VI

AT THIS POINT let us allude more specifically than we have so far to that peculiarly Aristotelian and technical conception the *anagnōrisis* (the recognition or discovery). Else has bypassed some difficulties for himself by omitting from his volume the plotty, even rather Hitchcockian, types of *anagnōrisis* (tricky mechanisms in the play) enumerated in Chapter XVI of the *Poetics.*[7] But Chapter XIV tells us, in effect, that a superior kind of *pathos* (tragic incident) occurs

Aristotle and Oedipus

when the protagonist commits a deed (a killing in the family) in ignorance and only afterwards recognizes what he has done. Nevertheless:

> The question is how the catharsis is operated, and the answer is that it is operated ... by the plot (the *mimēsis*). To some extent this is achieved by all that we see and hear about the hero in the play. All that we see of Oedipus assures us that he is a strong-willed, excitable, hot-tempered man, but also a kind, loving, and public-spirited one. Such a person cannot, we feel, have killed his father and married his mother in cold blood. But these reassurances are not enough. . . . It is Oedipus's self-blinding, his transport of grief and remorse when he learns the truth, that finally assures us of his 'purity' and releases our tears. Thus recognition is the structural device which makes it possible for the hero to prove that he did indeed act *di' hamartian tina* and so deserves our pity. (Else, p. 438)

In this crucial passage, Else has executed an extraordinary dual shift from the traditional view of *anagnōrisis*: (1) from a discovery of guilt (a horrible discovery) to a discovery of innocence; (2) from a discovery by the protagonist to a discovery by the audience. (Or, the result is a confusion of one kind of discovery with the other.) *Anagnōrisis* undergoes a kind of displacement which is the complement of that undergone by *katharsis*. *Katharsis*, which was once in the spectator, is moved into the play. *Anagnōrisis*, which was once in the play, is moved into the spectator.

The legal-judicial situation which Else invokes as his model is actually rather different from the situation in the drama. Let us consider these steps:

> 1. A man is awakened in the dark by a sound, as of an intruder. He reaches for his gun and shoots.

Hateful Contraries

2. He "discovers" that the person he has shot is not an intruder, but his own father.
3. The police come and take the shooter into custody.
4. At the trial he convinces the jury (they "discover") that he killed his father by mistake.

In the legal situation, the two moments of discovery are not simultaneous, and the jurymen (who have a real decision to reach) are not very much like spectators at a Greek play. The Greek play, by the peculiar economy and compression of its dramatic irony, managed things so that an audience who knew all along who Oedipus was and what he had done were ringside spectators of a moment when *he* was made to discover simultaneously both his own ignorance and his guilt—or the peculiar blend of ignorance and guilt which was his horrible lot. So far as the accent of the play is on discovery, it is on the discovery of horror.

How does Oedipus, at the end of the play, appear in his own world, to himself and the persons around him? Consult the words of Creon, of Oedipus himself. Consult the chorus. Clearly Oedipus is a ruined, a polluted man. "The unclean must not remain in the eye of day." "Cast me away this instant." "Behold, this was Oedipus. . . . Behold, what a full tide of misfortune swept over his head."

VII

ONE CONSIDERABLE MERIT of Else's book lies, I believe, in his militant recognition that Aristotle's theory was not merely descriptive—but normative and ideal—and rather rigorously so. Aristotle seems to intend this meaning:

Aristotle and Oedipus

That the ideal poetry is drama.

That the ideal drama is tragedy.

That the ideal tragedy is that having a complex plot (that is, a *peripeteia* or sharp reversal and an *anagnōrisis*).

The complex plot, we may add, is a kind that affords a maximum exploitation of the kind of painfully dubious *hamartia* envisaged in the theory of Butcher. Many plays, it is true, exhibit various sorts of merit. But very few plays qualify as examples of the ideal—*Oedipus the King* and *Iphigenia Among the Taurians* (in a rather different way—where the discovery is made in time to prevent the painful act), and perhaps a very few others.

Let us ask then a final question: What is the relation, what is the degree of correspondence, between Aristotle's *Poetics* and the actual play *Oedipus the King?* Or: How would Gerald Else's reinterpretation of the *Poetics,* if widely accepted, affect that degree of correspondence? Consider two alternatives. If Else is right, then either (1) *Oedipus* the play is far other than we have been thinking; or (2) Aristotle's *Poetics* is not so close to *Oedipus* as we may have been thinking. Else seems to believe that his theory of *hamartia* and *katharsis* fits both Aristotle and *Oedipus.* But, in a more general way, he would accept the second kind of alternative cheerfully enough.

Tragedy in its greatest days comported things that were not dreamt of in Aristotle's philosophy. (Else, p. 446)

This separatist idea—that a rather wide chasm opens between Aristotle and actual Greek tragedy—is one which I believe may be gaining a good deal of ground today. Bernard

Hateful Contraries

Knox (*Oedipus at Thebes,* 1957) and Richard B. Sewall (*The Vision of Tragedy,* 1959) are two advanced humanists who might be cited in support of this guess. But an even better instance is Cedric H. Whitman, in the second chapter, "Scholarship and Hamartia," of his *Sophocles, A Study in Heroic Humanism* (Cambridge, Mass., 1951). A noteworthy difference between Else and Whitman appears in the fact that Whitman (on the evidence of those same passages in the *Ethics* which we have been considering) believes that Aristotle's idea of *hamartia* is a simply moral one—*hamartia* is a blamable fault. For just *this* reason, Whitman argues that Aristotle does not correctly describe *Oedipus the King*. For, he says, this play moves on a different principle from that of guilt and punishment—on a principle, that is, of sheerly human morality—against a backdrop of an irrational and unjustifiable universe—a chaos, not a cosmos. The morality of Sophocles is not that of theology or theodicy, but precisely that of heroic humanism. The world view is Promethean. In such a context, the question about *hamartia* cannot even arise. Man is responsible for his acts only to himself. He comes to grief indeed—but without crime.

It would seem obvious that to a critic of Whitman's temper, even Else's view of *hamartia* and purgation (if offered in place of usual interpretations) would not make Aristotle any more available. Whitman's Sophoclean hero can do without the gods and their justice. He can surely do without Else's discovery of pain and innocence—his expenditure of pleasurable pity.

We have then a crisis in which the custodians of Sophoclean drama, on the one hand, and the custodians of Aristotelian poetics, on the other, may well be moving in such

Aristotle and Oedipus

opposite directions that they threaten to put the theory and the poetry irremediably out of touch with each other.

In one sense—on principle—I myself could hardly object to this. It is not my notion that the theory of a given age is ever necessarily a correct or best commentary on the poems of that age or adjacent ages.

Still, I see no advantage in needlessly or wantonly working to dissolve an association, a critical focus, which has for so long a time seemed to afford so strong an illumination. The adequacy (or inadequacy) of the contemporary trend toward heroic humanism as an explanation of the greatness of Greek literature (The *Iliad,* for example, or *Oedipus*) is not the topic of the present essay. I have been trying to expound, however, some reasons why the more complicated view of *hamartia* defined by Butcher in his classic of 1895 (and perhaps developed a little in my own account) is closer to the truth about Aristotle than the novel view of Gerald Else. This older view has the advantage—obviously—of bringing Aristotle much closer to the mystery (the complexity) of the Sophoclean *Oedipus* than either the simple theory of Aristotelian *hamartia* as innocent mistake (entertained by Else) or the equally simple theory of Aristotelian *hamartia* as moral guilt (entertained by Whitman and, in fact, imputed by him to Butcher). I have been trying to pay a fair tribute to a learned and acute, an immensely valuable new commentary on Aristotle's *Poetics,* but at the same time to utter a plea for conservatism in our revisions of a handsome and fruitful critical tradition.

THE CRITICISM OF COMEDY

Despite a classical tradition concerning miscarriage at the sight of Aeschylean furies, or bad conscience laid open, and despite a tearful indulgence that seems to have been fairly frequent with audiences in the eighteenth century, tragedy is nowadays hardly expected to produce even the commotion of tears. On the other hand, one of the most patent facts about comedy is that even the modern audience does laugh, and is apparently expected to. One recent writer on the subject has indeed considered it "very doubtful whether the end of comedy is to produce laughter." He observes that "many of the greatest comedies have a rather sobering effect." His argument may work especially well for the comic novel or the "comic" essay. Mr. Potts may be able to read *Emma* to himself without laughing.[1] But a comic play at which people do not laugh sounds like an odd success, and this no doubt helps to explain both why the literary comic tradition centers on the stage, and why comic theory has almost always been implicated in theory of laughter. The phenomenon of laughter does offer an easily locatable, if perhaps only superficial, point of reference for talking about a literary species.

At the same time, laughter has always been one of the chief embarrassments of the comic theorist. Theories of laughter, by definition, or by initial assumption and focus, are of course just that—theories of the laughing person and

The Criticism of Comedy

his pleasure. It is possible to reduce the subjectivity of the theory even to a simple tautology, saying: To laugh at something is just to throw your laughter at it, thereby *making* it laughable. The laughable is just what you laugh at. And so have said such disparate figures as Samuel Johnson (in his *Rambler* 125) and Max Eastman (in his guidebook *Laughter*) appealing to the psychology of McDougall for the concept of an innate laughing impulse, a primary humorous instinct.

Even laughter theories of a more special content are not so various as might be feared. They are all subject-centered in a double sense, in that they all stress not only a subjective feeling but the aspect of an egoistic gratification. The essential is always some form of either "triumph" or "liberty." Thus Plato said in the *Philebus* that stage comedies give us a malicious feeling of gratification at seeing bullies and braggarts revealed as harmless pretenders. And Hobbes conferred upon the early modern version of this theory the confident, bouncing name of "Sudden Glory." His formulation is always worth quoting:

Sudden Glory, is the passion which maketh those *Grimaces* called LAUGHTER; and is caused either by some sudden act of their own, that pleaseth them; or by the apprehension of some deformed thing in another, in comparison whereof they suddenly applaud themselves. (*Leviathan,* I, vi.)

During the later nineteenth century the theory of triumph became crudified through various physiological, psychological, and primitivistic analogies: the expression of the suckling infant, the laughter of children in barbarous games, the roar of the savage in victory, the smile on the face of tiger or Cheshire cat.[2] A more complex modern version appears in the group of "oscillation" theories, which, beginning with the grossness of tickle, move towards the refinements of alternating emotions, attitude mixing, or mental hopping, and of correspondingly ambivalent objects—for example, the woman, towards whom we entertain dominant feelings of affection often interrupted by feelings of hostility.[3] Hence an experience of mental tickling and laughter, and hence all those jokes about women which the theorist, who is usually a man, remembers so vividly.

Again, Plato in his *Republic* and *Laws* warns us that laughter is a dangerous kind of escape. And Shaftesbury, giving us a revaluation of the old idea, says laughter is a liberating force in political and religious debate and a kind of aid to finding the truth.[4]

The natural free spirits of ingenious man, if imprisoned or controlled, will find out other ways of motion to relieve themselves in their constraint; and whether it be in burlesque, mimicry or buffoonery, they will be glad at any rate to vent themselves, and be revenged on their constrainers. . . . 'Tis the persecuting spirit has raised the bantering one. (*On the Freedom of Wit and Humour*, I, iv.)

True, laughter as freedom or frivolity in politics is today only an occasional subject of concern.* But laughter as

* Consult, for instance, H. M. Kallen, "The Arts and Thomas Jefferson," *Ethics*, LIII (July, 1943), 282; and T. V. Smith, "The Serious Problem of Campaign Humor," New York *Times Sunday Magazine*, September 28, 1952, p. 11. Jefferson deplored the levity of the French and in 1789 worried about their capacity for a serious revolution. The most insidious modern attempts with laughter are perhaps being made in the comic strips. "Beneath the high notes of patriotism, we want to hear the low notes of laughter, always off-key, always true. Jagged, imperfect and lovely, the goal lies here. This is the estate of our independence" (Walt Kelly, *The Incompleat Pogo* [New York, 1953], p. 191).

The Criticism of Comedy

personal liberty has been much treated by psychological theorists. Certain very generalized and softened speculations are urged, for instance, by Auguste Penjon in the *Revue Philosophique* for 1893 and by his follower L. W. Kline in the *American Journal of Psychology* for 1907. A bit of bark in a fireplace blazes up, and persons seated dreamily about the embers smile. A big drop of rain falls into a pond, and boys sitting about gazing at the surface smile. Children snicker at nothing in the restraint of a school room. Spectators laugh at almost nothing in a court room. "The function of the humorous stimulus consists in cutting the surface tension, in taking the hide off consciousness."[5]

Can the triumph in laughter be distinguished from the liberty? Everybody will think of Freud's *Wit and Its Relation to the Unconscious*—the polite aggression, often sexual, of the tendentious joke, the psychic economy or easy irrational leaps of idea which explain the pleasure of even the harmless joke, the dreamy art form of comedy where grown-up people enjoy a regression to an infantile, arcadian *id* realm.

The euphoria which we are thus striving to obtain is nothing but the state of a bygone time, in which we were wont to defray our psychic work with slight expenditure. It is the state of our childhood in which we did not know the comic, were incapable of wit and did not need humor to make us happy.[6]

In a book called *The Origins of Wit and Humour*, published as recently as 1952, Albert Rapp argues that laughter is a demobilization, a *relief* from tension, upon sudden *triumph*, and his archetype is the supposed mirthful guffaw of very early savage man enjoying a victory in hand-to-hand conflict. Hence the laughter of ridicule, whether spontaneous or incited by words, and hence too the laughter of wit, which has an intermediate ancestry in such mental tussles or riddlings as may at one time have taken the place of more savage physical strife. Seeing the point of a joke is enjoying a sudden mental triumph. Jokes about sex or about Prohibition in America thirty years ago are easily enough explained as triumphs over suppression. Perhaps Mr. Rapp has more trouble when he tries to incorporate into his system the very common form of laughter which he calls "loving ridicule," or humor. The laughter itself remains just as aggressive as ever (the archetypal laughter of the mother at the child who toddles and falls, the laughter of the English audience at Falstaff), but in a happy transformation the selfish principle is fused, mixed, or merged with love. Thus a victory is gained by annexation or *Anschluss* with the opposing principle. The theorist has his own way by reasserting a definition. Laughter is just per se aggressive, no matter what you join with it, or in what nonaggressive forms it appears.

Why do I laugh when my opponent trumps his partner's ace? when the wind blows off the parson's hat? when an old blind peddler stumbles and spills his pencils all over the street? I don't know. Maybe I don't laugh. But a Fiji Islander would! He will laugh when a prisoner is being roasted alive in an oven! Confident proclamations about the nature of anthropoid laughter are invested with importance by equally confident assumptions that reduction to the lowest common factor is the right way of proceeding. Civilized society discourages cruel jokes and brutal laughter, but what primitive society does is more important. Not

The Criticism of Comedy

what I laugh at but what I don't laugh at is the critical clue to my laughter. Are such theories of hidden elements and forgotten origins supposed to increase my appreciation of jokes or comic situations? It would appear not. If I dwell on the explanations long enough, or let myself pretend to believe in them, I begin to be conscious of a distinct aversion to laughter.

Here, at this terminus of sheerly affective theory about laughter, we are a long way from being able to frame any critical discourse about works of comic literary art. Happily, we may turn—or at least we may, with some effort, work our way—to another tradition.

The more austere theories which have looked away from the laugher himself, or out from his consciousness or unconsciousness as a laugher, toward the things he may be supposed to laugh at, have always laid stress upon some kind of contrast. The Kantian incongruity between idea entertained and sensuously discovered object and the similar formula of Schopenhauer are among the most purified versions.[7] Obviously the basic notion calls for some kind of subtilizing. Yet attempts to subtilize it have often enlisted the aid of some markedly affective clause, as in the "tickle" and "oscillation" theories, where we have noted already that some ambivalent figure like the woman is the cognitive counterpart of a certain supposedly rapid alternation of feelings.

Arthur Koestler's *Insight and Outlook* (1949) draws a "Geometry" of wit somewhat as follows: Imagine that there are "Operative Fields" of ideas (groups or systems of ideas that go together), and imagine two of these fields adjacent to each other, and a train of thought traveling through one of them. The thought comes to the border and happens to encounter there one of those double-faced symbols or ambiguities so prominent in wit-work of all kinds—a "bisociated" link between the fields. Quick as a flash the thought jumps from one field to the other. But a load of emotion which was being carried along—more physical, lumpish, inert—is jolted off and left behind or shot to one side, discharged (recathected, as Freud would say) in laughter. And it is precisely the kind of emotion, the painful feeling of antagonism, which, being sidetracked by the witty jolt, determines the comic pleasure. If the emotion is of another sort, then the geometry of wit may just as well fit the case of "serious" poetry, or, for that matter, of scientific discovery. The thought structure is always the same. The emotions differ and determine comedy, tragedy, or science. Thus a resolute show of joining thought and emotion in the same diagram turns out to be a device of thoroughly affective implication.

More successful attempts to complicate a theory of ludicrous contrast have moved in the social and moral direction. The tradition begins when Aristotle observes that comedy deals with characters inferior to those in real life, but that the comic defect *(hamartēma)* is, unlike the tragic, not painful or destructive *(anōdunon kai ou phthartikon)*, and perhaps there ought to be a happy ending. The latter clauses are the cognitive counterparts to a notion of laughter as a somewhat kindly movement. (On these clauses, in the long run, may well depend the most reliable kind of distinctions between the tragic and the comic.) Molière, Pope, Swift, and Fielding spoke much, in harsh and punishing tones, about certain vices, follies, affectations, hypocrisies. But softer modern illuminations have occurred, as in German romantic criticism, or in Meredith's lecture (partly inspired

The Criticism of Comedy

by Jean Paul) celebrating the "thoughtful laughter" excited in a competent observer by the combat between the sexes in the high society game, or again in Bergson's view of the laughable as failure of the *élan vital,* the suspension of vitality in any form of mechanism or stereotype—the physical automatism of stumbling, for instance, or the mental rigidity of absent-mindedness or bad habits. (The comic character comes to be seen as incapable of moving toward discovery of himself—fixed in mere postures of self-exposure.[8]) Most recently appear the refinements of Mr. Potts, though he does not believe in the happy ending—nor in laughter, as we have seen. Aristotle said that in tragedy the fable is the first principle; the characters come in for the sake of the fable. He did not say the opposite for comedy. But Mr. Potts is able to make it look as if indeed he might have, as if a more or less necessary chain of temporal events following on some blunder may be essential to tragedy, while a "spatial" pattern of characters significantly opposed and acting to reveal one another may be equally essential to comedy. The action follows the free whim of the characters. The tragic character is unusual but normal, whereas the comic character is just the opposite, abnormal or eccentric, but all too usual (as the psychologist tells us today that most persons are neurotic). Comedy is the spirit of humility and of measurement by the norm. Thus far Mr. Potts.

In Aristotle, comedy does not enjoy a mythic status, for comedy is to deal not with heroes of myth but with low characters. It seems certain enough that any further Aristotelian remarks on comedy which may be lost did not argue a very cogent relation between comedy and symbol. Metaphor was for Aristotle a way of heightening poetic style—or it could be a joke, if deliberately misused. But these facts in the history of literary theory do not make it impossible that ancient comedy should be found actually symbolic in structure, or even mythic, with "comic Oedipus patterns" and the like. At any rate, modern critics of myth and symbol (among whom Northrop Frye[9] enjoys an extremely advanced position) practice a hugely expanded analogical mode which embraces with equal confidence both tragic and comic and their origins in ritual death or ritual resurrection, heroic quest and divine sacrifice, or carnival misrule and the "green world" of Robin Hood. Albert Cook's *The Dark Voyage and the Golden Mean* (1949) dichotomizes all human experience into mutually dependent "antinomic symbols," the wonderful—instanced in the tragic quest—and the probable—instanced in the social norm from which the comic deviates into existence. Comedy and tragedy are part of an almost transcendental opposition which includes, at different levels, such various pairs as concept and symbol, sex and death, the beautiful and the sublime, success and failure, bourgeois and aristocrat. This kind of criticism seems as vastly removed as it is possible to be from all that concern with the convulsions of laughter and its stimuli which we encounter in Mr. Rapp and the other psychological writers. The structures of significance indeed are so manifold and so extensive that even a small incautious laugh here might set off thunderous and toppling reverberations.

We have been speaking about theories of laughter itself and then about theories of what is laughed at so far as these two may be separately discernible. It must be admitted, however, that laughter and the laughable are not often

The Criticism of Comedy

discussed separately for very long. (And here the critic's task is going to be greatly complicated—though at the same time his opportunities may be marvelously enriched.) The two kinds of theory tend to come together—the automatized object of laughter in Bergson's theory, for instance, looking a great deal like the comatose or mechanized subject just before he is awakened by laughter in the theory of Penjon—the Platonic stage bully being, one fears, not so much unlike the ego of the audience which rises in the appropriate laughter of malice and triumph. There is much room in the laughing situation, much need, for "empathy." And this is especially true of the situation in comic art, for art is a reflexive work, a thing contrived of the human object only as this is caught in the light of responses thrown upon it. Comedy (to compress into one sentence a great deal that is important but in the climate of recent critical theory almost a truism) combines the accent of laughter and the accent of sympathy in a union of the laugher and his audience with the targets of laughter. Molière in his *Critique de l'École des Femmes* and Fielding, following him, in *Joseph Andrews*, say that comic and satiric "history" is a glass where "thousands in their closet" may see their own faces. Swift in his Preface to *The Battle of the Books* says just the opposite, that "Satyr is a sort of Glass, wherein Beholders do generally discover everybody's Face but their Own." Each of these views is of course correct.*

---

* This neither accepts nor rejects, though it does assert the critical irrelevance of, the classic apology made by the satirist or comic writer that his function is to ridicule and hence to correct vice or folly—*corriger les hommes en les divertissant*. The distinction confidently made by Meredith and others between satire and comedy, so much to the advantage of the latter, may or may not come in. And the critic may or may not believe

Hateful Contraries

The laugh of self-enhancement in the presence of the comic figure must always have been in danger of being itself the occasion of laughter to the nearest spectator—but that spectator has often, happily, been the self. The German romantic theorists dwelt much in the region where subject and object are one. And laughter was one of their best avenues for getting there. The theory of laughter was reflexively subtilized by Jean Paul in his *Vorschule*, by Friederich Schlegel, and by others into various shapes of self-criticism and sardonic transcendence. And after them comes Kierkegaard, in his double transcendence, by "irony" from the aesthetic to the ethical, and by "humor" from the ethical to the religious. "In order not to be distracted by the finite, by all the relativities in the world, the ethicist places the comical between himself and the world, thereby insuring himself against becoming comical through naive misunderstanding of his ethical passion."[10]

But a too close union between the laugher and his object may be one of the main dangers to which metaphysical laughing theory has been exposed. Laughter (because of its unreliable tendency to slide from the aloof to the sympathetic) is not a stern way of dealing with deviation. It is always somewhat too much like its object—undignified, friv-

---

—without special critical commitment in either case—that dunces and scoundrels were actually instructed or brought to repentance by the wit of Molière or Pope. It would seem that in some more or less primitive societies, satire has been thought to operate with a magically destructive force—killing rats, raising blisters on faces, driving Lycambes and his daughter to hang themselves. (Cp. Robert C. Elliott, "The Satirist and Society," *ELH, A Journal of English Literary History*, XXI [September, 1954], 237-48; and *The Power of Satire: Magic, Ritual, Art*, Princeton, 1960.) Terror of ridicule may be one of the most permanent human passions. But it is presumably not the same as aesthetic experience.

The Criticism of Comedy

olous, inferior. Hence it happened during the Renaissance that Aristotle himself was translated as saying that laughter is a form of baseness, a "fowling for the people's delight, or their fooling." And later on the romantic theorist in order to be superior had to be serious, looking at the comic in the light of the cosmic, and implicitly assigning to laughter a low place in his philosophy. "Reason does not joke," says Emerson in an essay on *The Comic*, "and men of reason do not."

The essence of all jokes, of all comedy, seems to be an honest or well-intended halfness; . . . The balking of the intellect is comedy; and it announces itself physically in the pleasant spasms which we call laughter.

Pleasant spasms! "Peculiar explosions of laughter . . ." "Muscular irritation . . ." "Violent convulsions of the face and sides, and obstreperous roarings of the throat."[11] A note of patronage is clear. Another writer in English who leans toward the same predicament is Meredith, whose poems, if not his famous lecture on the "Comic Spirit," make a heavy linkage between laughter and the positivistic fetishes of nature, earth, brain, and blood. And here too, enjoying a high rank among sober laughers, appears Bergson, for whom the comic literary form reflects the limitation of its stereotyped and superficial objects, just as tragedy or serious art does the individuality and vitality of its own proper objects. Laughter is "a froth with a saline base. Like froth, it sparkles. It is gaiety itself. But the philosopher who gathers a handful to taste may find that the substance is scanty, and the aftertaste bitter."[12]

And so we have swung back once more, rather toward

Hateful Contraries

the embarrassments than toward the riches which laughter produces for the comic theorist and critic. And we have now to confess one more reason—or aspect of reasons already named—why the critic should, for the moment of his criticism at least, look askance at the pleasure of laughing. This is related less to any lofty dilemma than to the need of criticism just to keep to its object. The critic has not come before his audience to tell jokes, to demonstrate to them in any way at all that he knows how to make people laugh. It has been mainly when he has been bent on taking direct hold on laughter itself rather than on its objects that he has felt impelled to some such foredoomed attempt. The lugubriously heavy Germanic jokes, about Jews, about sex, and the like, which encumber Freud's pages will come to mind. Even Meredith, alert intellect that he is, may be felt to stumble when he challenges the national mentality and tries to persuade us, at some expense of words, about two incidents where the British would not laugh but *should*, and one where they would laugh but should *not*. Time and again the writer on the comic should have had his warning.[13] No matter how successful he is in other arenas as a wit, or perhaps all the more especially if he is a noted wit, he ought not to attempt the illustrated lecture. The general truth that there is no such thing as a scientific demonstration of the poetic is specially pointed up in the case of comedy by the sanction of laughter.

II

ONE OF THE MAIN VIRTUES of the volume of essays *English Stage Comedy* (1954) for which I wrote this essay as

The Criticism of Comedy

Introduction is that no one of the six contributors* anywhere attempts to quote his materials in illustration of how funny they are. Mr. Barber's brief—and I believe inoffensive—allusion to laughter is a marked exception to the prevailing method of the volume. There is no implication, so far as I can see, in any of the essays that comedy should not or need not be funny. Yet a statement of the theses of the six authors (so far as their speculations admit being reduced to the simplicity of thesis) may sound severe enough: that Falstaff in the two parts of *Henry IV* is a character shaped on age-old lines of ritual meaning, a saturnalian king of misrule and then a scapegoat; that Shakespeare's final comedy *The Tempest* is a romanticized softening of certain Plautine lineaments of intrigue, the good old master, the clever willing servant, and the bungling oaf; that Ben Jonson's realistic comedies achieve their unity and meaning by organization around certain bizarre central symbols—the fanatically morose noise-hater, for instance, symbol of revulsion from the whole clattering business of metropolitan false living; that the after-gleams of English manners comedy, Sheridan and Wilde, are but pale affectations compared to the full social fire of Wycherley and Congreve; that the principle which makes Shaw's best comedies work, and which strives more or less ineffectually in his later comedies, is "Hegelian" dialectic; that T. S. Eliot's comedies, somewhat like his Euripidean models, aim at a religious conversion of secular, even farcical materials, but that, unlike Euripides, Eliot scarcely succeeds. Here, one might say,

* C. L. Barber on *Henry IV;* Bernard Knox on *The Tempest;* Ray L. Heffner, Jr., on Jonson's *Silent Woman;* Marvin Mudrick on English comedy of manners; Katherine Gatch on Shaw; William Arrowsmith on T. S. Eliot.

Hateful Contraries

are no laughing matters. The accent is scarcely that of the silvery laughter which Meredith partly manages to share with the Comic Spirit of his classic lecture. There is not even any of the somber-lurid funniness which exhales like a flickering gaslight along the ways of Bergson's metaphysical discussion, nor of the lumbering guffaw which may be heard heavily as from an inner chamber of the Freudian clinic. There are those who will point out quickly enough the prepared slant which the discussion has received from the Eliotic return to the quasi-tragic and quasi-religious melodramas of Euripides, from the dialectic habits of the conversational Shaw, even from the sandpapery rub of the didactic universe of Bartholomew Fair. There will undoubtedly be some who respond with indignation at the attempt to sublime Falstaff into anything so canonically primitive as a ritual scapegoat, and at the superior gaze turned by one of our authors upon the "good-natured sentimental dramas of comic intrigue" which Sheridan is said to have concocted for a "passive audience . . . bottle-fed on sermons."

All six of the essays are written in what may broadly be called the "classical" vein—as indeed every rebirth of English stage comedy has been in the classical vein. It was with a shrewd theoretical insight, if not with complete theatrical success, that T. S. Eliot in a plan to return verse comedy to the English stage went back to the point in the history of Greek drama where Euripidean melodramatized tragedy was falling off into the patterns of tender emotion, intrigue, mistaken identity, foundling and changeling plots from which the "New" Greek comedy, the form prevailing on the stage ever since, was to take its cue. In each new era

The Criticism of Comedy

the comic writer's talent has been to reinvent some neglected formula. Herakles tippling and joking among the servants at the home of the bereft Admetus becomes, as Mr. Eliot himself had to point out to his commentators, the unrevealed psychiatrist at the ruined cocktail party of Edward Chamberlayne—with a "Toory-ooly toory-iley, what's the matter with One-Eyed Riley?" Prospero and Ariel reenact, in a strange new context of island enchantments, the Plautine negotiations of the benevolent master and crafty slave. Make the slave a willing but subordinate and perhaps not brilliant charismatic personality, and the master a patient, far-scheming, priestly psychiatrist, and you have the interesting scene in Harcourt-Reilly's consulting room at the start of Eliot's second act:

REILLY: It was necessary to delay his appointment
To lower his resistance. But what I mean is,
Does he trust your judgment?

ALEX: Yes, implicitly.
It's not that he regards me as very intelligent,
But he thinks I'm well informed: the sort of person
Who would know the right doctor, as well as the right shops.
Besides, he was ready to consult any doctor
Recommended by anyone except his wife.

REILLY: I had already impressed upon her
That she was not to mention my name to him.

ALEX: With your usual foresight.

But the essays in *English Stage Comedy* are classical in a wider and deeper sense than that they are concerned with picking up such parallels, and indeed Mr. Arrowsmith on

Hateful Contraries

Eliot has not bothered that way at all. These essays are classical in the sense that they share the view which allows comic poetry and tragic poetry to be treated side by side in Aristotle's treatise on the *Art of Fiction*.[14] The implications of Aristotle's arrangement and of the Greek theatrical habit itself gradually shaded off into something different. As for comedy and satire, said Horace, we will inquire another time whether this kind of writing is really poetry or not. Of course he was joking, at least in part. But it has been along this line that later times, and especially our own, when laughter itself has become the object of a quasi-literary theoretical inquiry, have tended to assign comic theory its own special and inferior place, apart from serious poetics. Metaphysical wit and irony have been recent avenues of serious realliance with the laughing spirit of poetry. But to be yet more inclusive and venture a concern even for the comic (not as Emerson did it, not as Bergson, not quite perhaps even as Meredith, but in the manner of some new critic—more or less I think in the manner of the six critics in *English Stage Comedy*) may be the most urgent requirement for a progressive criticism of poetry today.

And lastly, there is another sense and a very important one in which the essays I have been alluding to are classical. Though they are all interested more or less overtly in symbols, and though two of them at least are in the full mythic and ritual mode, I believe that each of them keeps clear of that modern heresy which wants to make myth a new kind of canonical poetic subject matter or a guaranteed poetic idiom. As Jung at least (among the psychiatrists) has recognized, there is a difference between a graceful and a clumsy dream, a well-made and an ill-made

The Criticism of Comedy

myth or version of myth—between, let us say, a cliché myth and a real metaphoric utterance. This difference is carried over and written large in the world of poetry. At least two of the essays, the first and the last, are devoted to a formal insistence upon the critical significance of this kind of difference. It is through his recognizing and discussing this difference that the literary critic—whether of tragedy or of comedy—reveals that his concern is not specifically with anthropology and the analysis of myth but with criticism.

THE CONCEPT OF METER:
AN EXERCISE IN ABSTRACTION

Let us first of all confess that we do not have a novel view to proclaim. It is true that the view which we believe to be correct is often under attack today and is sometimes supposed to be outmoded by recent refinements. Its proponents too are often not sure enough of its actual character to defend it with accuracy. At the same time, a look into some of the most recent handbooks and critical essays reveals that there are some teachers and writers on our subject today who expound this view in a perfectly clear and accurate way. We have in mind, for instance, *A Glossary of Literary Terms* revised by Meyer Abrams for Rinehart in 1957 from the earlier work by Norton and Rushton, or the handbook by Laurence Perrine, *Sound and Sense: An Introduction to Poetry*, published in 1956 by Harcourt, Brace. In the lengthy *Kenyon Review* symposium on English verse, Summer, 1956,[1] we admire the niceties of Mr. Arnold Stein's traditionally oriented discussion of Donne and Milton. There is also Mr. Stein's earlier *PMLA* article (LIX [1944], 393-97) on "Donne's Prosody." In the *Kenyon* symposium there is, furthermore, Mr. Ransom. It would be difficult to frame a more politely telling, persuasive, accurate retort than his to the more extravagant claims of the linguists.

The Concept of Meter

We are, therefore, in a position to do no more than take sides in a debate which is already well defined. Still this may be worth doing. Our aim is to state as precisely as we can just what the traditional English syllable-accent meter is or depends upon, to rehearse a few more reasons in its support, perhaps to disembarrass it of some of the burdens that are nowadays needlessly contrived for it.

II

THIS ESSAY is about the scanning of English verse. We want to consider two influential current schools of thought about scanning, and to examine critically a fundamental mistake which we believe is made by both of them, though in different ways. These two deviations from what we consider good sense in metrics may be conveniently designated as on the one hand the linguistic and on the other the musical or temporal. The linguistic view, as it happens, has been authoritatively illustrated in the contributions to the *Kenyon* symposium of 1956 by Harold Whitehall and Seymour Chatman. The musical view has been very well represented in the more recent volume *Sound and Poetry, English Institute Essays 1956,* and especially in its introductory essay "Lexis and Melos," by the editor, Northrop Frye—and no less in the same writer's larger book *Anatomy of Criticism,* published at Princeton in 1957.

Mr. Whitehall gives us an admirable summary of the linguistic system of George L. Trager and Henry Lee Smith, in part a reprint of his 1951 *Kenyon* review of their treatise, *An Outline of English Structure* (1951). But his essay is more than a summary; it is a celebration. Indeed it makes a very large claim for what this system can contribute to the modern study of metrics:

> as no science can go beyond mathematics, no criticism can go beyond its linguistics. And the kind of linguistics needed by recent criticism for the solution of its pressing problems of metrics and stylistics, in fact, for all problems of the linguistic surface of letters, is not semantics, either epistemological or communicative, but down-to-the-surface linguistics, microlinguistics not metalinguistics. (*Kenyon Review*, XVIII, 415)

To Mr. Chatman falls the pioneer task of showing how these extraordinary claims are to be substantiated. He presents us with a careful and interesting analysis of eight tape-recorded readings of a short poem by Robert Frost, one of the readers being Frost himself. Mr. Chatman's essay is full of passages of good sense. Still we have some objections to urge against him: the gist of these is that through his desire to exhibit the stress-pitch-juncture elements in spoken English, he shows an insufficient concern for the normative fact of the poem's meter. It is true that he does not deny that the poem has an "abstract metrical pattern," and he acknowledges the "two-valued metrics of alternating stresses" (p. 422). But in his actual readings these seem to be of little interest.

We are not quite sure we understand Mr. Chatman's idea of the relation between meter and Trager-Smith linguistics. One subheading of his essay, "Prosody and Meaning Resolution," probably ought to read "Intonation and Meaning Resolution." ("An 'intonation pattern'," let us note well, "is an amalgam of features of stress, pitch, and juncture which occurs as part of a spoken phrase."—p. 422) Mr.

The Concept of Meter

Chatman has learned from Frost's reading of his poem the correct intonation and meaning of the phrase "scared a bright green snake." Very well. Correct understanding *produces* correct intonation, and correct intonation *reveals* correct understanding. And one may choose or may not choose to indicate the intonation by Trager-Smith notation. And this intonation (whether indicated by Trager-Smith notation or not) may or may not affect the meter in the given instance. In this instance there is nothing to show that what Mr. Chatman learned about the intonation did change the meter. The same observations hold for Mr. Chatman's discovery of the meaning and intonation of the concluding phrase of the poem, "and left the hay to make." Through recorded readings of a poem Mr. Chatman learns something that another person might know through boyhood experience on a farm, or through a footnote. But again no need for Trager-Smith. And no change in meter. The point is brought out even more clearly in another recent article by Mr. Chatman, in the *Quarterly Journal of Speech*. He makes a shrewd observation about a passage in Spenser's *Faerie Queene* (I.ii.13. 4-5): "And like a Persian mitre on her head/ She wore. . . ." "We must," he says, "resist the temptation to read *And líke a Pérsian mítre.*" The obvious meaning is rather: "Like a Persian, she wore. . . ."[2] Quite true. One stresses *Persian* a little more strongly, one pauses between *Persian* and *mitre*. But there is no change in meter, and no change in intonation that an old-fashioned comma will not provide for.

One of the good things about Mr. Chatman's *Kenyon* contribution is that, like Victor Erlich, whose *Russian Formalism* (1955) he aptly quotes (p. 438), Mr. Chatman prefers a "phonemic" analysis to the now somewhat old-fashioned total "acoustic" way of trying to study either language or metrics. (Phonemic differences, we can never remind ourselves too often, are those that make a real difference in the structure of a language, like the difference between *d* and *t* in English, rather than the difference between your pronunciation of *t* and mine.) Phonetic studies, observes Mr. Chatman, "before the discovery of the phonemic principle," were not really getting anywhere with the understanding of language. "It is unfortunately a truism that one cannot get more structure out of a machine than one puts in" (p. 422). We hold that for metrical study it is indeed necessary to remember the phonemic principle—in the broadest sense, the principle of linguistic significance in phonetic difference. But it is also necessary, while we work within that principle, to practice an even further degree of abstraction. Not just all or any phonemic features—not all or any intonational features—but a certain level of these is organized by the poet to make a metrical pattern.

Let us turn for a moment to our other authority and point of departure for the present argument, Northrop Frye. Mr. Frye's chief emphasis, both in his English Institute essay and in his *Anatomy,* is on the similarity or continuity between the pentameter line of Milton or Shakespeare and the older (and newer) English strong-stress meter, *Piers Plowman, Everyman, Christabel, The Cocktail Party.* "A four-stress line," he says, "seems to be inherent in the structure of the English language" (*Anatomy,* p. 251; cp. *Sound and Poetry,* pp. xvii, xx). It is true that Mr. Frye does not identify the four-stress pattern of the pentameter line with its meter; he clearly thinks of the "stress" pattern and the "meter" as two different things; for example, in a reading of Hamlet's soliloquy, "the old four-stress line stands out in clear relief against the metrical background" (*Anatomy*, p. 251). Nevertheless, it is also apparent from his neglect of any specific discussion of "meter" that he attaches little importance to it; he does not seem to believe that it has much to do with what he calls, in his special sense, the "music" of poetry. "To read poetry which is musical in our sense we need a principle of accentual scansion, a regular recurrence of beats with a variable number of syllables between the beats. This corresponds to the general rhythm of the music in the Western tradition, where there is a regular stress accent with a variable number of notes in each measure" (*Sound and Poetry*, p. xvii). Rather than object more emphatically to Mr. Frye's views at this point, we allow our difference from him to emerge, as we go along, in later parts of our essay.

Let us round out our preliminary account of strong-stress rhythm by a return to Mr. Whitehall. Mr. Whitehall is much impressed by Kenneth L. Pike's principle (e.g., *The Intonation of American English*, [Ann Arbor, 1945], p. 34) that in English "the time-lapse between any two primary stresses tends to be the same irrespective of the number of syllables and the junctures between them" (*Kenyon Review*, XVIII, 418). Mr. Whitehall distinguishes a type of "rhythm" which he calls the *isochronic:* it "depends on equal time-lapses between primary stresses" (p. 420). And he finds in a line of Gray's *Elegy* three "primary stresses" and hence three isochronic sequences of syllables. It is not wholly clear whether the term "rhythm," as Mr. Whitehall uses it, embraces, excludes, or nullifies the concept of "meter," for

Hateful Contraries

Mr. Whitehall eschews the latter term. But when we consider his other technical terms, we can assemble a view very much like that of Mr. Frye. He speaks of *syllabic* "rhythms" (p. 420) and among these the *isoaccentual,* and he says that in Pope's *Essay on Man* there is "undoubtedly isoaccentual counterpointed with isochronic rhythm," while "in much of Milton" there is "isochronic counter-pointed with isoaccentual rhythm." The nature of Mr. Whitehall's "prosodic" observations might be made clearer if we were to substitute for one of his terms an apparent synonym: for "isoaccentual rhythm" read "meter," i.e., syllable-stress meter of the English pentameter tradition, Chaucer to Tennyson. In Pope and Milton there is both syllable-stress *meter* and an occasional pattern of strong stresses which can, if one wishes, be taken as a moment of the older strong-stress *meter*.

Again: when Mr. Whitehall speaks of "isoaccentual" rhythms, and when he speaks of "isosyntactic" rhythms, he is talking about ascertainable linguistic features, and hence about ascertainable and definable metric patterns. But when he adds that "the other type [of non-syllabic rhythm] is isochronic," he has slipped into another gear. This term is not on all fours with the others. Isochronism, observes Mr. Whitehall himself on an earlier page, is "not mentioned in the [Trager-Smith] *Outline*"; it is "not directly a significant part of the English linguistic structure" (p. 418). It is something which may or may not occur in correct English speech.

At the same time, let us observe that if isochronism *were* a general principle, or even an approximate principle, of all English speech, it would clearly be a different thing from

The Concept of Meter

meter. It would not serve to distinguish the metrical from the nonmetrical. Isochronism, according to the Pike theory, is not a special feat of language, managed by the poet, but a common feature of language. So long as a poet's lines had some strong stresses, and they always must have, the isochronism would take care of itself. In the actual English meters of the poets, even in the old strong-stress *Beowulf* and *Piers Plowman* meter, something quite determinate and special always *is* added: an approximately equal number of weaker syllables between the strong stresses, "configurational" heightening of the stresses, as by alliteration, and the syntactic entity of the lines and half-lines.

III

SOME, though perhaps not all, of those who approach the sound of poetry from the two viewpoints we are here debating will want to reply to our argument by saying that we have lost sight of the primary poetic fact, which, they will say, is always this or that reading of a poem out loud—as by the bard with a harp, by the modern author for a tape-recording, or by actors on a stage. What our argument takes as the object of scansion will be referred to disrespectfully as a mere skeleton of the real poem. Mr. Chatman, for example, "attempts to describe the verse line as it is actually 'performed.'" And he likes the Trager-Smith system because it "demands a comparison between actual oral performances of poetry and traditional meters." "It incorporates both formula and performance" (p. 423). Let it be so. Let the difference between our view and that of the linguistic recorders be something of that sort.

Hateful Contraries

There is, of course, a sense in which the reading of the poem is primary: this is what the poem is *for*. But there is another and equally important sense in which the poem is not to be identified with any particular performance of it, or any set of such performances. Each performance of the poem is an actualization of it, and no doubt in the end everything we say about the poem ought to be translatable into a statement about an actual or possible performance of it. But not everything which is true of some particular performance will be necessarily true of the poem. There are many performances of the same poem—differing among themselves in many ways. A performance is an event, but the poem itself, if there *is* any poem, must be some kind of enduring object. (No doubt we encounter here a difficult ontological question; we are not inclined to argue it. It seems necessary only to expose the fundamental assumption which we take to be inevitable for any discussion of "meter.") When we ask what the meter of a poem is, we are not asking how Robert Frost or Professor X reads the poem, with all the features peculiar to that performance. We are asking about the poem as a public linguistic object, something that can be examined by various persons, studied, disputed—univocally.

The meter, like the rest of the language, is something that can be read and studied with the help of grammars and dictionaries and other linguistic guides. In this objective study, Trager-Smith principles, for instance, may be largely helpful. At the same time they may be in excess of any strictly metrical need. For the meter is something which for the most part inheres in language precisely at that level of linguistic organization which grammars and dictionaries

The Concept of Meter

and elementary rhetoric can successfully cope with. So far as Trager-Smith is a refinement on traditional ways of indicating intonation patterns (by punctuation, by diacritical marks, by spelling and word separation), Trager-Smith may well be a help to saying something about meter. On the other hand, it may well become only a needless fussiness of symbols by which somebody tries to be scientific about the ever-present, the ever-different disparities and tensions between formal meter and the linguistic totality. Our argument is not specifically against Trager-Smith, but against certain ways of combining Trager-Smith with multiple readings. It is interesting to study the tape-recording of various performances of Frost's "Mowing." But we must not let this mass of data blind us to the possibility that some of our readers have failed to get the meter right.

In the same way we argue against the temporal theorists, the timers. In the broadest sense, we define their theory as one which says that meter either consists wholly in, or has as an essential feature, some principle of recurrence in equal, or approximately equal, times—analogous to musical pulse. And we respond, in brief, that meter must be a character of the poem, but that timing is a character of performance: what is done or can be done by a reader, a chanter, or a singer. Mr. John Hollander, in a recent article ("The Music of Poetry," *Journal of Aesthetics and Art Criticism,* XV [1956], 232-44) has warned us against confusing a "descriptive" with a "performative" system of prosody. This is just what the timers have done since the beginning. Reciting poetry in equal times is a matter related to music, and there is no question that music can be imposed on verse—very readily on some verse—and that here and there in the history of poetic recitation music has been invoked to fill out what the meter did not do—where in effect the meter was insufficient. But the musician or the musicologist who comes in to perform these services or to point out their possibility ought to remember what he is doing.

Discussion of English meters seems to have been badly misled for a long time now by a prevalent supposition that the two main alternative, or complementary, principles of English meter are time and stress. Karl Shapiro's handy guide to modern English metrical theory (*A Bibliography of Modern Prosody*, 1948) reports that this is indeed the major split in the whole field of English metrical theory (of which the two great champions are Lanier for the timers and Saintsbury for the stressers), and Mr. Shapiro himself seems to welcome this alignment and to consider it more or less correct and inevitable. But the two main alternative principles of English meter, as we shall argue more in detail a little later, are actually two kinds of stress—strong stress (the Old English, the *Piers Plowman* tradition) and syllable stress (the Chaucer-Tennyson tradition). The difficulty of describing the difference between these kinds of stress meter and their occasional difficult relations with each other account in part for the experiments of the temporal theory.

The basic arguments against the temporal theories of English meter are now almost universally accepted so far as one main branch of these theories is concerned, namely, the "quantitative"—the theory of long and short *syllables*, on the classical analogy. The history of English prosody affords the futile instances of the Elizabethan "Areopagus" and in the eighteenth and nineteenth centuries the luxuriance of theories described in T. S. Omond's sympathetic *English*

The Concept of Meter

Metrists (1921). So far as the Greek and Latin patterns of long and short (dactylic hexameters, sapphics, hendecasyllabics or the like) have been *successfully* reillustrated in English, this has been done on strictly accentual (plus syllable-counting) principles:

> This is the forest primeval. The murmuring pines and
>   the hemlocks . . .

> Needy Knife-grinder! whither are you going?
> Rough is the road, your wheel is out of order—
> Bleak blows the blast;—your hat has got a hole in't,
>   So have your breeches.

> O you chorus of indolent reviewers,
> Irresponsible, indolent reviewers. . . .

Syllables, number of syllables, and stresses, primary, secondary, and weak, are linguistic features which you can find in the English dictionary. But long and short syllables are not found in the English dictionary. Some syllables are, of course, often, perhaps nearly always, spoken more rapidly than others. But the length of the syllable is not a part of correctness or incorrectness in speaking English. Quantity, so far as it appears in any determinate way, more or less rides along with stress. We can drag or clip the syllables of English words, and we may sound odd, affected, or funny, but still we shall not be *mis*pronouncing our words, or changing their meaning. Quantity is a dimension where you cannot make mistakes in pronouncing English. And where you cannot make mistakes, you cannot be right, as opposed to wrong. It follows that in such a dimension a writer in English cannot create a public pattern. The English language will not permit a quantitative meter.

It would seem, however, that some kind of quantitative assumption must inevitably reappear (or be added to the linguistic facts) whenever the other main kind of temporal theory, the "isochronic," is applied in an actual scansion of lines of English verse. Syllables which in themselves may be recognized as having no correct quantity, either long or short, now have quantity conferred on them by crowding or jamming ("accelerating and crushing together"—Mr. Whitehall's terms) or by stretching, to meet the demands of the isochronic assumption. This kind of processing or adjustment of syllables is taken as a justification for, and is symbolized by, the use of musical notation, and such notation is sometimes called "scansion."

Let us ask the question whether it is *actually the case* that readers of poetry always, or even generally, do perform their readings isochronically.[3] (That this *can* be done, by a sufficiently skilful, or a sufficiently musical, reader no one of course denies.) It may be that we have here to acknowledge a distinction between two rather different kinds of verse. Perhaps it *is* true that nursery rhymes and ballads, at least some ballads, are usually, and normally, and even *best*, read with an approximation to isochronism. (This may have something to do with their origin in close connection with music.) The most convincing examples of musical notation produced by the equal-timing prosodists are in this area: "Mary, Mary,"—"O what is that sound that so thrills the ear?"—"It was 'Din! Din! Din!'" But then a Shakespeare sonnet or *Paradise Lost* or a lyric by A. E. Housman is a very different kind of thing.

The Concept of Meter

When a poem is set to music, definite values have to be assigned to its notes and rests, and consequently to its measures and phrases. And however this is done, we are introducing an extralinguistic element, a precision of timing that does not belong to the linguistic elements, the words and syllables, as such. Consider, for example, the opening of Ralph Vaughan Williams' setting of a Housman poem:

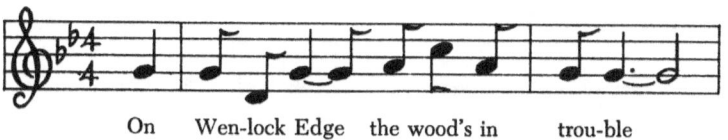

On   Wen-lock Edge   the wood's in   trou-ble

Thus we make "on" twice as long as "Wen-," or "Edge" three times as long as "wood's." For another good example, compare a normal *reading* of Edith Sitwell's poems in *Facade* with the way she recites them to the accompaniment of William Walton's music.

Both printed words and printed musical score are prescriptions, or directions, for performance. Our point is that they are different prescriptions—perhaps complementary and cooperating, but still different and independent. One, the musical score, is not an explication or explanation (like diacritical marks) of the other, the words, but an addition to it.[4]

Music—or at least music with bar-lines, which is all we are concerned with here—is precisely a time-measuring notation; it divides the time into equal intervals and prescribes a felt underlying "pulse."[5] It calls for the metronome or the tapping foot. If we ourselves wish to add to the poet's notation our own rhythmic pattern, say

Hateful Contraries

we are not scanning the verse, but either reporting on the way one reader performed it or else recommending that others perform it this way. Thus, Mr. Frye gives the following analysis of a line from Meredith's *Love in the Valley* (*Anatomy*, p. 254):

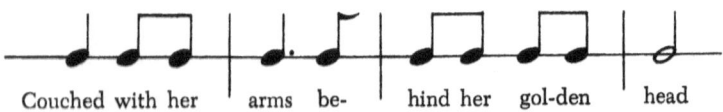

But another reader might, with equal plausibility, read it this way:

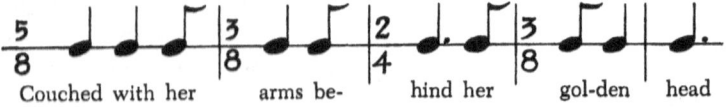

Meter involves measurement, no doubt, or it can hardly with much meaning be called "meter." But all measurement is not necessarily temporal measurement—even when the things measured occur in a temporal succession. If a person walks along the street hitting every third paling in a fence, he sets up a pattern, but he may or he may not do this in equal lengths of time. Better still, let every third paling be painted red, and we have a pattern which our person does not have to set up for himself but can observe objectively. He will observe or experience this pattern in time, but not necessarily in equal lengths of time. In either case, that of striking or that of simply seeing, we may further suppose the palings for some reason to be spaced along the fence at

The Concept of Meter

irregular intervals. Musical meter is a matching, or coordination, of two patterns, stress and time. But poetic meter is only one of these patterns. Why does one kind of measurement have to be matched with another kind? or translated into it? The measurement of verse is determined by some recurrent linguistic feature, peg, obstacle, jutting stress, or whatever. If we read this recurrence so as to give it equal times, this is something we do to it. Maybe we actually do, and maybe this is a part of our aesthetic satisfaction; still it is not a part of the linguistic fact which the poet has to recognize and on which he has to rely in order to write verses.

IV

THE METER inheres in the language of the poem, but in what way and at what level? We hold that it inheres in aspects of the language that can be abstracted with considerable precision, isolated, and even preserved in the appearance of an essence—mummified or dummified. An appropriate example is to hand and does not have to be invented. Back in the 1920's I. A. Richards was much concerned, and properly, to show that the movement or rhythm of poetry was closely inter-dependent with its other kinds of meaning. The movement, he argued, could hardly be said to occur at all except as an aspect of some linguistic meaning. Or at least it had no poetic value except as an aspect of some meaning. It is not quite clear which point Richards was making. But for the sake of his argument he exhibited, in his *Practical Criticism*, a contrivance which he called a "double or dummy"—"with nonsense syllables"—"a purified dummy." The dummy showed several things, perhaps a good deal more than Richards had in mind. For it certainly was not a *pure* dummy. How could it be? It was a linguistic dummy. And so this dummy did have a meter—perhaps even a kind of rhythm. If it did not have a meter, how could it be adduced as showing that movement, or meter, apart from sense did not have poetic value? You can't illustrate the poetic nullity of a certain quality taken pure by annihilating that quality. You do it by purging or purifying, isolating, the quality. And if you can do that, you prove that the quality can be isolated—at least from *certain* other qualities, in this case, the *main lines* of the linguistic meaning. In order to get even this dummy of a meter, Richards had to leave in a good many linguistic features.

>J. Drootan-Sussting Benn
>Mill-down Leduren N.
>   Telamba-taras oderwainto weiring
>Awersey zet bidreen
>Ownd istellester sween. . . .

"If any reader," says Richards, "has any difficulty in scanning these verses, reference to Milton, *On the Morning of Christ's Nativity*, xv, will prove of assistance."[6] There are, indeed, several uncertainties in Richards' composition which correspond to greater certainties in Milton's full linguistic archetype. Still the Milton is not necessary. Let us list some of the things we know about this dummy. The "nonsense syllables" are divided into groups (words). As English readers we find little difficulty pronouncing them. Some of the groups are English words ("Mill," "down,"); others are

The Concept of Meter

English syllables, even morphemes ("ing," "ey," "een," "er"). The capital initials, the monosyllables, the hyphens, the rhymes, give us very strong indications, absolutely sure indications, where some of the stresses fall. And there are some syllables, notably some final syllables, which are surely unstressed. If we don't inquire too closely how much any given stressed syllable is stressed more than another (and who is to say that we should make that inquiry?), we will indicate the scansion of Richards' dummy somewhat as follows:

J. Dróotan-Sússting Bénn
Míll-dówn Lédùren Ń.
 Telàmba-táras óderwáinto wéiring
Àwérsey zét bidréen
Ównd istèllèster swéen. . . .

The main uncertainties will be with the groups "Leduren," "Telamba," "Awersey," "istellester," where there will be a choice or guess in placing the stress. But the choice in no one of the four cases is crucial to the meter. You can choose either way and not destroy the iambics. And Richards' readers who have read this dummy and admired the ingenuity of the argument have certainly all along been giving the dummy the benefit of some implicit scansion.

The dummy does two things for the present argument. It illustrates or strongly suggests the principle that meter may inhere at certain rudimentary levels of linguistic organization, and, more specifically, that the kind of English meter of which we are speaking, so far as it depends on syllabic stress, depends not on any kind of absolute or very

Hateful Contraries

strong stress, but merely on a relative degree of stress—on a certain moreness of stress in certain positions. Of this latter we want to say something further before we finish. It is not a principle which is challenged by the linguists—though the exact sense in which they wish to apply it seems doubtful.

Let us now make some general prosodic observations. And first, that to have verses or lines, you have to have certain broader structural features, notably the endings. Milton's line is not only a visual or typographical fact on the page, but a fact of the language. If you try to cut up his pentameters into tetrameters, for example, you find yourself ending in the middle of words or on weak words like "on" or "the." Much English prose is iambic or nearly iambic, but it is only very irregular verse, because if you try to cut it regularly, you get the same awkward and weak result. Lines of verse are syntactic entities, though not necessarily similar or parallel entities. Depending on the degree of parallel, you get different kinds of tension between the fact of the lines and the fact of the overall syntax or movement.

Given the line then or the typographical semblance of a line (the possibility of a line) on the page, let us ask the question how we know we have a meter and know what meter it is. The line may indeed be only a syntactic entity and not metrical in any more precise way—as perhaps it is throughout Robert Bridges' *Testament of Beauty*[7] and in much so-called "free verse." With Mr. Whitehall we can call this a kind of "rhythm," *nonsyllabic, isosyntactic,* so long as the syntactic entities, the phrases or clauses, are "in strictly parallel sequence," as in Hebrew verse and in *some* "free verse." But this is in fact a very narrow restriction. It rules out all mere cutting of ordinary prose into its

The Concept of Meter

phrases or clauses (as in much free verse, and perhaps in Bridges or in parts of Bridges). For again, like Pike's isochronism, phrases and clauses are inevitable, and if they by themselves make a "rhythm" (or a meter), it is impossible not to write in this "rhythm" or meter. To get a meter, some other kind of equality has to be added to the succession of syntactic entities. (Even strictly parallel syntactic entities will be improved metrically by the addition of some more precise kind of equality.) The meter in the sense that it is internal to a given line or that it is something that runs through the series of lines is some kind of more minute recurrence—some exact or approximate number of syllables, with probably some reenforcement of certain syllables, some repeated weighting, what Mr. Whitehall calls a "configurational feature." Here if we take a wide enough look at the world's languages and literatures (at Chinese and classical Greek, as well as the Western vernaculars of our immediate experience), we can talk about pitch and quantity, as well as accent or stress. But for our discussion of English meters, stress is the thing. (Rhyme, assonance, alliteration too are auxiliary "configurational" and metric features—though Mr. Whitehall seems to count them out.)

The important principle of stress or accent in English verse is, however, a rather ambiguous thing, for there are in fact two main kinds of stress meter in English: the very old (and recently revived) meter of strong stress with indeterminate or relatively indeterminate number of syllables between the stresses, and the other meter, of the great English art tradition (Chaucer to Tennyson), which is a syllable-stress meter, that is, a meter of counted syllables and of both major and minor stresses.

Hateful Contraries

There are certainly some lines of syllable-stress meter which taken alone could be read also as strong-stress meter (four beats instead of five). To use one of Mr. Frye's examples:

> To bé, or nót to be, thát is the quéstion:
> Whéther 'tis nóbler in the mínd to súffer
> The slíngs and árrows of outrágeous fórtune . . .

But the precise number of syllables in syllable-stress meter is always somewhat against the strong-stress interpretation. One stress out of five in a pentameter line will inevitably be the weakest; still, because of the numbering of the syllables, and the alternation of the stresses, this fifth too calls out for some recognition.

> To bé, or nót to bé, thát is the quéstion.
> With lóss of Éden, tíll one gréater mán . . .

And then we have the matter of the whole passage, the whole act and scene, the whole book, the whole long poem to consider. And Mr. Frye admits that the strong stresses vary in number from eight (the maximum apparently possible within the conditions of the pentameter—a virtuoso feat achieved by Milton) and the scarcely satisfactory three (eked out in musical terms, for a line of Keats by Mr. Frye's assumption of a preliminary "rest"). But the "pentameter" in a long poem by Shakespeare, Milton, Pope, Wordsworth, or Keats is not subject to such fluctuations. The pentameter is always there. It is *the* meter of the poem. The strong-stress lines of four, of three, of eight, and so on, come and go, playing along with the steady pentameter—and it is a

The Concept of Meter

good thing they do come and go, for if every line of *Hamlet* or *Paradise Lost* had the four strong beats which Mr. Frye finds in the opening four or five lines, Mr. Frye would begin to detect something marvelously monotonous; he wouldn't be so happy about his "inherent" and "common" four-stress rhythm. One principle of monotony is enough; it is *the* meter of the poem. In "pentameter" verse it is the iambic pentameter.

A few lines of Chaucer, Shakespeare, Spenser, Pope, Wordsworth, Tennyson, read consecutively, can hardly fail to establish the meter. What makes it possible for the lighter stresses to count in syllable-stress meter is the fact that it *is* a syllable meter. Following French and classical models, but in an English way, the poets count their syllables precisely or almost precisely, ten to a pentameter line, and this measuring out makes it possible to employ the minor accents along with the major ones in an alternating motion, up and down. The precise measurement tilts and juggles the little accents into place, establishes their occurrence as a regular part of all that is going on.

Likewise, the clutter of weaker syllables in a strong-stress meter is against an accurate syllable-stress reading, most often prevents it entirely. A few lines of *Piers Plowman* or of *Everyman* ought to suffice to show what is what.

> In a somer seson, whan soft was the sonne,
> I shope me in shroudes, as I a shepe were,
> In habits like an heremite, unholy of workes,
> Went wyde in this world, wondres to here.

> Lorde, I wyll in the worlde go renne over all,
> And cruelly out-serche bothe grete and small.
> Every man wyll I beset that lyveth beestly
> Out of Goddes lawes, and dredeth not foly.

Hateful Contraries

This other kind of meter is older in English poetry and may be more natural to the English tongue, though again it may not be. Here only the major stresses of the major words count in the scanning. The gabble of weaker syllables, now more, now fewer, between the major stresses obscures all the minor stresses and relieves them of any structural duty. (Sometimes the major stresses are pointed up by alliteration; they are likely to fall into groups of two on each side of a caesura.) Thus we have *Beowulf, Piers Plowman, Everyman*, Spenser's *February Eclogue*, Coleridge's *Christabel*, the poetry of G. M. Hopkins (who talks about "sprung rhythm" and "outrides"), the poetry of T. S. Eliot, and many another in our day.[8]

Let us now return and dwell more precisely for a moment on the principle of relative stress. This is a slight but very certain thing in English; it is the indispensable and quite adequate principle for recognizing and scanning verses composed precisely of a given number of English syllables—or more exactly, for seeing if they *will* scan (for not all sequences of equal numbers of syllables show a measured alternation of accents). This is the main point of our whole essay: simply to reassert the fact of English syllable-stress meter, to vindicate the principle of relative stress as the one principle of stress which in conjunction with syllable counting makes this kind of meter. Mr. Chatman has already quoted the landmark statement about relative stress made by Otto Jespersen in his "Notes on Metre," 1900 (*Linguistica* [Copenhagen, 1933], pp. 272-74), and we need not repeat this. In speaking of this principle let us explain firmly, however, that we do not find it necessary to follow either Jespersen or Trager-Smith in believing

The Concept of Meter

in any fixed or countable number of degrees of English stress. We wish in the main to avoid the cumbersome grammar of the new linguists. For all we know, there may be, not four, but five degrees of English stress, or eight.[9] How can one be sure? What one can nearly always be sure of is that a given syllable in a sequence is more or less stressed than the preceding or the following. Or, suppose that there are, as Jespersen and Trager-Smith seem to agree, just *four* degrees of English stress. The discriminations are not needed for discerning the meter—but only the degrees of more and less. How *much* more is always irrelevant.

The main thing to observe about the principles of relative stress and counted syllables is that by means of these you can explain the necessary things about English syllable-stress verse. For one thing, quite starkly, you can tell an iambic line from one that is not iambic.

> Preserved in Milton's or Shakespeare's name.

When a student misquotes this Popean line in a paper, it is not our perfect memory of the poem but our sense of the meter (and our belief in meter) which tells us he has left out a word. The four-beat theory of the pentameter could not make this discovery.

To take another kind of example: let us suppose that Pope had written:

> A little advice is a dangerous thing.

Persons who say that the line is one of Pope's four-beat lines will be hard put to explain why it isn't a good line; it still has its four strong beats. Yet nobody can actually say that the revised line is a good Popean line and goes well

Hateful Contraries

with the other lines of the *Essay on Criticism*. And all we have changed is the position of one relative accent, which makes it impossible that the syllable "is" should receive a stronger accent than the preceding syllable, and hence impossible that there should be five iambs in the line.

A lít́tle advíce is a dángerous thíng.

That one shift of accent throws us immediately into the anapestic gallop, and we have a line that belongs in Anstey's *Bath Guide*.

Another kind of example:

Ah, Sunflower, weary of time.

Hardly the Goldsmith or Anstey anapestic gallop. Yet unmistakably an anapestic line. The strong syllables "Ah," and "flow-," coming where they do, create a heavy drag. Nevertheless, "sun" is even stronger, at least stronger than "flow-," a fact which is crucial. A reader can take the two opening syllables as he likes, as iamb, trochee, or spondee (if there is such a thing), and still not defeat the subsequent anapests. The very weak syllables "er" and "y" in two key iambic stress positions make it unthinkable that the line should be read as iambic.

Again: the beginning of the line is a characteristic place, in both iambic and anapestic lines, for the full inversion.

> Ruin hath taught me thus to ruminate.

> Whether 'tis nobler in the mind to suffer . . .

> Softly, in the dusk, a woman is singing to me;
> Taking me back down the vista of years, till I see . . .

The Concept of Meter

But:

Hail to thee, blithe spirit!

This is something different. The unquestionably iambic movement following the very strong first syllable[10] might, if we were desperate, be accounted for by saying that the word "Hail" breaks into two syllables, "Hay-ul," with a resultant needed extra weak syllable and the familiar opening pattern of iambic inversion. But a much more energetic and irrefutable assertion of the iamb appears in the progressive rise or stress increase of the three syllables "thée, blíthe spírit." (Note well: the slack of a given foot can be stronger than the stress of the preceding foot.) For a trochaic reading of this line, you would have to have "thée, blíthe," a rhetorical impossibility, making a nonsensically hopping line.

The notion of an accentual spondee (or "level" foot) in English would seem to be illusory, for the reason that it is impossible to pronounce any two successive syllables in English without some rise or fall of stress—and *some* rise or fall of stress is all that is needed for a metrical ictus. This fact produces in English iambic meter two kinds of ambiguous situations or metrical choices, that of two weak syllables coming together, and that of two strong syllables coming together. In each of these situations, the iambic principle is saved merely by the fact that certain unhappy choices are impossible.

Rocks, caves, lakes, fens, bogs, dens, and shades of death.

Certainly it is impossible to pronounce the first two, the first three, the first six syllables of this line with a perfectly

Hateful Contraries

even stress. On the other hand, no determinate pattern of stresses seems dictated. No doubt several are possible and are actually employed or experienced by various readers of this Miltonic passage. To us the most plausible seems as follows:

Rŏcks, cáves, lákes, fĕns, bógs, dĕns . . .

The more regularly iambic reading,

Rócks, căves, lákes, fĕns . . .

seems forced. The only reading which will clearly defeat the iambic movement is absurd:

Rŏcks, cáves, lăkes, féns . . .

Two weak syllables together present perhaps the more difficult problem. But all cases will not be equally difficult.

In profuse strains of unpremeditated art.

Here certainly the crucial fact is that "strains" is *more* stressed than "-fuse." Only observe that much—come out on the fourth syllable with an ictus, and the first two syllables can be stressed any way anybody wants. There are only two possible ways: "Ĭn pro-" or "In pró-". The second way, invoking a kind of Miltonic indult for the disyllable beginning with "pro-," makes the line more regularly iambic, but it is not necessary.

Upon the supreme theme of Art and Song . . .

This is the same thing, only pushed ahead to the second and third feet of the line. The situation of the four syllables here, two weak and two strong, has been described as a kind of compensation, a "hovering" of the accent, or as a "double or ionic foot" (Ransom, *Kenyon Review*, XVIII, 471). And doubtless some such notion does something to help our rationalizations. But we may observe also that only the coming together of the two strong accents makes possible the coming together of the two weak. "The" and "su-" are so weak only because "-preme" is so strong; and because "-preme" is so strong, "theme" has to be yet stronger. (Imagine a group of persons arguing about themes. One says theme X is good. Another says theme Y is good. Another says, "Yes, but the suprém̋e théme is Zeta." Just the reverse of the stress required in the Yeats line.) In a system where the only absolute value, the ictus, consists only in a relationship, we needlessly pursue a too close inquiry into the precise strength of the stronger point in the relationship. A somewhat more difficult, double, example of the two-weak, two-strong pattern is provided by Marvell.

To a green thought in a green shade.

One may begin by observing that whatever we do with the two pairs of weak syllables, it remains absolutely certain that "thought" is stronger than "green," and that "shade" is stronger than "green." (The relative strength of the two "greens" produces of course the peculiarity of the logico-rhythmic character of the line—the interaction of its sense with its meter. But here we speak precisely of the meter.) "To a," because of its introductory position, presents no difficulty. "In a" is more curious just because of its medial position. Probably a rather marked caesura, in spite of the

Hateful Contraries

continuing syntax and the shortness of the line, is created by the head to back juxtaposition of the two ictuses "thought" and "in." This again is part of the peculiar gravity of the line. The most plausible reading seems to us:

$$\text{Tó a gréen thőught ín a gréen sháde.}$$

If anybody wants to read:

$$\text{To a gréen thőught in a gréen sháde,}$$

arguing for two anapests compensated for by two single-syllable strong feet, there is probably no triumphant way to refute the reading. Still the lack of pause between "green" and the nouns which follow it is against the single-syllable foot. The single-syllable foot occurs in lines that sound like this: "Weave, weave, the sunlight in your hair."

Some of the most perplexing problems confronting the theorist of English meter—no matter to what school he belongs—are those arising in connection with the "dipody" or double-jump single foot ($x \acute{x} x \acute{\acute{x}}$). This foot was much used by narrative poets of the late Victorian and Edwardian eras and also, because of its accentual difficulties and ambiguities, has been a favorite ground for exercise in several kinds of temporal scansion. Regular or nearly regular instances of the dipody are perhaps easy enough.

$$\text{I wőuld I wére in Shőreham át the sétting óf the sún.}$$

A recent handbook remarks very sanely: "Although the meter is duple insofar as there is an alternation between unaccented and accented syllables, there is also an alternation in the degree of stress on the accented syllables . . .

The Concept of Meter

the result is that the two-syllable feet tend to group themselves into larger units" (Laurence Perrine, *Sound and Sense* [New York, 1956], p. 160). "You will probably find yourself reading it as a four-beat line." It is a kind of strong-accent meter, with number of syllables and minor stresses tightened up into a secondary pattern. An easy enough substitute for the dipody will be of course the anapest (x x x́). The iamb also (x x́) is available, and also the single strong-stress syllable, either at the start of the line, or just after a medial pause.

Broöding o'er the gloöm, spíns the broẃn eve-jar̋.

Thus dipodic meters can occur where no single line has more than two dipodies, and many lines have only one, and in these latter the reader may well have a choice just where to place the dipody. Meters of this sort are very slippery, elusive. One's first feeling on reading them may be that a strong lilt or swing is present, though it is hard to say just how it ought to be defined. A recurrent feature may be that the line seems to start on a strong stress, with falling meter, but then, with the aid of the agile dipody, swings up midway into a rising meter to the finish. The number of syllables in the line will vary greatly, and the principle of relative stress operates with a vengeance—the weaker syllable of the dipody showing all sorts of relations to the stresses of the other feet. It is a tricky, virtuoso meter, very apt in nursery rhymes and in the rakish, barrack-room, madhatter, pirate-galleon narratives of the era to which we have alluded above. Meredith's pleasant little monstrosity "Love in the Valley" is a striking instance of the difficulties. It seems safe to say that no *great* English poems have been accomplished in any variant of this meter. The theory of meter which we are defending is, we believe, better fitted to explain—and reveal the ambiguities of—the dipodic meter than any other theory. But the illustration and arguing of the point are perhaps beyond present requirements.

V

IT IS ONE of the hazards of an argument such as this that it is often on the verge of slipping from questions about something that seems to be merely and safely a matter of "fact" to questions about value. It is quite possible that some prosodists of the linguistic and musical schools would grant that meter, as we have described it, is a fact, but in the same breath would put it aside as of little consequence, at least when compared to the strong-stress pattern or some principle of equal timing. This was, for instance, the spirit of D. W. Prall's attack on the traditional metric in his *Aesthetic Analysis* (New York, 1936, esp. pp. 117, 130). Such a metric was trivial, "artificial," misleading. Our own difference from some recent writers may partly be reduced to a difference in emphasis, which reflects a different estimate of significance. We maintain not only that meter, in our sense, does occur, but that it is an important feature of verse.

To make out a broad-scale case for this claim might require much space and effort. Fortunately, we can do perhaps all that is necessary at the moment if we work upon an assumption that is now quite widely entertained, or indeed is a commonplace with students of poetry today: that there are tensions between various poetic elements, among

The Concept of Meter

them meter and various aspects of sense, and that these tensions are valuable.

One of the good features of Mr. Chatman's *Kenyon* essay is his constant appeal to an idea of "tension" between the full spoken poem and some kind of metrical pattern. "I believe that the beauty of verse often inheres in the tensions developed between the absolute, abstract metrical pattern and the oral actualization of sequences of English sounds" (p. 436). A student in a seminar presided over by one of the present writers was stumped, however, in scanning a line at the blackboard and refused to put the next stress mark anywhere at all. "I don't see how to show the interaction between the meter and the sense." As if by scanning he *could* show the interaction. As if anybody expected him to. As if the meter itself could be the interaction between itself and something else. This interest in tension, or interaction, is excellent. But how can there be a tension without two things to be in tension?

> Wóndring upón this wórd, quáking for dréde.
> (*Clerk's Tale*, 1. 358)

Here is a very special relation of phrase to meter. The double inversion, at the start of the line and again after the caesura, gives the two participial verbs a special quiver. But this depends on the fact that there *is* a meter; the inversions otherwise would not be inversions.

You can write a grammar of the meter. And if you cannot, there is no meter. But you cannot write a grammar of the meter's interaction with the sense, any more than you can write a grammar of the arrangement of metaphors. The interactions and the metaphors are the free and individual and unpredictable (though not irrational) parts of the poetry. You can perceive them, and study them, and talk about them, but not write rules for them. The meter, like the grammar and the vocabulary, is subject to rules. It is just as important to observe what meter a poem is written in (especially if it is written in one of the precise meters of the syllable-stress tradition) as it is to observe what language the poem is written in. Before you recognize the meter, you have only a vague apprehension of the much-prized tensions.

Perhaps it needs to be said that there is a difference between deviations from a meter (or "exceptions," as Mr. Ransom calls them) and the constant strain or tension of a meter (as an abstract norm or expectancy) against the concrete or full reality of the poetic utterance. The deviations are a part of the tension, but only an occasional part. The deviations occur only here and there—though some of them, the inverted first foot, the dropping of the first slack syllable, the extra slack syllable internal to the line (elided, or not elided in the anapest)—occur so often as to assume the character of an accepted complication of the norm. But the tension in the wider sense is always there. Here one might discourse on the "promotion" and "suppression" of syllables to which both the linguists and Arnold Stein refer. These are useful terms. There is no line so regular (so *evenly* alternating weak and strong) that it does not show some tension. It is practically impossible to write an English line that will not in some way buck against the meter. Insofar as the line does approximate the condition of complete submission, it is most likely a tame line, a weak line.

And thus: "scanning" a line is not a dramatic, or poetic,

The Concept of Meter

reading of a line. Scanning a line is reading it in a special, more or less forced, way, to bring out the meter *and* any definite deviations or substitutions. Scanning will not bring out the other parts of the tension; it will tend to iron them out. On the other hand, a good dramatic, or poetic, reading will tend to bring out the tensions—but note well that in order to do this it must be careful not to override completely and kill the meter. When that is done, the tensions vanish. (Another reason why the meter must be observed is, of course, that if a line is truly metrical, a reading which actually destroys the meter can only be an incorrect reading —by dictionary and rhetorical standards.) A good dramatic reading is a much more delicate, difficult, and rewarding performance than a mere scanning. Yet the scanning has its justification, its use. We would argue that a good dramatic reading is possible only by a person who *can* also perform a scansion.

"The trouble with conventional metrics," complains Mr. Chatman, "is that because it cannot distinguish between levels of stress and intonation, it often cannot distinguish meaningful from trivial performances" (p. 436). The answer is that metric is not required to do this, though it is needed for it. Mr. Chatman or another reader will have to make his own reading as meaningful as possible, but he will be in a better position to do this if he recognizes the meter. We are speaking all along, if not about a sufficient, yet about a necessary, rule for poetic reading.

If we may insert a brief pedagogic excursus: Schoolteachers nowadays, beginning in grade school and going right up into graduate school, probably try much too hard to prevent their students from a "mechanical" or thumped-

Hateful Contraries

out scansion, telling them rather to observe the variations, the tensions—telling them in effect to promote all tensions as much as possible. But the fact is that the tensions and the variations will pretty much take care of themselves if the student lives long enough and provided he is equipped with just one principle (of no precise application) that the variations and tensions are there and ought somehow to be recognized. The variations and tensions tend to assert themselves. The meter, because it is artificial, precisely measured, frail if meticulous, tends to be overridden and, if not actually destroyed (as it cannot be in any correct reading), at least obscured. This you can see if you ask college freshmen to scan a passage of Milton or to write fifteen lines in imitation. The probability is that the student of average gifts, if he has never at any stage of his schoolroom education been required or allowed to whang out the meter, is not aware that it is there and hence has very little notion of what the teacher means by the tensions.

For the word "tension," let us substitute at this point, in a concluding suggestion, the word "interplay"—meaning the interplay of syllable-stress meter with various other features of linguistic organization, but especially with those which are likely to set up other quasi-metric or rhythmic patterns. One of the disadvantages of the old strong-stress meter is doubtless its limited capacity for interplay. The stress pattern of the meter is so nearly the same as the stress pattern of the syntax and logic that there is nothing much for the meter to interplay with. The same must be true for all meters depending on patterns of repeated or parallel syntax—such as the meter of the Hebrew Psalms and the free verse of Walt Whitman. Where such meters gain in

The Concept of Meter

freedom and direct speech-feeling, they lose in opportunity for precise interplay. Conversely, where syllable-stress meters lose in freedom and naturalness of speech-feeling, they gain in the possibility of precise interplay. Perhaps this suggests a reason why the greatest English poetry (Chaucer, Shakespeare, Milton, Pope, Wordsworth) has after all been written in the more artful syllable-stress meter—not in the older, simpler, more directly natural strong-stress meter.

It is no doubt possible to think of many kinds of interplay, with many resulting kinds of total poetic feel. Maybe some of the languor and soft drag of Tennyson's verse, for instance, comes sometimes from the interplay between the rising iambic motion of the line and the falling trochaic character of a series of important words.

> It little profits that an idle king . . .
> To follow knowledge, like a sinking star . . .

Again, and very frequently in English verse of the tradition, the special rhythmic effects arise from the fact that the stress pattern of the iambics either more or less coincides with or more or less fails to coincide with the pattern of the stronger logical stresses, thus producing a movement either slow or fast, heavy or light.

That, like a wounded snake, drágs its slów léngth alóng . . .
Flies o'er th'unbending corn, and skíms alóng the máin.

The same kind of thing combines further with the number and length of the words involved in a line to produce contours of tension so special as perhaps better not translated into any other kind of meaning but simply regarded

Hateful Contraries

as shapes of energy. The 10,565 lines of Milton's *Paradise Lost*, all but two or three of them iambic pentameter lines, abound in illustrations of Milton's virtuosity. To show two extremes in one respect, recall a line we have already quoted and set beside it another.

> Rocks, caves, lakes, fens, bogs, dens, and shades of death . . .
> Immutable, immortal, infinite . . .

Eight strong stresses in one line; three in the other. But five *metric* stresses in either. And if that were not so, there would be nothing at all remarkable about the difference between eight and three.

It is, finally, possible, as we have already observed, that a given line in a given poet may invite scanning in either the older strong-stress way or in the Chaucer-Tennyson syllable-stress way—four beats by the old, five beats by the new. If a poem written on the whole in syllable-counting pentameters happens to show here and there lines which have one somewhat lighter stress and hence four stronger stresses, this is not very remarkable. For in the nature of things, as we have already observed, five stresses will always include one weakest. We have already sufficiently illustrated this phenomenon. But if a poem written on the whole in a meter of four strong stresses, with indeterminate number of syllables, at some point tightens up, counts syllables, and tilts minor accents into an iambic pentameter, this is something else. A wise and shifty modern poet, always in search of rhythmical invention, writes a stanza containing in the middle such a line as:

> Her hair over her arms and her arms full of flowers,

The Concept of Meter

and at the end:

> Sometimes these cogitations still amaze
> The troubled midnight and the noon's repose.

This is playing in and out of the metrical inheritance. Part V of *The Waste Land* begins:

> After the torchlight red on sweaty faces
> After the frosty silence in the gardens
> After the agony in stony places . . .

Coming after four parts of a poem written largely in strong-stress meter, these lines, with their marked swinging parallel of construction, will most likely be read at a fast walk as strong-stress meter, four stresses to the first, three each to the second and the third. But each is also a perfectly accurate pentameter line, each complicated in the same two traditional ways, the inverted beginning and the hypermetric ending. ("Whether 'tis nobler in the mind to suffer . . .")

It is probably not until about the time of Mr. Eliot and his friends that the free and subtle moving in and out and coalescing of strong-stress and syllable-stress meters in the same poem, the same stanza, begins to appear with any frequency. This is something remarkable in the history of metrics. But the understanding of it depends precisely upon the recognition of the few homely and sound, traditional and objective, principles of prosody upon which we have been insisting throughout this essay. Without recognition of the two distinct principles of strong-stress and of syllable-stress meter, it seems doubtful if anything at all precise or technical can be said about Mr. Eliot's peculiar rhythms and tensions.

Three

THE AUGUSTAN MODE IN ENGLISH POETRY

ONE OF THE MOST serviceable routines of "scientific" literary criticism is the proem which points to the deficiencies of earlier workers in the field. Yet this is a form which, often enough inept, would be especially so in the present instance. More than a little criticism of English neoclassical poetry, and in my opinion some excellent criticism, has been written in our own century and by critics who are still alive. From the work of the last ten years I select two essays which appear to me to converge very cogently in an argument which I now make my own. These two essays are "The Mask of Pope," by Professor Austin Warren, and that on Pope's verbal style entitled "Wit and Poetry and Pope," by Professor Maynard Mack.

Professor Warren's thesis is that English neoclassical poets wrote their best poetry under the sanction of the "play principle." They professed a strong allegiance to a standard of nature and reason, and to lofty ideals, the heroic and the sublime. They had a vision of an "ultimate and inclusive order" and inside that, sitting pretty, the smaller order of a modern civilization.[1] But guided by this vision they managed an *Annus Mirabilis* or a *Carmen Saeculare*, or erected the crystal palace of *An Essay on Man*, or conferred an elaborate new decorum upon the Virgilian and

Hateful Contraries

Homeric narratives. It was only on vacation from the vision and the ideal—with a ticket of satiric and burlesque license—that they engaged in the serious fun which an expressionist theory would call being true to themselves—an *Absalom and Achitophel*, a *Cadenus and Vanessa*, a *Shepherd's Week*, a *Rape of the Lock*, an *Arbuthnot*, or a *Dunciad*. As another modern critic has expressed it, "only an age of reason would put so much beauty into burlesque or would feel it needed the protection."[2] Perhaps the earliest writer to make the point was Samuel Johnson, with his remark that Gay's pastorals, though intended for burlesque, had the "effect of reality and truth." Swift's defection from the ideal, after his juvenile Pindarics, took the form of a relentlessly disgusted antisublime. Gay's mockery was chronic and frivolous. Prior's attempts to be serious are hardly important. Only Dryden and Pope, the greatest of the neoclassical poets, show important alternations between the modes, and if the effort of Pope's *Essay on Man* was nearly simultaneous with some of his most mature laughter, and if his Horatian poems are shaded between straight sober morality and satiric fun, this does not so much refute our theory as compel the admission that the challenge met by the neoclassical and in particular the Augustan poet was a complex one and the adequate response by no means an easy burlesque nihilism.

There is an accent of the genetic about this account which I think differs a little from what one might look for in a description of neoclassical poems constructed with a strictly critical purpose. Nevertheless, the insight seems to me accurate, and one that we ought to accept with gratitude. Working in another quarter, on the very surface of the poetry itself, in the rhetorical and ambiguous colors where

The Augustan Mode

the poet's conscious plans can perhaps be read with least certitude and least profit, Professor Mack reaches a conclusion that strikes me as the accurate counterpart of Professor Warren's. Augustan poetry, observes Professor Mack, was once called prose and more recently, in a more complimentary spirit, has been called "poetry of statement." In some sense it obviously is a kind of "poetry of statement." It sounds more like statement than much other poetry we can think of—the poetry of metaphysical violence, for instance, or that of romantic passion. Augustan poetry seems to sound like or to wish to sound like a statement about literary criticism, about ethics, or about cosmology, or perhaps like just a good clear statement of a story or a good clear description of a foolish or wicked character. As another recent critic has put it, the thing that normally "comes first" in the poetry of Pope and his friends is the "thought."[3] Or, it is the poetry of "coherence,"[4] or "intellectual" poetry. Or it solves "the aesthetic problem of reasoning in poetry."[5] A recent anonymous writer in the London *Times Literary Supplement* has revived with approval the notion entertained by Carlyle that Pope's use of language was a "cold-blooded use of language."[6] But Mr. Mack's thesis, demonstrated beyond cavil in a series of finely distinguished and graded examples, is that if Pope was a poet of "reason" or "statement," he had a very peculiar way of showing this. It is true that he had a verbal style which was to some extent limited and determined by the apparent aim of seeming reasonable and clear, by the neat couplets ending the thoughts of neat length, the exactly divided parallels and oppositions. Nevertheless—and this may seem extraordinary —it was also a style which in virtue of the same rules and

Hateful Contraries

limits had special invitations and encouragements to be unprosaic, even unreasonable. Only a passion for exact alignment, for precision work with words—so the argument runs—made possible the Augustan repertory of pregnant junctures, metaphoric insinuations, covert symbols, hinted puns, sly rhymes, cheating jingles and riddles. The tight frame of logic and meter kept words in their places, but in so doing forced them to exert all the more their interactive energies. The Augustan couplet at its best earned the displeasure of a severe critic, Mr. Dennis, in the same way—by wit and puns—that poetry in general earned the displeasure of a serious philosopher, Mr. Locke. This couplet poetry might look like a surrender to prevailing norms of clarity, distinctness, sweet reasonableness, science, and the order of nature. It was actually a polite evasion of all that. One might have thought it curious, on the face of the matter, that the great age of classical order should be at ease only in the Gothic and mystical shackles of rhyme.

II

THERE HAVE BEEN other ways of approaching the thesis which I am urging. The way of morbid psychology, for instance. English neoclassicism is the "expression through frivolity of concealed anxieties."[7] Or the sociological, which is perhaps in this instance more rewarding. Thirty years ago Professor Griffith remarked that the Augustan man of letters wished at any cost to appear as a wit and hence had to abhor pedantry, which meant any show of learning. Still he had to have knowledge and had to use it in his poetry. And this was one reason for the vogue of poems in the mode

The Augustan Mode

we call the Progress Piece, especially the burlesque kind, like *Dunciad III*. These poems permitted the poet to dramatize a tract of knowledge, to get it in "surreptitiously, as it were, and without prejudice."[8] The sociological color of this argument has come out more strongly in recent explorations of the "war" waged by middleclass sensible men—"men of sense"—Blackmore, for instance, and the elder Wesley—against aristocratic "men of wit," the "debauched crew" who followed Dryden.[9] Wit in this view became a "sin" ("no venial crime")[10] against normal sobriety—if not against normal dullness—and the more it was a point of pride among the Tory literati, the more it was resented by their antagonists. Wit glanced irreverently at the heights; the wit of Swift even presumed to be "reconciled" with "divinity."

One of Mr. Empson's less difficult analyses of the structure of "complex words" deals with the word "wit" as it appears for the well-known forty-sixth time in Pope's *Essay on Criticism*. We have three "wits," the poet, the critic, and the smart society man or elegant salon conversationalist. Rate one or another of these three "wits" plus or minus (honored or degraded) as he is compared one way or another with one of the others. But the main implication is that a poet ought to be not a pedant but a polished gentleman.

This is a different sort of sociological poetics from the upperclass celebration of security which is sometimes imputed to Augustan poets and their patrons.[11] That connected presumably, on the philosophic side, with the cosmic complacency to which we have already alluded, with a "spacious baroque optimism"[12]—to use an older phrase, with "The Peace of the Augustans." Nature, in such loftier reaches, seemed to refuse the garment of "wit," presumably looking upon it as *dis*advantageous. Near the end of the *Essay on Man* Pope himself makes what seems to me a lamentable recantation of a classical doctrine received in childhood.

> I turn'd the tuneful art
> From sounds to things, from fancy to the heart;
> From Wit's false mirror held up Nature's light.
> IV. 391-93

The pity is that he was more or less telling the truth. If, for example, the unearned optimism of the "ruling passion" which runs through Epistle II of the *Essay on Man* falls a bit short of being Pope's most impressive poetry, as I at least am inclined to think it does, one way to suggest the character of the shortcoming is to say that the lines would have trouble passing the salon test.

> See some strange comfort ev'ry state attend,
> And Pride bestow'd on all, a common friend.
> II. 271-72

This may be somewhat tedious, somewhat too comforting. A more tart expression, one that took proper advantage of human vanity and was safe from being found a partisan with it, would no doubt have been inappropriate in the context. Yet in a different context Pope had once before shown the witty side of the same platitude.

> Whatever Nature has in worth denied,
> She gives in large recruits of needful Pride.
> *Essay on Criticism*, ll. 205-206

Lord Chesterfield's advice to his son about cultivating poetic diction and his advice about cultivating the precise, unpretentious speech of a gentleman are equally in earnest, but these utterances do not occur in the same letter.[13] They represent a split in the Augustan ideal of eloquence—between a social side and a purely literary side—an opposition which the greatest of the Augustan poets was able to harmonize no more completely than the greatest of the salon conversationalists.

III

ONE GREAT DIFFERENCE between Augustan serious poetry and Augustan poetry for fun lies in how the poet has dealt with reality. The classical tradition of the mirror joined with the new rationalism and scientific standards of observation made Augustan professions of describing the reality very high. The classic metaphysical view that the most real is what is most basic and permanent—what is in a sense "ideal" —determined to a large extent the kind of reality that was aimed at in the loftier poems. The religious and literary standard of the "sublime" fitted in readily here too. The recognition of deviation and deformity—of evil, ugliness, and suffering—was hitched into such idealism by an argument about parts going into the whole, private into public (vices into larger virtues). "Whatever is, is right." That was one kind of reality—cosmic and total. The opposite sort of reality —commonplace and fragmentary—the unexplained, supposed real of literal everyday life, was something that Augustan poets did not much try to handle. Swift scores a moderate triumph because he has the wit to see that even the drollness of burlesque will sustain a "Description of the Morning" or a "Description of a City Shower" for only a limited number

Hateful Contraries

of lines. The subject is too drab and too innocent to be susceptible of much perversion. It is not clever of Gay to ramble on for three longish parts of a poem that gives mainly good advice on how to walk the streets of London without getting splattered. I believe his *Trivia* is a poem highly prized by historians of the city.

It is true that a classical theory of the comic stood ready to support a certain kind of realism. The Aristotelian characters of lower life became characters of ordinary life in the Roman formulas: *speculum consuetudinis, imitatio vitae*. The objects of comedy were supposed to be the recognizable characters of everyday experience (the more difficult to portray as the portrait was more subject to verification). In the specially Roman genre of satire also, the theory was realistic. The language of satire, a thing emphasized by Horace, was to be plain and unambitious, *sermo pedestris*. This clause gave much leeway for breaking poetic rules and having fun in a parvenu and not strictly titled genre. Horace summed up the situation in a passage of highly suspicious modesty.

I will strike my own name from the list of those I call poets. It is not enough to turn verses—especially if the thoughts are prosy *(sermoni propiora)*, as mine are. A poet has to have some real talent and inspiration, a big mind, and great powers of expression. That explains why some critics have been very much inclined to question whether comic drama is real poetry or not. It doesn't have enough strength and brilliance—either in its message or in its style. It is ordinary prose conversation put into meter. . . . Rearrange the words so as to break up the meter, and the character in the play is speaking the same as he would in real life.
Satire I, iv, 39 ff.

The Augustan Mode

It would remain for Joseph Warton to make an earnest application of this argument against the poetry of Pope, and for Percival Stockdale to undertake a demonstrative refutation.[14] Nothing, however, forbids our supposing that the Augustan poet himself on occasion found in this classic view some assistance for his rationalizations.

> And this unpolished, rugged verse, I chose,
> As fittest for discourse, and nearest prose.
> Dryden, *Religio Laici*, ll. 453-54

Yet classical comic realism had never dealt out straight, ordinary reality—any more than any other successful realism ever has. To explain what it did do is not easy. The universal meaning attributed to poetry in Aristotle's *Poetics* is one thing if related to the tragic hero and pushed in the direction of Aristotle's *Metaphysics,* but it is another thing if related to the comic deviational "character" which is defined in the *Poetics* and sketched in Aristotle's *Ethics.* The thirty *Characters* of Aristotle's pupil Theophrastus are all eccentrics— cranks, degenerates, misfits. They are a gallery of diseases, a nosology. Where then is the classic universal in any sense which one may relate to the metaphysical exemplar? It may be said that classical comedy teaches us ideals of human behavior by the method of contrasted deformities. And to this it may be added that Aristotle's *Ethics,* with its compliment to the ready-witted, ironic gentleman conversationalist and its alignment of him with the refined innuendo of "New" Comedy, shows that the rule in the *Poetics* that comic characters must be inferior was far from the whole truth. The classical comic, and after it the Restoration Molièresque comic, included along with the inferior butt the superior witty critic of the butt. This indeed was necessary—to escape the dullness of subnormality and to cast a lustre of the ideal (wit and intellect are always ideal) over the comic supposedly everyday real.

IV

MY VIEW IS that the English Augustans were, at their best and at their most characteristic, laughing poets of a heightened unreality. The world which the Augustan wit found most amusing and into which he had his deepest visions was an inverted, chaotic reality, the unreality of the "uncreating word,"—the "true No-meaning" which "puzzles more than Wit." The peculiar feat of the Augustan poet was the art of teasing unreality with the redeeming force of wit—of casting upon a welter of unreal materials a light of order and a perspective vision.

That is the truth despite all the intimations to the contrary which Augustan poets themselves may have uttered, all the rules which later scholars may have identified, to the effect that Augustanism is the direct incorporation of ideal reality, of reason and light—"one clear, unchanged, and universal light." That passage on Nature in Pope's *Essay*, like the rules for every poetic emergency urbanely recited by Horace, is perhaps best taken as a part of the author's mask. Augustan poets (along with the critic Dennis) could talk about the rules, they could in various ways introduce the rules as material into their poetical Arts of Poetry; but Augustan poets could not formally demonstrate the rules without being chilly. The *Essay on Criticism* furnishes posi-

The Augustan Mode

tive examples only of how to accommodate the sound to the sense. The best these poets could do for the rules—and it was uncommonly good—was to give burlesque examples of how the rules are violated. This explains why the liveliest Augustan prose criticism (it is not found in the Longinian terms of a Preface to Homer or of notes to Homer) sounds so much like the actual performance of Augustan poetry.

Thus, there was a rule derived from Aristotle and Horace that a literary character portrayal should be consistent and plausible—it should observe its "decorum."

> ... si forte reponis Achillem,
> impiger, iracundus, inexorabilis, acer.
> *Ad Pisones*, ll. 120-21

But this rule is not very exciting. It does not invite extra-illustration. Or at least the Augustans were not really so much interested in illustrating it as a Scaliger or a Vida might have been. The only way to make such a rule interesting is to subvert it. Chapter V of Pope's Scriblerian *Peri Bathous* prescribes how a modern poet of the "profund" might do this.

In the very *Manners* he will affect the Marvelous; he will draw *Achilles* with the Patience of *Job*; a Prince talking like a Jack-pudding; a Maid of Honour selling Bargains;[15] a Footman speaking like a Philosopher; and a fine Gentleman like a Scholar.

With the important difference in consciousness that made wit, this kind of garbled character was what the Augustan poet himself would execute in his poems.

> Rufa, whose eye quick-glancing o'er the Park,
> Attracts each light gay meteor of a Spark,

Hateful Contraries

> Agrees as ill with Rufa studying Locke,
> As Sappho's diamonds with her dirty smock. . . .
>
> Now deep in Taylor and the Book of Martyrs,
> Now drinking citron with his Grace and Chartres.
> Now Conscience chills her, and now Passion burns:
> And Atheism and Religion take their turns.
> *Moral Essay* II, 21-24, 63-66
>
> Now high, now low, now Master up, now Miss,
> And he himself one vile Antithesis.
> *Epistle to Arbuthnot,* ll. 324-25

The principle of unreality comes out in Pope's *Peri Bathous* even more starkly when he talks about outdoor nature. And here let me cite a curious parallel to a modern philosopher's view of the whole meaning of our modern Western art. In his *Dehumanization of Art* Ortega y Gasset remarks:

> It would be interesting to find out whether in the new artistic inspiration, where they fulfill a substantive and not merely a decorative function, images have not acquired a curious derogatory quality and, instead of ennobling and enhancing, belittle and disparage poor reality. I remember reading a book of modern poetry in which a flash of lightning was compared to a carpenter's rule and the leafless trees of winter to brooms sweeping the sky. The weapon of poetry turns against natural things and wounds or murders them.[16]

Beside that place the following passage of *Peri Bathous.*

He [the poet of the profund] ought therefore to render himself master of this happy and *anti-natural* way of thinking to such a degree, as to be able, on the appearance of any object to furnish his imagination with ideas infinitely *below* it. And his eyes should be like unto the wrong end of a perspective glass, by which all

The Augustan Mode

the objects of nature are lessened. For Example; when a true genius looks upon the Sky, he immediately catches the idea of a piece of blue lutestring or a child's mantle. . . . If he looks upon a Tempest, he shall have an image of a tumbled bed.

Chapter V

Ortega y Gasset begins his essay by professing a neutral descriptive purpose. Yet his description is so sympathetic as to sound much like an apology. Say what you will, he argues in effect, these *are* the modern values in art. See what you can make of them. Pope, on the other hand, is putting a finger on deviations from the norm of classical sanity. "Nobody can write that way without being ridiculous." The similarity of the two critiques, however, is striking, as is the general correspondence of *Peri Bathous* to the lavish subversions which characterize Pope's own poetry.

> In cold December fragrant chaplets blow,
> And heavy harvests nod beneath the snow.
> *Dunciad* I, 77-78

> The forests dance, the rivers upward rise,
> Whales sport in woods, and dolphins in the skies.
> *Dunciad* III, 245-46*

In all this there appears, I believe, more than a slight affinity between Augustan burlesque and the kind of unreality which during the period of Ortega's survey flourished in various forms of "expression" and "surrealism." The parallel between *Peri Bathous* and the conceptions of Ortega reaches its most exquisite in Ortega's introduction of the

---

* Cp. Horace, *Ad Pisones*, 1. 29: "Delphinum silvis adpingit, fluctibus aprum" (the negative rule) with Horace, *Odes*, I, ii, 9-12: "Piscium et summa genus haesit ulmo / Nota quae sedes fuerat columbis, / Et superjecto pavidae natarunt / Aequore dammae."

term "infrarealism." The English translation of the sentence by which this term is defined could scarcely sound more like a borrowing from Pope's ironic treatise. "Instead of soaring to poetical heights, art may dive beneath the level marked by the natural perspective."

V

THE SUBLIME VIEW of the world had, as we have seen, a way of facing and comprehending evil by assimilating it— the part into the grander whole, the definite ugly detail into the large mystery. This hypertheodicean tendency showed a fairly close sympathy for the less precise versification of the Miltonic influence, for the "philosophic" vocabulary, the newly pervasive benevolence, the apple-bearing landscape without original sin. And all these things had a comfortable relation with the softening, the tenderly emotive trend of the age, the sentimentalizing of comedy, the subsiding of tragedy (after the inflation of heroics) either into poetic justice or into a counterpart which we may call poetic injustice—the thing that Dennis disliked in Addison's *Cato*. Distinct from all these things and in many instances opposed to them, stood the aristocratic vice of wit—a different way of coming to account with evil.

If one looks about among the Augustans for a theory of laughter, one may come across some version of self-enhancement, the Hobbesian "sudden glory" (as in Addison's *Spectator* no. 47) or the more refined Shaftesburyan connection of laughter with freedom and hence with intellectual debate.[17] There was also the well-known satirist's apology: that men are willing to be thought scoundrels, but afraid of

The Augustan Mode

being thought fools, that satire is a public corrective of vice, that it "heals with morals what it hurts with wit." (Some allowance on our part for satirical disingenuousness would seem in order when the emphasis falls upon "healing.") In general these theories of laughter are antithetical not only to the psychologisms known to us of a later day but to the somber forms of transcendentalism and intuitionism where laughter itself and the comic literary genre have been seen as participating in the inferiority of the laughable object, in its mechanization, absent-mindedness, or conceptualized rigidity. The classical tradition of laughter, aside from the Platonic nervousness about comic contagion, in general honored and relished the act of laughter, though disparaging its object.* Augustan wit, in particular, was both very lively-serious (or lively-gloomy)[18] and very well aware of its own powers—even though, as we have seen, it was on holiday from poetic rules. Not in Swift, however, nor in Pope, nor in any of their friends, I believe, does one find so direct a statement about the relation of laughter to "serious" literature as this of Fielding's in the *Covent Garden Journal:*

It is from a very common but a very false Opinion, that we constantly mix the Idea of Levity with those of Wit and Humour. The gravest of Men have often possessed these qualities in a very eminent Degree, and have exerted them on the most solemn Subjects with very eminent Success. These are to be found in many Places in the most serious Works of Plato and Aristotle, of Cicero and Seneca. Not only Swift, but South hath used them on

* The misapprehension of Aristotle that appears in Ben Jonson's free translation of a Platonic passage in Heinsius' commentary on Horace ("As *Aristotle* saies rightly, the moving of laughter is a fault in Comedie"—*Timber,* no. 131, ed. Maurice Castelain [Paris, 1906], p. 133) represents, I believe, not so much a really agelastic attitude on the part of Jonson as a protest against certain forms of farce and slapstick.

the highest and most important of all subjects. In the sermons of the Latter, there is perhaps more Wit than in the Comedies of Congreve. . . . No. 18, March 3, 1752

Fielding's conception of a serious "wit" and "humour" may be understood from his own prose of the *Covent Garden Journal* as well as from his comic prose histories. He is the last of the triumphantly comic Augustans. (Dr. Johnson was very deeply touched by the strain of solemnity and feeling that overcame the Augustan laughter.) And Fielding's conception is above all exemplified in the mode of poetry—that established by Dryden and perfected by Pope —which it has been the aim of this paper to define. Augustan poetry at its best—let me recapitulate my argument—was the last stand of a classic mode of laughter against forces that were working for a sublime inflation of ideas and a luxury of sorry feeling. It did its work under a kind of disguise, by a kind of licensed escape or leave of absence from serious rules which it could not wholly afford to repudiate. It was a way of declining a prevalent and respectable disorder of the age—the now notorious "dissociation of sensibility"— while appearing to participate. Augustan poetry was a retirement from areas of "nature" that were beginning to look sterile, a spirited rearguard action in the retreat of Renaissance humanism before the march of science. It may have been the poetry of a "Silver Age," but when Shelley's friend Peacock later gave it that name, he did so without understanding either the challenge with which the poets were confronted or the character of their response.

THE FACT IMAGINED:
JAMES BOSWELL*

It would be difficult to argue which is the more striking thing—Boswell the man, living a certain eager and violent kind of life; or Boswell the author, writing a certain deeply engaged kind of journal. The *Journal* could not have been written without the life. The life will not actually be diminished or removed from focus if we consider it as the conscious enactment of a story for a journal, the more or less deliberate and daring involvement in an experience that came quite near, in alternating phases, to both the comic and the tragic of the literary categories. ("My avidity to put as much as possible into a day makes me fill it till it is like to burst." "It has occurred to me that a man should not live more than he can record. . . . I have so long accustomed myself to write a diary that when I omit it the day seems to be lost.")

Both Johnson and Boswell set great store by the very fact. "The value of every story," said Johnson (and Boswell recorded it), "depends on its being true. A story is a picture of either an individual or of human nature in general: if it be false, it is a picture of nothing." Boswell had been brilliantly successful, at the time of his first *London Journal,* in employing the dramatic perspective that came with some deliberate lag in "posting" his entries. Nevertheless, it was

* Copyright 1959 by Yale University.

Hateful Contraries

always a matter of moment to him that his *Journals* should have the kind of accuracy which came from his writing down some kind of record when the events were very "recent" in his mind. He would dispute the point with warmth and conviction against anybody who from *mere* memory, "at a distance of several years," ventured to question a statement he had published. "No man's memory can preserve facts or sayings with such fidelity as may be done by writing them down when they are recent." Sometimes a sketch of only a few words would later serve as a clue which he would confidently, and, we have reason to believe, accurately, expand into a detailed scene. At other times, when he was in fact writing up his *Journal* "from memory," after a lapse of even so short a space as three or four weeks, he might suffer from a feeling that what he wrote was "very imperfect." Let the literary critic be ready to concede that for diaries and journals the conviction of the individual historic verity does count heavily. Given a certain degree of fictive, of symbolic, of universal interest in a writing, if then the fact be known also to be present, a great enhancement does occur. A measure even of dead weight in the design, of mere fact, will be tolerated and will work in its own way to fortify the imaginative substance.

II

ON AN AUGUST AFTERNOON in Edinburgh, six judges of the High Court of Justiciary sit looking down upon a miserable man, a peasant butcher and drover of cattle who has been tried the day before on a charge of sheep-stealing. The jury of Edinburgh businessmen brings in a unanimous verdict of

The Fact Imagined

guilty. The counsel for the defence, James Boswell, steps forward and makes a plea to the judges that in view of certain circumstances which he believes are present, he be allowed a few days to muster an argument for mitigation of sentence. One of the judges is Boswell's father; another is a friend and encourager, but no less senior and sarcastic critic on occasion, the hanging judge and literary theorist Lord Kames. A third is the parvenu Ayrshire neighbor of the Boswells, Thomas Miller, Lord Justice-Clerk and Acting President of the Court, a man whose already publicly expressed attitude toward the defendant (and perhaps toward his counsel) may be taken as lethal in this situation. Each of these judges, starting with Alexander Boswell and ending with Thomas Miller, delivers his opinion. They mention the younger Boswell as well as his client. "I'm for indulging [the] young man." "Your counsel . . . has exerted all his talents and abilities. . . ." "Nothing remains to me now but to pronounce . . ." We have the very words of all six judges, or most of their words. Of the substantial sense and the key phrases, there can be no doubt—because Boswell, deeply intent, sympathetic, persevering counsel that he is, sole advocate of the woefully lost cause, at the same time does not in the least lose his awareness of himself as an experiencing, recording personality. On the margins of a printed petition in an inheritance cause a week old he scribbles the words—even the largely pompous and needless speech of Lord Coalston making the point that in industry and learning he himself is not unworthy to be sitting on that bench. Would this scene, as we partly edit and reconstruct it for Boswell, adding to his words some of the official documents—the verdict, the dreadful sentence (". . . by the hands

Hateful Contraries

of the common executioner upon a gibbet . . . pronounced for doom")—pass muster in a novel by Sir Walter Scott or R. L. Stevenson? How much would a free creative storyteller wish to alter the materials? In the face of what we have, the question becomes irrelevant. A certain powerful element of the universal, of symbolic interest—present beyond question—is here merged with the known and equally unquestionable historic fact. Something sombre and pathetic was enacted, by certain agents, of whom we know enough to conceive them in a deeply substantive way, as real persons—by Boswell, by his father, by the Justice-Clerk, by the doomed man. Add, too, our reflection on the remarkable chance, the wild improbability of our actually having this record. This true drama refuses to be measured completely by the norms of the fictional.

Having said that, however, we return to the categories—because these are all we can pretend to expound or criticize.

There is a certain kind of thing which Boswell is not very good at talking about. This is the external physical object or scene, especially if it is in some way curious and has to be described or explained. Place Boswell before a rude country gate, an old tower, a prehistoric arrangement of big stones, a cave, a landscape in the Hebrides, a machine for leveling a very steep hill, and he perhaps labors greatly, but not with much effect. He was well enough aware of this. "I am a very imperfect topographer." "I find I can do nothing in the way of description of any visible object whatever. Whether it is owing to my not seeing with accuracy, or to my not having the use of words fitted to such sort of description, I cannot say." Well then, if Boswell is unable to describe physical objects, how is it that certain scenes in

The Fact Imagined

his *Journals* stand out so vividly in our memory? "I walked down the high street of Edinburgh, which has a grand appearance in the silence and dusky light of three in the morning, and felt myself like an officer in a campaign." "I waited a little and then heard the great man. . . . The sound of his feet upon the timber steps was weighty. . . . He had on an old purple cloth suit, and a large whitish wig." "I was . . . conducted by a person in the Ambassador's livery to a seat just before the organ and fronting the altar. The solemnity of high mass, the music, the wax lights, and the odor of the frankincense made a delightful impression upon me. I was divinely happy." ". . . to the Temple Gate. Mr. Johnson could not stop his merriment. . . . 'Ha, ha, ha,' making all Fleet Street resound at the silent midnight hour. I went with him to his door, when he embraced me and blessed me." The principle of inner human relevance which works in these city scenes can hardly be disguised, even when they are cut down to such glimpses; it scarcely needs direct laboring. Still they are external scenes too, and this defines and gives edge to the inner relevance. Perhaps we may borrow some special illumination for the enquiry if we permit ourselves to turn aside and pursue Boswell for a moment of the year 1773 into the less characteristic outdoor and scenic paths of his Hebrides Tour—the environment which elicits from him those misgivings as to his descriptive power which we have quoted.

Most often there is not, in fact, any description at all—at least not anything that Sir Walter or Flaubert would have considered a description. The chief medium is the names of the characters, their grouping, and their words—always their words. There will be also, in some instances, something like a stage direction, in the most ordinary specific terms, concerning how things looked. This element may seem severely restricted, almost perfunctory. It too, however, can be quite important. Consider: "a large boat with eight oars," "a fine autumn Sunday morning" on the sea between Raasay and Skye, a party of seven passengers which includes the Raasay chief and a minister of the Gospel; and Samuel Johnson "with manly eloquence" delivers "a short discourse worth any sermon," on facing death, on punishment or annihilation, on a "trust in the mercy of God, through the merits of Jesus Christ." Immediately after, we come into the harbor of Portree and alongside a vessel "lying in it to carry off the emigrants" to America. A hinted seascape, a minimum of properties, a reminder of local history compose a contrasting frame of earthly circumstance which accents and marvelously deepens this lay sermon on the waves, gives to the snapshot gesture the definition of a drama. Not "paint," but the idea is Boswell's descriptive technique. Few readers, one may hazard, will fail to imagine this scene vividly—and it will scarcely matter that their images will differ as widely as their experience of seascapes, of boats, of sermons.

III

HUMAN BEINGS in the act of speech are always Boswell's focus, his medium, his idiom. This fact is ambivalent: on one side spontaneous and autobiographical, on the other, traditional and literary. On the one hand, Boswell himself is an active, an eager, a perpetual, a chronic conversationalist —never happy unless in company, scarcely even alive unless

The Fact Imagined

in company. He cannot remember what happened on a certain single day, he will say in writing up a back stretch of *Journal*. "I am pretty certain that I passed it in the plain course of business without being in company." On the other hand, the literary tradition from which both Boswell and his great mentor Samuel Johnson stem is that of the "apophthegm," the anecdote, the collection of *Ana*. "I love anecdotes," says Johnson. "I fancy mankind may come in time to write all aphoristically, except in narrative; grow weary of preparation and connexion and illustration and all those arts by which a big book is made." And Boswell thought "that there should be half a dozen of Ménages in every age to preserve the remarkable sayings which are often lost."

At certain times, especially when he was in the company of the London great ones, Boswell was content to play a very modest, though he believed an important, conversational role. "I have an admirable talent of leading the conversation; I do not mean . . . by playing the first fiddle, but . . . as one does in examining a witness." We notice, however, and perhaps with some dismay, that the conversational anecdote is very closely connected in Boswell's mind with the *bon mot*, the witticism, the ingenious simile, and especially the pun—the kind of thing which he records so extensively in his *Boswelliana*. And this again is very close to a more active and agressive side of Boswell himself as a conversationalist, heard most loudly at the Edinburgh supper and drinking parties among his Scottish advocate and writer friends. "I said I would rather see *Sir* George and the *goose,* than *St.* George and the *dragon;* and the garters of *onion* I called the collars of the order. . . . I was in admirable spirits from having spoken as I did." "Lord Alemoor . . . asked me if I ever studied beforehand the good things which I said in company. I told him I did not. I was really excellent company." And all this again is very close to those deliberate and ingenious similes which Boswell so often interrupts his *Journal* to develop—the mind of the essayist ("The Hypochondriack") at work excogitating materials. "Nothing worth recording was either said or done. But I shall here put down a simile which I made at Alnwick. . . . Facts . . . particular causes . . . are to principles, like sticks to peas in a garden. . . . This is a good idea, and upon some occasion . . . I may expand it."

We discover furthermore that Boswell has the opinion—or at least professes this opinion in a prominent place, at the end of the *Hebrides*—that the only conversation worth putting down for posterity to read is the brilliant sayings of the great and celebrated. "Few, very few, need be afraid that their sayings will be recorded." This formula works well enough, for the most part, so long as we are in the company of Johnson or some of the other members of the Club. The conversations of the Johnsonian circle, and especially of course Johnson's own thrusts, often give us the *bon mot* (the trenchant figure, not the pun) in its full size and might. Even in these conversations, however, the quality is often not brilliance, but something more homely—perhaps even the opposite of brilliance, as in the ambitious bungles, the habitual *étourderie* of Goldsmith. Think too of the more staple scenes of human intercourse, innumerable and varied —the tender, the sorrowful, the wrangling, the anguished— which fill the *Journals* and are their unremitting kind of merit. Boswell was oppressed in the presence of really dull

The Fact Imagined

persons. A certain energy and honesty of converse seems to have been his requirement in a companion. But it is hardly true that he always talked with brilliant persons or waited for brilliance before beginning to remember and record. He hardly could have.

Magazine writers of Boswell's day now and then employed, half in earnest, a kind of "Poetical Scale" or tabular score-board for comparing the merits of English poets. Under the head of some such term as "invention," we may imagine one of them, if required to compare Boswell's prose with the work of the poets, giving him only about five points (out of the possible twenty). He invents nothing, at least not in the literary sense; his invention comes just in the way he lives. Under some head like "arrangement" this critic, if he looked carefully, might have given Boswell perhaps eighteen or nineteen points ("The twentieth was never yet attained to"). The way he puts his persons and places together—arranges his scenes—we have noticed in the *Hebrides*, might well seem to be his greatest skill. And then the head of "diction"? Here the critic might have been nonplussed. In a certain sense it would have appeared to him that Boswell was not using diction at all—just words of no special kind or distinction, except perhaps for a moment now and then of essay style, when he tries to be like his hero Johnson. In the main, and in the best passages (when he is writing directly from the observed and felt life), he seems to think that the ordinary, the correct, name for every object and action suits his purpose better than any other. His narrative enjoys a kind of effortless immediacy of contact with his subject matter. No periphrase, no poetry, no tints in the medium, no bubbles. All is "plate glass," or looking through contact lenses. A compliment which Boswell elicited when he showed Johnson parts of the *Hebrides Journal* referred specifically to his avoiding Scotticisms, but it may be stretched a little to suggest Boswell's chief and most constant stylistic gift, his native and perhaps hardly conscious talent for saying things straight. "I said I wished he would translate it. 'How?' said he. BOSWELL. 'Into good English.' JOHNSON. 'Sir, it is very good English.'"

But that critic of the "poetical scale" who had set out to place Boswell according to the neoclassic categories might very conceivably not have pursued his discussion of the diction in this way. After noting that the words were plain and undistinguished, he would almost certainly have added that they were often "low." (Diction, 3!) There was hardly any object so low that Boswell would not name it by its correct name ("four combs, a pair of scissors, and a stick of pomatum," "a pot of lenitive electuary"). This was part of that fidelity which he cultivated. (It was an aspect of the actual difficulty, the anfractuosity, of life as seen, perhaps deceptively, through the simple and plain style.) It was not as if Boswell had theories about literature that were in advance of the prevailing taste and theory of his day. So far as he followed theory, he followed one branch, the biographical or the anecdotal, rather than the full-dress poetic. But in his practice he followed the biographical all the way, to its full consequences, without any of the buffering of implicit poetic decorum, of elegance, which appears, say, in the biographical writing of Mason's *Gray* or even in Johnson's *Lives of the Poets*. Boswell's autobiography, after being pillaged by Boswell himself of certain special parts for the *Life of Johnson*, dropped out of sight

The Fact Imagined

in its boxes and bundles. It comes to notice again in the middle of the twentieth century and sounds astonishingly like a segment of the fictional prose of this era.

IV

WE HAVE Samuel Johnson's advice to Boswell on how to keep a journal, delivered in the very swim of events during one of Boswell's London "jaunts." "The great thing is the state of your own mind; and you ought to write down everything that you can. . . . Write immediately while the impression is fresh." (Aristotle to Menander on how to get a laugh, to the tadpole on how to become a frog.) This advice can scarcely have seemed novel to Boswell, yet one part of it was impressive enough for him to repeat it in his *Journal* more than a year later. "Mr. Johnson said that the great thing was to register the state of my own mind." Years earlier, Boswell, in a moment of indolence and misgiving about his *Journal*, had argued with himself, "Does it not contain a faithful register of my variations of mind?" If we wish to understand why some of Boswell's narrations, even some of the most seemingly routine or perfunctory sketches of the shape of a given day, have their own interest and carry us on easily to the next day and the next, it is because Boswell is always talking about how his days and nights felt to him. It is always a cardinal point with him to be searching for happiness, to keep testing himself to see if he is finding it, to take his own emotional temperature, to look forward to his opportunities, and backward to estimate his successes and his failures. He tries hard to state explicitly; he is busy also arranging details to suggest. ("Words cannot describe our feelings. The finer parts are lost, as the down upon the plum." "The state of my mind must be gathered from the little circumstances inserted in my Journal.") The great days of London life when he hugs himself for joy, certain skillfully managed Edinburgh days of just enough work, just enough sociability, just the right kind and amount of food and the warming wine carefully "sucked," and on the contrary the days of madness and rampaging, of gross boldness, of violence and intemperance in convivial life, in drinking, in making love, and the subsequent days of oppressive melancholy and desolation—these stand forth conspicuously enough in the record. At the same time he is attentive to the days of quieter tone, the intermediate values. "I rose from the table quite cool, and several of us drank tea with the ladies. This was an inoffensive day." "We three drank a bottle of claret each, which just cheered me."

V

THE STORY of Boswell is the story of man's disobedience and its fruit, as that fruit grew ripe in the experience of a man who lived both marvelously in accord, and marvelously at variance, with the life of his contemporaries. Sing, terrestrial muse. . . . The literary mind of the age would have had the story, if not heavenly poetic, at any rate reasonably smooth and elegant or majestically grand. As a precocious Eton schoolboy in the year 1787 wrote in his Addisonian essay: the poet Chaucer "lived in a period little favourable to simplicity, and several meannesses occur throughout his work. . . . The state of equipoise between horror and laughter which the mind must here experience may be

The Fact Imagined

ranked among its most unpleasing sensations." Boswell himself records for us his friend Dempster's report on the historian Orme, who occupied himself reading "Euripides in Greek because his mind had to have something hard to chew." But "over one door [he had] a drawing of a boy painting. Over the opposite door, a boy playing on a flute. 'There,' said he, 'is my opinion of poetry; beautiful images and fine sounds.'" There was a part of Boswell's mind which was largely in rapport with this kind of taste and interest. "When fancy from its bud scarce peeped, and life's sweet matins rung," he wrote in a youthful poem, and he defended the lines in his *Journal:* ". . . I think them two beautiful allusions." "Auchinleck," he wrote later to a friend who was planning to enrich a progress poem with an allusion to the family and estate, "is a most unpoetical name. But it may be mentioned at the foot of a page." His favorite image for what delights him in verbal composition is the edible sweet—the "delicious" pineapple, "the dessert of rich flavor." Among his most frequent terms of praise for the conversation of Samuel Johnson are "majestic," "musical," "melodious."

Such expressions, however, do not bring us very close to the real imaginative principle in Boswell. Surely the most extraordinary thing about his management of human conversation and feeling in his life and in his *Journals* is his capacity (defying good taste) to entertain the jostling opposites—in alternation, in conjunction: good and evil, prudence and rashness, and all their attendant range of pleasure and pain, delight and woe. There is a special kind of reflective or aesthetic feeling—an accent of realization— which arises just out of the clash of the primary or immediate life feelings. One of these accents, a major one, is the laughable. Boswell was hitting to one side of the truth about this when in a *Hypochondriack* essay he recommended for the comic stage a certain "character compounded of two qualities, *each* of which may be the foundation of ridicule." The principle is actually somewhat wider, surely wide enough, for instance, to embrace Boswell himself standing before the bar of the House of Lords, Boswell recording of himself: "'My Lords,' said I, 'I speak with warmth for this schoolmaster who is accused of too much severity. I speak from gratitude, for I am sensible that if I had not been very severely beat by my master, I should not have been able to make even the weak defence which I now make. . . .' Lord Mansfield smiled." Boswell for the defence: comic mode.

A second major accent of realization is, with Boswell, not quite the classic counterpart or tragic opposite of the laughable, but rather a near neighbor living in certain interestingly uneasy relationships. Any kind of feeling at all, any internal commotion, may be enjoyable and may be deliberately sought and deliberately nursed in memory. He reads in a newspaper about the death of an earl whom he had long considered a great man of the world. "There is a pleasure in being to a certain degree agitated by events." And thus his repeated interviews with condemned men, his executions, and his funerals. ("I can never resist seeing executions. . . . One of weak nerves is overpowered by such spectacles.") And thus his own curiously flickering and detached, both complacent and assured, self-awareness on such occasions. His unselfish and anguished engagement in behalf of a doomed client merges with a quite satisfactory consciousness

The Fact Imagined

of his own role as eloquent defender and a prolonged exploitation of his opportunity as observer. "I was in a kind of agitation, which is not without something agreeable, in an odd way of feeling. . . . I enjoyed the applause." "I said, 'I suppose, John, you know that the executioner is down in the hall.' . . . Two o'clock struck. I said, with solemn tone, 'There's two o'clock.'" Boswell for the defence: quasi-tragic mode.

Such are his experiences in partisanship and sympathy. But an even more central theme of the *Journals* is the daily endurance of his own most personal and immediate version of the human tragi-comedy. One of the most constant things that Boswell knows is the vibration between indulgence and remorse—or their near simultaneity and union. "Drinking never fails to make me ill-bred. . . . I recollect having felt much warmth of heart, fertility of fancy, and joyous complacency mingled in a sort of delirium. . . . my wife was waiting all the time, drowsy and anxious." Sometimes the awareness is more tired and casual. In those nonce reflections, incidental and effortless observations, after a day or after a supper, of which the *Journals* are so full, often there appears a kind of puzzled estimate of dissatisfaction, its causes, its feeble remedies. "After every enjoyment comes weariness and disgust." "Our grave reflections on the vanity of life are part of the farce—like the grave ridiculous in comedy—for, after making them, we take a jovial bottle as if we never had thought."

Suppose that we ourselves, a modern reader of Boswell, had been living about the year 1755 and had been mature enough and shrewd enough, or clairvoyant enough (a kind of Rousseau or Voltaire with a vision of the future) to have been asked by some young Scot what kind of man he should strive to become in order to write a daily record of his life that would have a strong claim on the attention of a wide audience a hundred and fifty years later. To be honest, we should have had to give a combination of advice and diagnosis which would have ended with a preachment, something like this: "Let it be understood, then, that your eager pursuit of the varieties of human experience will necessarily entail much imprudence, much moral turpitude ('fornication . . . lasciviousness . . . emulations . . . strife . . . drunkenness, revellings, and such like'), much consequent debilitation and remorse. You will know moments of joyous realization, others of only feverish excitement, and many others of intense anguish, of black despair and oppression. The latter will become more frequent and settled as you grow older. Your life will not be long, and its closing years will not be happy.

"In short, the advice (even though we are *philosophes* and urge no theological scruples) is far from an exhortation that you do attempt to lead the kind of life that will be desirable, in some measure necessary, if you are to be the writer of a certain kind of engrossing journal. Other generations of readers, many years later, will gain by your enterprise. You yourself will pay a heavy price; so will your wife and your children."

Or, let us resume our actual vantage of the present moment and look back as seriously as we can. We ask the question, inevitably, how is this frank, this prideful, at moments even exultant record, not offensive? What is the quality or degree of Boswell's awareness of evil? ("Yet I am a very sensible, good sort of man." "I have one of the most

The Fact Imagined

singular minds ever was formed.") Does he really understand what he is? Does he enjoy the kind of perspective needed to shape such experiences as he endures into a record that commands our serious regard? We have to acknowledge first of all that this record proceeds throughout upon a kind of perception which is demonstrated in the expression. It is not a record or a confession by accident. When Boswell joins with the very jury at a tavern in a species of celebration on the coffin of a client, there is, it is true, no embarrassment, just a certain odd elation. Still it is Boswell himself who has acknowledged and joined these impressions for us. Another sensibility might well have screened, might well have bowdlerized and simplified—bidding for a higher degree of propriety, of the supposed tragic or sublime, of purity of "diction." The endless naiveté of Boswell, his profoundly childlike mentality, comes in here as a force in the self-dramatization. If only the writer have the accuracy, the courage, to portray his childlikeness! Childlikeness directly displayed is not like what leaks out unhappily around the edges of the dishonest attempt at self-concealment. Boswell is the man who does not blench at revealing that in a fit of domestic rage he threw an egg or a banknote in the fire, that in a moment of hilarity he lowed like a cow in the Drury Lane playhouse, that another time in London, mistaken for Wilkes, he was willing to pretend to be Wilkes, that in the provinces, at York, he talks to a man about Boswell's *Corsica* without letting on that he *is* Boswell. A pun or wild sally enveloped in Boswell's complacent report of it is a more interesting thing than the bare joke, presented on its own as a gem, in *Boswelliana*.

Boswell almost never, perhaps never for any extended

stretch, writes in complete ignorance or moral obtuseness. Even the exuberant whoring passages are likely to have their edging of apology, of rueful humor, their introspective accent, their partly foreseen and dreaded aftermath of remorse. ("In the midst of divine service I was laying plans for having women. . . . I imagine that my want of belief is the occasion of this.") The awareness of evil perhaps seldom or never reaches degrees of great reflective intensity. Still Boswell has a sense of evil—a feeling of it, the kind of painful impression which Johnson, after a day of fatiguing hospitality at Aberdeen, acknowledged in the words: "Sensation is sensation."

The analogy between Boswell and the sentimental hero of his day, the rake with the heart of gold in the picaresque or comic epic novel, is too striking to be resisted. Doubtless Boswell himself felt the resemblance, and he must have felt some special distress in the realization that his own true story could not end like the fiction of *Tom Jones*. ("Such a cloud of hypochondria. . . . I wish it may not press upon me in my old age.") The sentimental novels were a species of hagiography. They presented the rake as the hero of the new morality of the good heart. Boswell himself exemplifies that morality, but no author ever took less pains to glorify his hero than Boswell in his autobiography, less pains to make his readers *like* that hero.

Boswell and his *Journal* sometimes today do encounter the criticism that it is difficult to like Boswell. The question is hardly more relevant than a question whether we can *like* Hamlet or Heathcliff. Boswell writes a true story—beyond question—and this, as we have observed, is one undoubted source of its peculiar power. (In real life no doubt he did

The Fact Imagined

care very much whether he was liked. He tried hard to be liked.) At the same time, in the detachment of his writing, in the subtle ranges and conflicts of feeling which he manages, in his firmness of detail and purity of verbal style —in his general artistry as a journalist—Boswell projects himself as a figure of unique fictive significance. If we know what we are about as we read and respond to this extraordinary saga of self-portrayal, we shall hardly stop to wonder whether we do like Boswell, whether we ought to like him. (The very possibility of puzzlement is a clue to the situation.) In part no doubt we will like him. Who can fail to like the lover of Margaret Montgomerie, the patient correspondent of the neurotic Temple, the friend in need of Paoli, the devotee and biographer of Johnson, the desperate opponent of the Justice-Clerk, the counsel for the defence of the abandoned John Reid? At the same time there will doubtless be many respects in which we find it very difficult to like him. Why should we not admit this? What kind of purity, of whitewash, do we look for in the protagonists of our most impressive stories? The correct response to Boswell is to *value* the man through the artist, the artist in the man.

ELIOT'S COMEDY:
THE COCKTAIL PARTY (1950)

... be prepared for the coming of the Stranger,
Be prepared for him who knows how to ask questions.

IT IS CLEAR by now that *The Cocktail Party*[1] is an unusual success—at least in America. Eliot has performed the considerable feat of getting the Broadway audience to listen to a comedy of manners in which the manners are criticized. Making due allowance for the difference between criticism and sentiment, poetry and prose of a sort, Eliot and Cibber, we may say that *The Cocktail Party* shows the same relation to the work of Noel Coward as in 1696 *Love's Last Shift* showed to the work of Etherege or Wycherley or to the immediately subsequent *Relapse* of Vanbrugh. Eliot's play has had generous applause from the popular press but is so far anomalous among contemporary smart comedies as to have aroused at the same time, in some more fastidious organs, distinct expressions of unhappiness—the strident disapproval of the *Partisan Review*, the tolerant dismay of the *New Yorker* and reluctant reservations of the *Nation*, the courteous anguish of the New York *Times*.[2] Mr. Brooks Atkinson, who might be allowed to represent this select chorus of voices, after the fair-minded preliminaries speaks with the accent of the professional who knows his drama

Eliot's Comedy

and knows what it is not—missing the "fiery imagery" of Robinson Jeffers and satisfied that Eliot's "verse in this play derives from a sanctimonious attitude toward life rather than from the superior spiritual vitality of a poet."

The play has certain faults, the most startling of which seems to me to occur at the pinnacle, in Act III, where one part of the double outcome, that of martyrdom, aiming at something the opposite of tame, shoots both too far above the comic and too far wide of it, into the sensationally gruesome. The fate of Celia as reported by the nuntius Alex, returning from the antipodes to horrify and edify his cocktail circle with the news, insists far too explicitly on the meaning of her name—a girl indeed "enskied and sainted." "We found that the natives. . . . Had erected a sort of shrine for Celia Where they brought offerings of fruit and flowers." And I can see no excuse for the manner of her death (even though, as I understand, Eliot has considerably softened this since his rehearsal draft). "It would seem that she must have been crucified Very near an ant-hill." The failure of tact is only underscored by an elaborate introductory patter about monkeys, heathens, and Christian natives. It is no doubt proper to elicit and to answer the complaint of the Philistine: "Just for a handful of plague-stricken natives Who would have died anyway." But something more muted, nearly accidental, unheroic, was surely required. It could have been disagreeable enough. A later passage in the same scene seems closer:

> hunger, damp, exposure,
> Bowel trouble, and the fear of lions.

I think of the grim fantasy of immurement in the Amazonian

Hateful Contraries

jungle which ends Waugh's *Handful of Dust,* or a death in Conrad's *Heart of Darkness:* ". . . some man—I was told the chief's son— . . . made a tentative jab with a spear at the white man—and of course it went quite easy between the shoulder-blades." The most successful part of Act III is the other half of the double outcome, the reward of mediocre acceptance. The homely, patched-up felicity of the Chamberlaynes, glimpsed at the moderately more than average moment as they prepare for the second party, is beyond cavil convincing and just dramatic enough to be interesting. The problem of Act III was expository, how to level off. The climaxes of decision had been reached in Act II in Harcourt-Reilly's consulting room.

But the general objection raised by the naturalistic left is that the play is emotionally thin and cold, substantively skeletal and brittle, and the most special and well defined form which this objection has taken runs to the effect that the alternatives discovered in the priest-psychiatrist's confessional—either sanctity or resignation—exclude the joyful "fullness of natural life," or at least that this exclusion is implicit in the fact that so "boring and empty" a couple as the Chamberlaynes are allowed to represent "the ultimate possibilities of human love." Here I believe one has to go to the trouble of pointing out the *données* upon which, after all, the alternatives of the action are based, of distinguishing between literal statement and intensive symbolic dimensions, of defending Eliot for having been true to the materials with which he is working. The play makes no implications whatever, so far as I can see, about the limits of natural love (though it may intimate that these will be the fuller for being opened by something supernatural).

Eliot's Comedy

Two people who know that they do not understand each other,
Breeding children whom they do not understand
And who will never understand them.

No doubt the psychiatrist is talking of something which in its crude concreteness he believes to be fairly common, and no doubt we are asked to recognize something more elusive, a kind of loneliness which is ultimate and universal—though naturalists may be shy of mentioning it. But none of this is to make Edward and Lavinia paragons. "It is *a* good life," says the psychiatrist. The play opens with a modern mess, a set of people, an atmosphere, and a diseased situation which has grown, not surprisingly, out of this atmosphere. The psychiatrist too is a typical figure. The reunion of Edward and Lavinia under his auspices is not the marriage of Romeo and Juliet by Friar Laurence. We have to go out of our way to miss or disallow in Eliot's play a kind of allusion or general reference to what is traditionally done in the comedy of manners, a comedy, that is, dealing with the corrupt mores of the fashionable set. And at this level, the intrigue is managed perfectly. The last shift of Edward and Lavinia, even if it works a little better than they deserve, is yet but a shift and produces the kind of happiness which is the most that may be expected from the initial situation. (The choice of sanctity made by Celia, the translation of her limitless desire, is also plausible enough and has been determined in part through the same situation. If on the one hand she has "really had a vision," on the other her affair with Edward has been an unlucky effort to realize it. "I found . . . that we had merely made use of each other." It is not her choice, only the sensationalism of the outcome, at which, as I have argued, one may boggle.) The comedy of the Chamberlaynes must be taken in the extensive dimension, as what the play is talking about, immediately and literally. If we wish to find universal meanings, about the fullness of life, they are there too, plainly enough, but they relate only incidentally to the maximum possibilities of married love. The cocktail world, with its peculiar problems relating to marriage or to dedication, is one of numerous worlds, among which love and marriage themselves are but others, the career of the Great Gatsby another. The cosmos is a microcosm. We may be altogether out of it and yet meditate the difference between expansive self-realization and the humility of acceptance.

> When you find, Mr. Chamberlayne,
> The best of a bad job is all any of us makes of it—
> Except of course, the saints. . . .
> you will forget this phrase,
> And in forgetting it will alter the condition.

At this point I leave consideration of difficulties to say something in general praise of the language and rhythms of the play. "Heightened" and "perfected conversation," another reviewer has called it, "a new birth of eloquence in the theatre."[3]

> The word neither diffident nor ostentatious, . . .
> The common word exact without vulgarity,
> The formal word precise but not pedantic.

Nobody has described this any better than Eliot himself. It is straight-shooting language, scrupulously right, making possible the little joke tied in at the end of the phrase as if without effort:

Eliot's Comedy

> Finding your life becoming cosier and cosier,
> Without the consistent critic, the patient misunderstander.

Or the sinister incompleteness:

>   Mr. Peter Quilpe
> Was a frequent guest.

Or the flattened gnomic summation (far echo of "Prufrock," "Gerontion," or *The Waste Land*):

> Each way means loneliness—and communion.
> Both ways avoid the final desolation
> Of solitude in the phantasmal world
> Of imagination, shuffling memories and desires.

Shall we say that Eliot, in his determination to put poetic drama honestly within reach of an audience, has uttered a thinner and plainer version of the themes and images of his major and more densely implicated poems? To say so need not, I believe, be a disparagement. A play is something which an audience is to follow from sentence to sentence and understand in the main—though certain auras of significance may be missed. Even these auras will be thinner than the suffused coloration of "Gerontion" or a meditation in *Four Quartets*. In a comedy of manners they will be scarcely so smoky or lurid as in the choruses of *Family Reunion*. There are poetic virtues of chasteness, restraint, terseness, precision. These are the presiding virtues of Eliot's comedy.

Concerning the verse, Eliot has explained that in the less intense parts "the purpose . . . should be to operate upon the auditor unconsciously so that he shall think and feel in the rhythms imposed by the poet, without being aware of what these rhythms are doing." But this may be understatement. I find the meter, or at least the rhythm, a very marked thing throughout. At times, as in the first exchange between Edward and Harcourt-Reilly, it seems to have got the better of the actors, inducing a kind of antiphonal barking or rasping. The most remarkable thing about Eliot's meters has always been their heavy reliance on the logic, the word repeated and modulated (the *traductio*, the "turn"), the phrase paralleled and contrasted, the analogies of overflow from line to line—against these the prosody in the sense of syllables or stresses often seeming at a sunken level. Some of the most rhythmically original passages of *The Waste Land* might be described in this way—"After the torchlight red on sweaty faces After the frosty silence in the gardens. . . ." *Sweeney Agonistes* showed the method at its sharpest and jazziest clip. "I don't care. You don't care! . . . Well some men don't and some men do Some men don't and you know who." And so in *The Cocktail Party:*

> It's such a nice party, I hate to leave it.
> It's such a nice party, I'd like to repeat it.
>   *I* don't know.
> *You* don't know! And what's his name?

Brassy, chattery rhythms like these from Julia, or, in contrast, more intricate motions of strategy.

>   If another woman,
> She might decide to be forgiving
> And gain an advantage. If there's no other woman
> And no other man, then the reason may be deeper
> And you've ground for hope that she won't come back at all.
> If another man, then you'd want to remarry. . . .

Eliot's Comedy

EDWARD
But I want my wife back.

The lacing and variation of parallels develops the psychiatrist's insidious intent, hypnotically—to the point where Edward's bark is elicited. I suppose a very distinct set of rhythms might be analyzed for each of the important characters. One other, for instance, surely characteristic of Celia, might be termed the "And if this" climax of sweet, austere discountenance, toward Edward or toward herself.

> And if this is reality, it is very like a dream.
>
> And if that is the sort of person you are—
> Well, you had better have her.
>
> And if that is all meaningless, I want to be cured
> Of a craving for something I cannot find. . . .

Or the expression may appear split.

> Because, if there isn't, then there's something wrong, . . .
> With the world itself—and that's much more frightening.

This in a manner epitomizes the rhythm of Celia's experience and utterance.

But to resume our more tentative inquiry into the larger features of the play: Certain likely sources of irritation may be ranked under the opposite heads of too great and too little verisimilitude. But these may have an inverse importance for the reader of the text and the audience at the play. The opening cocktail chatter—a story about tigers and there *were* no tigers, Lady Klootz at a wedding but "I wasn't at her wedding"—strikes me as rather painful realism, a society version of what Dryden would have called "mechanic humour," or what today might be charged with the fallacy of "imitative form," the imitation of inanity becoming itself inane. On the stage, however, it works very well. The passage has an important exordial function as the effort of four guests led by a talkative old harridan to keep things going through a mysteriously awkward emptiness—on one flank the savage red expression of the host without his wife and on the other the deadpan of the Unidentified Guest. It is a very fine dramatic conception. But later in the same scene, when the chatterers have departed and Edward turns to face the residual stranger, values are reversed. Along with a mildly amusing triple pattern of mixing gin and water, we have the first fine speeches of Harcourt-Reilly, the poetic interest of which can scarcely be in doubt but which as dramatically realized may strain our suspension of disbelief somewhat beyond the voluntary. "Now for a few questions. How long married?" It is difficult not to be sidetracked in the reflection that a professional psychiatrist (or a mysterious stranger) would not go at it like this in a man's drawing room, and that if he did he would most likely be kicked out. Later again in the same scene, when through the return of Peter seeking advice in his bafflement about Celia, Edward himself is drawn into the role of confessor, we may think he has picked up a great deal from his brief encounter with the psychiatrist. "As the fever cooled You would have found that she was another woman. . . ." There is a sort of ventriloquism here which the unfriendly will attribute to Eliot himself.

Several other uncertainties, and these of a kind more structural for the whole play, ought to be mentioned. How could so superior a girl as Celia ever fall for a mutt like

Eliot's Comedy

Edward? Or, if we like, an alternative question (the two may not be simultaneously permissible): What is there about Celia that prepares us for the prophecy "She will go far"? Again, would Edward and Lavinia accept the blunt advice given by Harcourt-Reilly in the consulting room, or wouldn't they be precipitated into the nervous breakdowns on the verge of which they are already teetering? And, most obviously: How can two such fatuous cocktail characters as Julia and Alex be translated between the first and second acts into Guardian Angels?[4] I believe these questions do represent a real weakness in the play, a certain thinness of flesh and blood, though to some extent the reason for them is the same as that always behind improbabilities of the poetic drama—the demands of drama and poetry. How could Othello be so brutally gullible? Grant a certain implausibility, a veto on the questioning faculty, and see what happens. Nevertheless, the last of these questions, that relating to Julia and Alex, is one which I am particularly interested to look at, for it relates in a special way to the play's most internal, characteristic, and ticklish arrangements, the interaction of the plain meaning, the comedy and psychology of manners, with the more or less hidden and hinted meanings of morals and theology. Literal, moral, and anagogical, a medievalist might say, are the three levels of the play. It may be a nice critical task to say how well they are erected upon one another and how well consolidated. But one of the troubles for the critics may have been that the name of Eliot has made them look for something esoteric in places where the literal mechanics of the plot are mainly to be noted. At any rate there are places where it seems necessary to insist on the latter. Julia and Alex, for instance, turn out to be Guardians not just because this is needed for the symbolic progression, but also for the very solid reason that it is a main part of the intrigue. They are Guardians from the start, from the first strained moments of the cocktail party, where they are present because Edward has been unable to head them off (presumably, that is, because their telephones would not answer). They have brought with them two of the principals to Edward's uncomfortable quadrangle, Celia and Peter Quilpe—and, of course, they are connivers in the presence of the unidentified psychiatrist. A concerted plan (or perhaps at some points only a complication) is in progress and continues steadily that evening in their several visits to the flat on the excuse of searching for umbrella or spectacles or of feeding Edward, and the next day as they use the fiction of telegrams to marshall Peter and Celia to the flat at the moment of Lavinia's return. This continues through Act II in the carefully timed arrivals of Edward, Lavinia, and Celia at the psychiatrist's office and the auxiliary hovering activities of Julia and Alex. The preliminary conference between Alex and Harcourt-Reilly is in the best tradition of comic plot—the informative, unctuous, self-gratulatory exchange between the master plotter and his confederate (Lady Sneerwell and Snake).

One might of course put the question about Julia and Alex in this way: If they were not really silly, how could they act so silly, and for that matter, are they not acting a part which all their friends accept as normal? Julia alludes to this duplicity in the first scene, with an avowal rather like Prince Hal's while rioting with Falstaff.

> I know you think I'm a silly old woman
> But I'm really very serious.

Eliot's Comedy

This will hardly do by any grim standard of plausibility. But Julia and Alex no doubt deserve some indulgence as descendants in the honorable line of good-hearted irregulars —Falstaff, for instance, Tony Lumpkin, Charles Surface, Mrs. Erlynne, and the Devil's Disciple.

But it will be appropriate to insist somewhat further on the difficulty of drawing a clean contour for the plot of this play, apart from the symbolism, or of separating the comic and psychiatric from the penumbra of the supernatural—the Jungian from the actually religious. Edward's drab invention of a sick aunt in Essex (a topic about which, incidentally, he is ribbed too often and too late) might be taken as a lame prefiguration, coming from the prosy side, of more pregnant uncertainties. Perhaps it is part of Eliot's triumph that he has been able to disguise or soften the lines of his plot to the degree that the comedy may be looked on seriously. Or perhaps this goes too far. One might like to inquire, for instance, more precisely into the relation of Alex and Julia to Harcourt-Reilly. What kind of establishment does he run?—with cars at the patient's door at nine, and his hotel (called sanatorium by the naïve) and his real sanatorium, a house of religious retreat or what? I suspect that Mr. Yvor Winters will have a field day here in the discovery of "pseudo-references." Toward the end of Act II, Julia and Harcourt-Reilly speak of Celia in terms which slip over, though by ever so little, from the spiritual to the neo-Platonic or mysterious. "You and I don't know the process by which the human is Transhumanized. . . . Will she be frightened by the first appearance of projected spirits?" This is a little in the manner of the glosses to *The Ancient Mariner*, from Iamblichus, *De Mysteriis*. Harcourt-Reilly on first meeting

Hateful Contraries

Celia saw behind her chair the image of a Celia "whose face showed the astonishment Of the first five minutes after a violent death." Here Shelley has been invoked to some effect: *The magus Zoroaster. . . . Met his own image walking in the garden.* ("If this strains your credulity, Mrs. Chamberlayne, I ask you only to entertain the suggestion That a sudden intuition, in certain minds, May tend to express itself at once in a picture.") Perhaps the most successful of these passages, refraining from the mysterious but standing on choral and ritual tiptoe, is that which closes Act II in the consulting room, the two Guardians and the psychiatrist drinking their "libation" and reciting the formulas for hearth, roof, and bed, and for the journey. This sequence is neatly returned to comedy by the recollection of Peter Quilpe, "one for whom the words cannot be spoken." "Others," says Alex, "perhaps, will speak them. You know, I have connections—even in California."

There are several allusions to Harcourt-Reilly as the "Devil." "I was rather afraid of him," says Celia. "He has some sort of power." "If it's a machine," says Lavinia, "someone else is running it. But who? Somebody is always interfering. . . . I don't feel free." One may sense here a kind of presidency familiar in a wide range of admired fables, a fairy-tale capacity and absoluteness like that of Duc Theseus, or Duke Vincentio, or Sherlock Holmes, or The Man Who Was Thursday. This is something which many stories cannot get along without, and which we ought to move cautiously in trying to discredit. Harcourt-Reilly is the more interesting too for the hints that after all it is not he who is ultimate in his machine, but the silly and dreadful (or at moments charming) old person Julia. Julia "is always

Eliot's Comedy

right," says someone in Act I. But it is a surprising juncture in Act II when Harcourt-Reilly, fatigued from his double triumph, asks Julia for reassurance, and she says: "Henry, you simply do not understand innocence."

>   . . . when I say to one like her,
> 'Work out your salvation with diligence,' I do not understand
> What I myself am saying.
>
>   JULIA
>   You must accept your limitations.

What I take to be the most elaborate figuration of this partly occult motif occurs in Act I on Julia's return in search of her spectacles, when the Unidentified Guest wheels suddenly from the mantel and with monocle fixed in his eye sings tipsily the song of One Eyed Reilly.

>   As I was drinkin' gin and water,
>   And me bein' the One Eyed Reilly,
>   Who came in but the landlord's daughter
>   And she took my heart entirely.

At this stage of the game they are not admitting their acquaintance, and the apparent significance of the business is that the stranger is having a little fun and disguising his serious purpose from a fatuous and inquisitive old woman. But his cue for the one-eyed foolery is her preceding line about the lost spectacles (in her purse, incidentally, all the while): "I'd know them, because one lens is missing." Teiresias, I shall venture, has suffered a split, into the male half and the female, each blind in one eye, but seeing mighty well in concert. (We may read this if we like as a joke, a flourish, an Eliot signature.) The same order of symbolism, though less intricate and amusing, appears in the indigestible supper cooked up by Alex—in this scene mainly a nuisance, and apparently an imbecile. It appears later in the cinematic world of "images" where Peter Quilpe has found the *métier* which he understands.

The Cocktail Party is a play which for complete realization requires a friendliness toward certain semiallegorical ways of statement. And it will be better not to look to it for the kind of real-seeming fullness which we may have been taught to equate with poetic drama—because poetic drama has most often been tragedy. Comedy we know has always been privileged to present the flat or even the cliché character. And one other kind of drama has too—the morality. (Much will depend on whether, like Mr. Brooks Atkinson, we affix the term "morality" as a conclusive stigma, or, more circumspectly, employ it as the name of an interesting if remote tradition of our drama.) Eliot's play is perhaps the best morality play in English since *Everyman,* and the only comical-morality. The late Victorian problem comedy, one may add in passing, is a kind of middle plane hinted by analogy, and in one or two passages having the tables smartly turned upon it.

CELIA
Well, my bringing up was pretty conventional—
I had always been taught to disbelieve in sin.

The conversation between Harcourt-Reilly and his clients in Act II, especially that with Edward, may be said to establish a comic mode of its own, the high psychiatric. ". . . letting you talk as long as you please, And taking note of what you do not say." And this too may be a turning of

Eliot's Comedy

the tables, in that Harcourt-Reilly's advice to his patients, though not perhaps orthodox psychiatry, may yet be very good advice.

Eliot has before this, in his *Murder in the Cathedral,* successfully employed the conventions of the morality, aligned with tragedy and the chorus. In his *Family Reunion* he has joined tragic choral poetry and a contemporary setting ("Argos and England"), and in pursuit of an issue very similar to that of *The Cocktail Party.* The choice of Celia is essentially the same as that of the martyr Becket in *Murder in the Cathedral* and the same as that of Harry Lord Monchensey, the expiator of ancestral guilt, in *Family Reunion.* A quotation from the hectic closing scene of the latter play may make this sufficiently clear.

> I have not yet had the precise direction.
> Where does one go from a world of insanity?
> Somewhere on the other side of despair.
> To the worship in the desert, the thirst and deprivation,
> A stony sanctuary and a primitive altar. . . .
> A care over the lives of humble people,
> The lesson of ignorance, of incurable diseases. . . .
> I must follow the bright angels.

The difference between *The Cocktail Party* and both the earlier plays lies in the treatment of the alternative worldly choice. In *Murder in the Cathedral* this is a temptation the rejection of which costs intense spiritual effort but is clearly indicated. In *Family Reunion* it is curtly assigned to the dolt. "John shall be the master. . . . What would destroy me will be life for John." But in *The Cocktail Party* Eliot has had the wholesome inspiration of exploring the moral and comic possibilities of the humbler choice. Had he kept the complementary choice of sanctity somehow closer to the same key, he would have written on the whole a better play. But in any case *The Cocktail Party* is both a more contemporary and a more cohesive play than either of the others, rising in its most assured moments moderately and decorously from the comedy of manners to the levels of morality and theology.

PRUFROCK AND *MAUD:*
FROM PLOT TO SYMBOL

No CRITIC of Eliot, so far as I am aware, has yet ventured any comment upon the many passages in Tennyson's *Maud* which sound like antecedents to the poetry of Eliot and especially to *Prufrock*. The resemblances are partly disguised by the rollicking meters and the melodramatic plot in which Tennyson's themes and images are carried. Yet the main features of Tennyson's lyric monodrama, its themes of hesitation, removal, and frustration, its brooding melancholy, and its technique of pathological soliloquy, constitute a generally sustaining frame of reference, and if one begins to read with an alerted ear, the reward may be astonishing.

The images in *Maud* which I find most suggestive of Eliot fall into three main groups: (1) certain garden images of innocence and ecstasy occurring apropos of the protagonist's halcyon moments as a hopeful and then accepted lover; (2) certain confused images of a death in life, of a dream world, and of yet another realm of death, running through the immediately succeeding darker phase of the action; (3) miscellaneous images of weariness, suspicion, and fear occurring at various points.

> A voice by the cedar tree,
> In the meadow under the Hall!
> (I, v, 1)

Hateful Contraries

> Birds in the high Hall-garden
> When twilight was falling,
> Maud, Maud, Maud, Maud,
> They were crying and calling
> (I, xii, 1)

The birds, the voice, the tree, and the meadow, the vague and economically suggestive use of the prepositions *by, in, under,* convey an intimation of mysterious ecstasy much like that which may be heard in several passages of Eliot's poetry —in *The Hollow Men,* in *Marina,* in *Burnt Norton.*

> *There, is a tree swinging*
> *And voices are*
> *In the wind's singing . . .*
>
> *And the bird called, in response to*
> *The unheard music hidden in the shrubbery.*

Both in *Maud* and in *Ash Wednesday,* in *Burnt Norton,* and in *The Family Reunion,*[1] as well as in other poems of Eliot, these garden images are centered in that of the rose.[2] In *Maud* the "rose-garden" theme is insistently reiterated during the happier phase of the action, up to the moment when Maud steals out from the dance to the lovers' ill-fated meeting.

> For I know her own rose-garden,
> And I mean to linger in it
> Till the dancing will be over. (I, xx, 4)
>
> *Down the passage which we did not take*
> *Towards the door we never opened*
> *Into the rose-garden.*

In the next phase of Tennyson's story, the protagonist, separated from Maud by his own violent deed in the duel

Prufrock *and* Maud

with her brother and then by her death (sombre events which have been presaged in the theme of ancestral feud and in his own morbid broodings), endures the torment of a half-dreaming hallucinatory state and then a madness of death in life.

> In a wakeful doze I sorrow
> For the hand, the lips, the eyes.... (II, iv, 5)
>
> She comes from another stiller world of the dead.
> (II, v, 7)
>
> To have look'd, tho' but in a dream, upon eyes so fair.
> (III, vi, 1)
>
> *Eyes I shall not see unless*
> *At the door of death's other kingdom*
>
> *Eyes I dare not meet in dreams*
> *In death's dream kingdom*
> *These do not appear:*
>
> *Lips that would kiss.*[3]

The protagonist in *Maud* wakes, to a sullen roll of "thunder," as "a tumult shakes the city." In the "shuddering dawn," he beholds by the curtains of his bed, the cold, white "phantom" of his love,

> Without knowledge, without pity.... (II, iv, 7)
>
> *After such knowledge, what forgiveness?*
>
> Get thee hence, nor come again,
> Mix not memory with doubt. (II, iv, 8)
>
> ... *mixing Memory and desire.*

With these images and themes—the frustrated and maddened lover, the ghastly city, the living death and dreamlike

Hateful Contraries

commerce with a spectral figure—we arrive at the areas of meaning where *Maud* most closely anticipates *Prufrock*. Early in his monologue the protagonist of *Maud* shows the symptoms of fatigue, uncertainty, worry about his future, and dream-living which are so conspicuous in *Prufrock*.

> Ah, what shall I be at fifty
> Should Nature keep me alive,
> If I find the world so bitter
> When I am but twenty-five? (I, vi, 5)

> Did I hear it half in a doze
> Long since, I know not where?
> Did I dream it an hour ago,
> When asleep in this arm-chair? (I, vii, 1)

> *I grow old . . . I grow old . . .*
> *I shall wear the bottoms of my trousers rolled.*

> *Till human voices wake us, and we drown.*

Even at the peak of the protagonist's success and joy, the notion of a death in life appears.

> I have climb'd nearer out of lonely Hell.
> (I, xviii, 8)

> *giammai di questo fondo*
> *Non tornò vivo alcun.*

In the phases of the action which follow, during the protagonist's exile and madness, images of the infernal are blended with those of the ghastly city—a Baudelairean *fourmillante cité pleine de rêves*—in a way that anticipates both *Prufrock* and Part I of *The Waste Land*. The protagonist lies "Dead, long dead . . ."[4] Only a yard beneath the street,"

Prufrock *and* Maud

> With never an end to the stream of passing feet
> . . . .
> Ever about me the dead men go
> . . . .
> For it is but a world of the dead. (II, v, 1, 3)

And just before this, before madness sets in:

> (. . . *décor semblable à l'âme de l'acteur,*
> *Un brouillard sale et jaune* . . .)
>
> . . . the yellow vapours choke
> The great city sounding wide;
> The day comes, a dull red ball
> Wrapt in drifts of lurid smoke
> Of the misty river-tide. (II, iv, 9)
>
> *The yellow fog that rubs its back upon the window panes*
> *. . . the yellow smoke that glides along the street . . .*
>
> *Under the brown fog of a winter dawn,*
> *A crowd flowed over London Bridge, so many,*
> *I had not thought death had undone so many.*

As Tennyson's protagonist moves through his nightmare (in the phase just before his madness) he is afflicted with emotions more violent than those of Prufrock, but involving nevertheless much the same accents of dislike, misgiving, and suspicion.

> Should I fear to greet my friend
> Or to say, 'Forgive the wrong'? (II, iv, 12)
>
> And I loathe the square and streets,
> And the faces that one meets . . . (II, iv, 13)
>
> *Should I . . .*
> *Have the strength to force the moment to its crisis?*

Hateful Contraries

"Do I dare?" and, "Do I dare?"

There will be time, there will be time
To prepare a face to meet the faces that you meet.

The couplet which we have last quoted from *Maud* (probably the most precise resemblance to *Prufrock*) is part of the germinal lyric (II, iv) which Tennyson published first in 1837 in *The Tribute*. In 1853 (two years before the nearly coincidental publication of *Maud* and of the first of the *Fleurs du Mal*) Arthur Hugh Clough, anonymously reviewing several volumes of verse, among them the Glasgow "mechanic" Alexander Smith's spasmodic *Life Drama* and Arnold's *Strayed Reveler* and *Empedocles*, quoted Tennyson's lines (without attribution) in a passage so richly prophetic of the Eliotic *décor* that it may perhaps be quoted here with relevance.

There is a charm . . . in finding . . . continual images drawn from the busy seats of industry; it seems to satisfy a want that we have long been conscious of, when we see the black streams that welter out of factories, the dreary lengths of urban and suburban dustiness,
   the squares and streets
 And the faces that one meets,
irradiated with a gleam of divine purity . . . the true and lawful haunts of the poetic powers . . . [are] if anywhere, in the blank and desolate streets, and upon the solitary bridges of the midnight city, where Guilt is and wild Temptation, and the dire Compulsion of what has once been done— . . . there walks the discrowned Apollo, with unstrung lyre.[5]

If one cares to bolster the parallel between Tennyson and Eliot by an appeal to external records of intention, the materials lie ready enough to hand, both on the side of

Prufrock *and* Maud

Tennyson and on that of Eliot. One would point out, I suppose, that *Maud* carries the subtitle *A Monodrama,* and that Tennyson himself observed that the poem is "a little *Hamlet.*" And that he further observed that "the peculiarity of this poem is that different phases of passion in one person take the place of different characters." (*Let us go then, you and I* . . .) One would point out, with even more assurance, that Eliot has given several restrained testimonials of homage to Tennyson, and even of admiration for parts of *Maud.* In an essay of 1942 he has written:

A third long poem which was very much admired is 'Maud': a poem, I think, of forced and unreal violence, but containing two or three great lyrical passages which will last as long as the language.[6]

In his longer essay on Tennyson, a version of which he used as Introduction to his edition of Tennyson in 1936, Eliot had actually named the two or three lyrics in *Maud* which he so much admires. Two of these are lyrics of ecstatic lover's yearning: "O let the solid ground Not fail beneath my feet Before my life has found . . ." (I, xi, 1), and "Go not, happy day . . . Till the maiden yields" (I, xvii). A third is that garden song which we have already quoted: "Birds in the high Hall-garden When twilight was falling . . ."

Let us say, however, that the discussion should not dwell on such betrayals,* or on whatever inferences about Eliot's

---

* I myself should be quite unwilling, for instance, to make Tennyson the final interpreter of his own poem. The account which appears in the *Memoir* and the annotations seems to me off center in at least three respects, the emphasis on "the holy power of Love," that on the "blighting influence" of a commercial age, and the idea that the poem demonstrates any final redemption through "unselfishness." The main force in the poem is the protagonist's riot of unhealthy emotion. The jingo theme which is planted

Hateful Contraries

sources of inspiration might be wrung from them. It will better serve both critical and historical purposes if we inquire whether there are any ways in which these parallels between Tennyson and Eliot (as they are observable in the poems themselves) can actually instruct our reading of the later poet. Is it possible or profitable to think of Tennyson's *Maud* as a part of the complicated perspective of allusion to which we have already learned to look, the gallery of echoing panels against which we have already learned to throw our voices, in the reading of a poem by Eliot? It appears to me that a case may be made at least with respect to *Prufrock*. We have all along recognized Hamlet, Lazarus, John the Baptist, and Marvell's eager lover as Prufrockian analogues. A few years ago Professor Pope added the tortured figure of Raskolnikov with his impotence, indecision, and solitude, his faltering and revulsion as he climbs the stairs of the police office toward the confession of his murder. "He felt as though the fateful moment was still far off, as though he had plenty of time left for consideration."[7] (*Time to turn back and descend the stairs . . .*) Perhaps the example that comes closest to providing a model for the present argument is Prufrock's tired allusion to Marvell's pursuit of the "Coy Mistress." "Let us roll all our strength and all Our sweetness up into one ball."

> Would it have been worth while . . .
> To have squeezed the universe into a ball . . .

---

in several early parts of the poem and provides the resolution is quite gratuitous. Tennyson's partial misreading of his own poem corresponds to the imbalance which appears in the emotions of the poem itself. His original title *Maud or the Madness* was a better reading.

Prufrock *and* Maud

If it is relevant here that we think about Marvell, perhaps too, when we read Prufrock's reflections upon the yellow fog, the streets, and "the faces that you meet," there may be a gleam of relevance in our remembering the sufferings of Tennyson's protagonist along "the squares and streets," through the same yellow fog and amid "the faces that one meets." The contrast between *Prufrock* and Marvell is one between slumbrous indecision and highly purposive action. The contrast between *Prufrock* and *Maud* is one between that same indecision (a state of delicate introspection) and an action which erupts momentarily and disastrously out of a background of clouded and stormy brooding. Tennyson's *Maud* and to some extent the very similar *Locksley Hall* are poems of melancholy introversion. The heroes, like so many of Browning's soliloquizers and like Arnold's Empedocles,* are self-dramatizers. Yet the melancholy of the hero in *Maud* is so flamboyantly expressive as to seem almost entirely innocent of self-appraisal. It is clearly without any saving grace of irony. It is what the school of scribblers with whom Tennyson was temporarily in rapport deliberately aimed at being—"spasmodic." Marvell gives us the erotico-metaphysical antecedent to the Prufrockian love song; Tennyson, the "spasmodic." The cultural moment represented in *Prufrock* is one of decline—of strenuous emotion (we may venture to call it "spasm") fatigued, relaxed, retrospective.

"A set of objects, a situation, a chain of events which shall be the formula of that *particular* emotion," writes Eliot in

---

* "The dialogue of the mind with itself has commenced; modern problems have presented themselves; we hear already the doubts, we witness the discouragement, of Hamlet and of Faust" (Arnold, Preface to *Poems*, 1853).

Hateful Contraries

his essay on *Hamlet*. But in that essay he makes it far from clear in fact whether the "objective correlative" of which he is speaking has to be a set of events, like murder or incest, which are motives for emotion, or whether that correlative may not be just a set of images and "musical" intimations, the verbal expression of an emotion for which the motive may be very obscure. A compromise between these alternatives is what appears in Tennyson's "little *Hamlet*," a poem part plot and part sheer expression of emotion. The second, or symbolic, alternative, carried to a subtle excess, is what appears in Eliot's poem about a man who is "not Prince Hamlet—nor was meant to be." If we make allowance for Eliot's now customary (though I think often unfortunate) translation of such distinctions into terms of the poet's own person, we may see our point about *Maud* made in the negative part of Eliot's critique of that poem.

> I think that the effect of feeble violence, which the poem as a whole produces, is the result of a fundamental error of form. A poet can express his feelings as fully through a dramatic, as through a lyrical form; but *Maud* is neither one thing nor the other... In *Maud*, Tennyson neither identifies himself with the lover, nor identifies the lover with himself: consequently, the real feelings of Tennyson, profound and tumultuous as they are, never arrive at expression.[8]

To continue the discussion in Eliot's terms, we should have to say that in *Prufrock* the poet has so well identified himself with the dramatic figure as to confer on the emotions expressed the benefit of superior ironic intelligence. This makes *Prufrock* clearly a better instance than *Maud* of that "intellectual narcissism," or "advance of self-consciousness,"

Prufrock *and* Maud

which Eliot has more recently celebrated in a Progress of Poesy from Poe to Valéry.[9]

But to attempt a conclusion on a ground apart from such speculations: if we are to say that "symbolism" is anything which is present in Mallarmé and Eliot but is not present, or at least not in just the same way, in Tennyson or Shakespeare, we shall have to say that "symbolism" is a use of symbols in a largely "qualitative"[10] way, that is, with a logic which is independent of the story or set of motives on which, until late in the nineteenth century, the logic of symbols had ordinarily been very much dependent. The older mode of poetry exhibited a literal meaning (the story of Maud and her lover) and, coloring or interpreting this, a texture of metaphorically invoked symbols or of actual but symbolic properties (the "black bat night" and the rose-garden). But the newer mode (perhaps fulfilling a profound tendency of the older) exhibits a telescoping of the "vehicle" and "tenor" of the metaphoric structure, a fusion of story and symbol, so that all of the poem is one symbolic texture, much more comprehensive but also much less determinate than any structure built on an explicit story.[11] (*"Nommer* un objet, c'est supprimer les trois quarts de la jouissance . . .") In *Prufrock* it is nearly possible, tantalizingly plausible, to suppose a basic story of a little man approaching a tea party at which there is a woman to whom he might, except for his morbid hesitancy, propose marriage, or to whom he stands, rather, in such a casual relation that his very thoughts of proposal are almost hallucinatory. But the story frays out disconcertingly at the edges into its larger symbolic intimations—of indecision, of sterility, of a manifold and indefinable spiritual malaise. Are these the theme, and is Prufrock the symbol? Or is it the other way? The very vagueness of the feelings, of the "Idea," with which the hypochondriac and schizophrenic soliloquist is afflicted, the reflexiveness, the deep internality, the untranslatable "musicality" of the whole experience, are of course a counterpart of the formal or structural uncertainties. Both in what it says and in how it says this (both as expression and as craft) *Prufrock* is a poem which typifies the symbolist and postsymbolist era in poetry. As a monodrama of frustration and melancholy *Maud* is one of the many precursors of *Prufrock* and is a minor analogue. At the same time, in its more strongly motivated and overtly asserted yet violently exaggerated sentiments, *Maud* offers a typically Victorian contrast both to the denser yet less certain symbolic structure and to the introspectively shifty meaning of *Prufrock*.

Four

WHAT TO SAY ABOUT A POEM

What to say about a poem. How to say something special about a poem, different from what is said by the ordinary reader, different quite likely from what would be said by the poet himself. Our professional preoccupation as teachers, scholars, critics, sometimes conceals from us the fact that our kind of interest in poems is after all a very special thing—a vocational or shop interest, somewhat strained perhaps at moments, even somewhat uncouth. Poems, a cultivated person might suppose, are made to be read and enjoyed. If I read a poem and enjoy it, why should I then proceed to dwell on it as an object about which something deliberate and elaborate has to be *said*—unless in a surreptitious effort to borrow or emulate some of the self-expression enjoyed by the poet? What a critic or a teacher does with a poem is not, certainly, the main thing the poem is intended for or fit for. The poem is not the special property of these professionals. What they do with it in any deeper sense, what their purpose and methods are, we had better not try to say too quickly. It is the problem of this essay.

II

Many centuries of literary theory have equipped us with a large array of now more or less standard topics, handles or labels, for the analysis of poems. We are disciplined to speak of the *theme* (the most abstractive and assertive kind of meaning which the poem has), and we wish to distinguish this from its realization or more concrete definition in various expressive features conceived as denser, more real, than theme, and yet translucent with meaning. We speak of *diction, imagery, metaphor, symbol* (above all symbol); we sometimes resurrect such older terms as *personification, allegory, fable*. And in our most ambitious, or in our vaguer and more portentous, moments, we sum up such terms and magnify them into the name of *myth*. At the same time, we speak of the movement of the poem in time, its *rhythm,* and more precisely its *meter,* its *lines, stanzas, rhymes, alliteration* and *assonance,* its echoes, turns, agnominations, and puns, and also the more directly imitative qualities of its sound, the *onomatopoeia,* representative meter, and sound symbolism, the orchestration, and all that. Sound tangles with meaning. A whole poem has a *pattern,* both of meaning and of sound, interacting. It is an act of speech and hence a *dramatization* of a meaning; it is set in a landscape or a decor, an *atmosphere,* a world, a place full of flora and fauna, constellations, furniture, accoutrements, all "symbolic" of course. It is spoken by some person, fictitious, or fictive, if we rightly conceive him, a *persona*, a mask, a mouthpiece, and hence it has a point of view and a variety of emotive endowments, an attitude toward its materials, and toward the speaker himself, a self-consciousness, and a *tone* of voice towards you and me the readers or *audience*. And often we too, if we rightly conceive ourselves, are a part of the fiction of the poem. Or at least we read only over the shoulder of some person or group that is the

What to Say about a Poem

immediate and fictive audience. The poem is furthermore (especially if we are historical critics) a poem of a certain type or *genre* (tragic, comic, epic, elegiac, satiric, or the like), and this conception implies certain *rules*, a tradition, a decorum, convention, or expectancy. The genre and its aspects are in truth a part of the language of the sophisticated poet, a backdrop for his gestures, a sounding board against which he plays off his effects. Often enough, or perhaps always, the exquisite poem presents a sort of finely blended or dramatically structured opposition of attitudes and of the meanings which lie behind them—their *objective correlatives*. Hence the poem has *tension* (stress and distress), it lives in conflict; its materials are warped, its diction strained, dislocated. Catachresis is only normal. That is to say, the poem is *metaphoric*. The metaphoric quality of the meaning turns out to be the inevitable counterpart of the mixed feelings. Sometimes this situation is so far developed as to merit the name of *paradoxical, ambiguous, ironic*. The poem is subtle, elusive, tough, *witty*. Always it is an indirect stratagem of its finest or deepest meaning.

I have been running over some of the main terms of our inherited grammar of criticism and attempting just a hint at some of their relationships—the pattern, if not of the poem, at least of criticism itself. I hope it is evident that I am in no sense unfriendly to this grammar of criticism or to any one of the terms of which it is composed. I am all in favor of a grammar of criticism and of our making it as sober, tight, accurate, and technically useful as may be possible. The grammar, for instance, must be especially firm in the areas of syntax and prosody, where the poet himself has, at various times in various languages and poetic traditions, been compelled to be, or has allowed himself to be, most tight and technical. It is important, for instance, to know that *Paradise Lost* is written in iambic pentameter, and if we let ourselves be pushed around at the whim of random musical or linguistic theory into finding three, four, or seven or eight metrical beats in a Miltonic line of blank verse, we are making sad nonsense of literary history and of what this particular poet did and said. An analogous difficulty would be the enterprise of talking about the poet John Donne without the use of any such terms at all as paradox, metaphysical wit, irony.

On the other hand, grammar is grammar. And I will confess to a decided opinion that the kind of technical and quasi-technical matters which I have been naming ought to be discussed mainly at the level of generalization—they ought to be taken mainly as the preliminaries, the tuning-up exercises, the calisthenics of criticism. An essay on the theme of metaphor, of symbol, of lyrical dramatics, of irony, of meter, of rhyme or pun, is one sort of thing—it is likely to be extremely interesting and useful. But an interpretation or appreciation of a specific poem by the means mainly of an appeal to categories expressed by such terms is another sort of thing—this is likely in my opinion to be somewhat less interesting.

The purpose of any poem cannot be simply to be a work of art, to be artificial, or to embody devices of art. A critic or appreciator of a poem ought scarcely to be conceived as a person who has a commitment to go into the poem and bring out trophies under any of the grammatical heads, or to locate and award credits for such technicalities—for symbols, for ironies, for meter. These and similar terms will likely

What to Say about a Poem

enough be useful in the course of the critic's going into and coming out of a given poem. But that is a different thing. To draw a crude analogy: It would be an awkward procedure to introduce one human being to another (one of our friends to another) with allusions to commonplaces of his anatomy, or labels of his race, creed, or type of neurosis. The analogy, as I have said, is crude. Poems are not persons. Still there may be a resemblance here sufficient to give us ground for reflection.

I am supposing that the specific thing we are discussing is what to say about a given poem—rather than how to make a survey of poetry in general in order to write a grammar of poetry. Not the most precisely definable and graded features of poems in general, the accepted grammar, but something in a sense even more generic, the basic activity of our own minds by which we examine a given individual poem—this is what I now wish to talk for a while about. This activity of our own in examining a poem, let me add immediately and firmly, does suppose that an object, with definable features, is there, independent of us, for us to examine.

III

LET US, for one thing, remember, and observe in passing, that as teachers, for instance, we are likely to put ourselves in a Socratic relation to our pupils—setting them exercises, asking them questions. So that our own first question, what to *say* about a poem, is likely enough to assume the shape: what to *ask* about a poem. This I think is a very special, intrinsic and difficult aspect of our professional problem. If we assume that we do know, roughly, the correct things

Hateful Contraries

to say about a poem, how can these be transposed into good questions? Sometimes the very attempt will reveal the emptiness of what we thought we had to say. This question about questions is obviously a matter of art and tact, our own personality and that of our pupils, and I believe that nobody ought to presume to write any manuals about it. But let me stay long enough to suggest that a good question about a poem should have at least two qualities—it should stand in a middle ground between two kinds of fault. That is, in the first place, it should have in mind an answer that is better than arbitrary or prescriptive. It should not mean in effect merely: "Guess what I am thinking about. Or, tell me what I ought to be thinking about." "How does the imagery, or the meter, in this poem accomplish its purpose?" We may look on such a question, if we like, as setting an exercise, a way of eliciting or demanding an overnight paper. It is scarcely a part of a Socratic discussion. But then in the second place, the question ought not to be so good that it betrays or implies its own answer or the terms of its answer. "Is the imagery of the dead trees in this poem well suited to express the idea of mortality?" The answer that is being angled for ought to be more than simply *yes* or *no*—unless perhaps as a mere preliminary to some further and more real question. Sometimes, oddly enough, the two faults of question-making turn out to be the same thing—or at least some of our more careless questions will invite being taken in either of two ways, both empty. Rather accurate parodies of the world of discourse we teachers are capable of creating appear sometimes in the jokes, gags, or riddles (learned I suppose mostly over breakfast radio) which become the favorites of our youngest pupils. "What is large

What to Say about a Poem

and red and eats rocks?" A certain father tried to be the ingenious pupil and answered, "A large poem by William Blake." But that of course was wrong. The answer was: "A large red rock-eater." A good question should have a definite answer—different from the question and yet entailed by it. Some questions the teacher will ask mainly for the sake of giving himself the occasion for reciting the answer. (I do not say that is always bad.) A good question about a poem will be less like the example I have already given than like this other from the same source—though not exactly like this either. "What is the difference between a lead pipe and an infatuated Dutchman?" The father, though a teacher of poetry, gave up. The answer of course is that one is a hollow cylinder, the other is a silly Hollander.

IV

AT THE OUTSET what can we be sure of? Mainly that a poem says or means something, or ought to mean something (or ought to if we as teachers have any business with it—perhaps that is the safe minimum). The meaning of the poem may be quite obscure and difficult (rough, opaque and resistant to first glance), or it may be smooth and easy, perhaps deceptively smooth and easy, a nice surface and seemingly transparent. For either kind of poem, the simplest, but not the least important, kind of observation we can make, the simplest question we can ask, is the kind which relates to the dictionary. What does a certain word or phrase mean? We are lucky enough, I am assuming, to have a poem which contains some archaic, technical, or esoteric expression, which the class, without previous research, will not under-

Hateful Contraries

stand. If we are even luckier, the word has another, a modern, an easy and plausible meaning, which conceals the more difficult meaning. (Ambiguity, double or simultaneous meaning, our grammar instructs us, is a normal situation in poems.) In any case, we can put our question in two stages: "Are there any difficulties or questions with this stanza?" "Well, in that case, Miss Proudfit, what does the word *braw* mean?" "What does *kirkward* mean?" "When six braw gentlemen kirkward shall carry ye." We are lucky, I say, not simply that we have a chance to teach the class something—to earn our salary in a clear and measurable way. But of course because we hereby succeed in turning the attention of the class to the poem, to the surface, and then through the surface. They may begin to suspect the whole of this surface. They may ask a few questions of their own. This is success. A person who has been a teacher for a number of years masters the problem of knowing his lesson only to experience the more difficult problem of trying to remember what it is like not to know it.

V

THE ANSWERS to the kind of questions we have just noticed lie in a clean, dictionary region of meaning. This kind of meaning is definitely, definably, and provably there—some of our pupils just did not happen to be aware of it. Let us call this *explicit* meaning. I believe it is important to give this kind of meaning a name and to keep it fixed. The act of expounding this meaning also needs a name. Let us call it *explanation*—explanation of the explicit.

Obviously, our talking about the poem will not go far at

What to Say about a Poem

this level—not much farther than our translation of Caesar or Virgil in a Latin reading class.

And so we proceed, or most often we do, to another level of commentary on the poem—not necessarily second *in order* for every teacher or for every poem, but at least early and fundamental, or in part so. This level of commentary may usefully be called *description* of a poem—not explanation, just description. There is no way of describing the weather report, except to repeat what it says—describing the weather. A poem, on the other hand, not only says something, but *is* something. "A poem," we know, "should not mean but be." And so the poem itself especially invites description.

The meter of a poem, for instance, is of a certain kind, with certain kinds of variations and certain relations to the syntax; one kind of word rhymes with another kind (*Aristotle* with *bottle*, in Byron; *Adam* with *madam*, in Yeats); some conspicuous repetition or refrain in a poem shows partial variations ("On the Ecchoing Green. . . . On the darkening Green." "Could frame thy fearful symmetry. . . . Dare frame thy fearful symmetry"). Some unusual word is repeated several times in a short poem, or a word appears in some curious position. Some image (or "symbol") or cluster of images recurs in a tragedy or is played against some other image or cluster. Shakespeare's *Hamlet,* for instance, may be described as a dramatic poem which concerns the murder of a father and a son's burden of exacting revenge. At the same time it is a work which exhibits a remarkable number and variety of images relating to the expressive arts and to the criticism of the arts—music, poetry, the theater. "That's an ill phrase, a vile phrase; 'beautified' is a vile phrase." "Speak the speech, I pray you . . . trippingly on the tongue."

"Govern these ventages with your finger and thumb . . . it will discourse most eloquent music."

Description in the most direct sense moves inside the poem, accenting the parts and showing their relations. It may also, however, look outside the poem. *Internal* and *external* are complementary. The external includes all the kinds of history in which the poem has its setting. A specially important kind of history, for example, is the literary tradition itself. The small neat squared-off quatrains of Andrew Marvell's *Horatian Ode* upon Oliver Cromwell go in a very exact way with the title and with the main statement of the poem. Both in ostensible theme and in prosody the poem is a kind of echo of Horatian alcaics in honor of Caesar Augustus. The blank verse of Milton's *Paradise Lost* and the couplets of Dryden's translation of the *Aeneid* are both attempts to find an equivalent for, or a vehicle of reference to, the hexameters of Greek and Latin epic poetry. A poem in William Blake's *Songs of Innocence* is written in simple quatrains, four rising feet or three to a line, with perhaps alternate rhymes. These are something like the stanzas of a folk ballad, but they are more like something else. A more immediate antecedent both of Blake's metric and of his vocabulary of childlike piety, virtues and vices, hopes and fears, is the popular religious poetry of the eighteenth century, the hymns sung at the evangelical chapels, written for children by authors like Isaac Watts or Christopher Smart.

VI

WE CAN INSIST, then, on *description* of poems, both *internal* and *external*, as a moment of critical discourse which has its

What to Say about a Poem

own identity and may be usefully recognized and defined. Let us hasten to add, however, that in making the effort to define this moment we are mainly concerned with setting up a platform for the accurate construction of something further.

The truth is that description of a poetic structure is never simply a report on appearances (as it might be, for instance, if the object were a painted wooden box). Description of a poetic structure is inevitably also an engagement with *meanings* which inhere in that structure. It is a necessary first part of the engagement with certain kinds of meaning. (*Certain kinds*—in the long run we shall want to lay some emphasis on that qualification. But for the moment the point is that there is meaning.) In the critic's discourse "pure description" will always have a hard time taking the "place of sense."

Perhaps we shall feel guilty of stretching the meaning of the word *meaning* slightly, but unless we are willing to leave many kinds of intimation out of our account of poetry, we shall have to say, for example, that Byron meant that criticism had fallen on evil days—and that it didn't matter very much. "Longinus o'er a bottle, Or, Every Poet his *own* Aristotle." We shall have to say, surely we shall wish to say, that Milton in the opening of his *Paradise Lost* means, "This is the language and style of epic, the greatest kind of poetry; and this is the one theme that surpasses those of the greatest epics of antiquity." ("This"—in a sense—"is an epic to end all epics." As it did.) Alexander Pope in his *Epistle to Augustus* means, "This is a poem to the King of England which sounds curiously like the Epistle of Horace to the Emperor Augustus. Let anybody who cares or dares notice how curious it sounds." Shakespeare means that the action of *Hamlet* takes place on a stage, in a world, where relations between appearance and reality are manifold and some of them oddly warped.

Through description of poems, then, we move back to meaning—though scarcely to the same kind of meaning as that with which we were engaged in our initial and simple explanation of words. Through description, we arrive at a kind of meaning which ought to have its own special name. We can safely and usefully, I think, give it the simple name of the *implicit*. What we are doing with it had better too be given a special name. Perhaps *explication* is the best, though the harsher word *explicitation* may seem invited. The realms of the explicit and the implicit do not, of course, constitute sealed-off separate compartments. Still there will be some meanings which we can say are clearly explicit, and some which are clearly but implicit.

I believe that we ought to work to keep ourselves keenly aware of two things concerning the nature of implicit meaning. One of these is the strongly directive and selective power of such meaning—the power of the *pattern*, of the main formally controlling purpose in the well-written poem (in terms of Gestalt psychology, the principle of "closure"). It is this which is the altogether sufficient and compelling reason in many of our decisions about details of meaning which we proceed, during our discussion of the poem, to make quite explicit—though the dictionary cannot instruct us. In the third stanza of Marvell's *Garden*: "No white or red was ever seen / So am'rous as this lovely green." How do we know that the words *white* and *red* refer to the complexions of the British ladies?—and not, for instance, to white and red roses? The word *am'rous* gives a clue. The

What to Say about a Poem

whole implicit pattern of meaning in the poem proves it. In these lines of this poem the words can mean nothing else. In Marvell's *Ode* on Cromwell: ". . . now the *Irish* are asham'd to see themselves in one Year tam'd. . . . They can affirm his Praises best, And have, though overcome, confest How good he is, how just, And fit for highest Trust." How do we show that these words do not express simply a complacent English report, for the year 1650, on the ruthless efficiency of Cromwell in Ireland? Only by appealing to the delicately managed intimations of the whole poem. The cruder reading, which might be unavoidable in some other context, will here reveal (in the interest of a supposedly stolid historical accuracy) a strange critical indifference to the extraordinary finesse of Marvell's poetic achievement. "Proud Maisie is in the wood, Walking so early. . . . 'Tell me, thou bonny bird, When shall I marry me?'—'When six braw gentlemen Kirkward shall carry ye.' " How do we know, how do we prove to our freshman class, that the word *proud* does not mean in the first place—does not necessarily mean at all—conceited, unlikable, nasty, unlovable, that Maisie does not suffer a fate more or less well deserved (withered and grown old as a spinster—an example of poetic justice)? Only, I think, by appealing to the whole contour and intent of this tiny but exquisitely complete poem.

> "Who makes the bridal bed,
>   Birdie, say truly?"—
> "The gray-headed sexton
>   That delves the grave duly.
>
> "The glow-worm o'er grave and stone
>   Shall light thee steady.
> The owl from the steeple sing,
>   'Welcome, proud lady.' "

Hateful Contraries

The second thing concerning implicit meaning which I think we ought to stress is exactly its character as implicit —and this in reaction against certain confused modes of talk which sometimes prevail. It was a hard fight for criticism, at one time not so long past, to gain recognition of the formal and implicit at all as a kind of meaning. But that fight being in part won, perhaps a careless habit developed of talking about all sorts and levels of meaning as if they all were meaning in the same direct and simple way. And this has brought anguished bursts of protest from more sober and literal scholars. The critic seems all too gracefully and readily to move beyond mere explanation (Being a sophisticated man, he feels perhaps the need to do relatively little of this). He soars or plunges into descriptions of the colors and structures of the poem, with immense involvements of meaning, manifold explicitations—yet all perhaps in one level tone of confident and precise insistence, which scarcely advertises or even admits what is actually going on. The trouble with this kind of criticism is that it knows too much. Students, who of course know too little, will sometimes render back and magnify this kind of weakness in weird parodies, innocent sabotage. "I am overtired / Of the great harvest I myself desired," proclaims the man who lives on the farm with the orchard, the cellar bin, the drinking trough, and the woodchuck, in Robert Frost's *After Apple-Picking*. "This man," says the student in his homework paper, "is tired of life. He wants to go to sleep and die." This we mark with a red pencil. Then we set to work, somehow, in class, to retrieve the "symbolism." This monodrama of a tired applepicker, with the feel of the ladder rungs in his instep, bears nearly the same relation to the end

What to Say about a Poem

of a country fair, the end of a victorious football season, of a long vacation, or of a full lifetime, as a doughnut bears to a Christmas wreath, a ferris wheel, or the rings of Saturn. *Nearly* the same relation, let us say. A poem is a kind of shape, a cunning and precise shape of words and human experience, which has something of the indeterminacy of a simpler physical shape, round or square, but which at the same time invites and justifies a very wide replication or reflection of itself in the field of our awareness.

>   Till the little ones, weary,
>   No more can be merry;
>   The sun does descend,
>   And our sports have an end.
>   Round the laps of their mothers
>   Many sisters and brothers,
>   Like birds in their nest,
>   Are ready for rest,
>   And sport no more seen
>   On the darkening Green.

What experience has any member of the class ever had, or what experiences can he think of or imagine, that are parallel to or concentric to that of the apple-picker? of the Ecchoing Green?—yet the words of the poem do not *mean* these other experiences in the same way that they mean the apples, the ladder, the man, the sport and the green. The kind of student interpretation which I have mentioned may be described as the fallacy of the literal feedback. Proud Maisie translated into conceited Maisie may be viewed as a miniature instance of the same. And this will illustrate the close relation between the two errors of implicit reading which I have just been trying to describe. The uncontrolled reading is very often the over-explicit reading.

Hateful Contraries

VII

EXPLANATION, then—of the explicit and clearly ascertainable but perhaps obscure or disguised meanings of words; description—of the poem's structure and parts, its shape and colors, and its historical relations; explication—the turning of such description as far as possible into meaning. These I believe are the teacher-critic's staple commitments—which we may sum up, if we wish, in some such generic term as *elucidation* or *interpretation*.

It is difficult to illustrate these matters evenly from any single short poem. Let me, nevertheless, make the effort. Not to show the originality of my own critical judgment, but to keep within the area of what is readily available and plausible, I choose the four quatrains of William Blake's *London* in his *Songs of Experience*.[1]

> I wander thro' each charter'd street
> Near where the charter'd Thames does flow,
> And mark in every face I meet
> Marks of weakness, marks of woe.
>
> In every cry of every Man,
> In every infant's cry of fear,
> In every voice, in every ban,
> The mind-forg'd manacles I hear.
>
> How the Chimney-sweeper's cry
> Every black'ning Church Appalls;
> And the hapless Soldier's sigh
> Runs in blood down Palace walls.
>
> But most thro' midnight streets I hear
> How the youthful Harlot's curse
> Blasts the new born Infant's tear,
> And blights with plagues the Marriage hearse.

What to Say about a Poem

Let me remark briefly that Blake engraved and printed and illuminated this poem as part of a pictorially designed page. But I believe that this poem (if perhaps not all of Blake's similarly illustrated poems) can be fully understood without any picture.

A further special remark is required by the fact that an early draft of this poem, which is available in Blake's notebook, the celebrated Rossetti manuscript, gives us several variant readings, even variants of key words in the poem. Such avenues of access to the poet's process of composition, a favorite kind of resort for the biographical detective, may also I believe be legitimately enough invoked by a teacher as an aid to exposition. Surely the variant reading, the fumbled and rejected inspiration, makes a convenient enough focus on the actual reading. We suppose that the poet did improve his composition, and usually he did. So if word A is worse, *why* is word B better, or best? Comparison opens inquiry, promotes realization. Sometimes the discovery of such an unravelled thread, in our learned edition of the poet, will save a classroom discussion which was otherwise moving toward vacuity. Nevertheless I choose here not to invoke the interesting variants to Blake's poem, because I believe the existence and the exhibition of such genetic vestiges is not intrinsic to the confrontation of our minds with the poem. Not that to invoke the variants would be unfair—it is simply unnecessary. If we really need inferior variants, we can make up some of our own. And perhaps we ought to.

Perhaps there is no single word in this poem which calls for the simple dictionary work which I have defined as the level of mere explanation. But the word *charter'd*, used twice in the first two lines, is nearly such a word. At any rate, its emphatic and reiterated assertion, its somewhat curious ring in its context, as well as its position at the start of the poem, make it a likely word to begin with. How is a street chartered? How is the Thames chartered? A charter is a written document, delivered by a governmental authority, and granting privileges, recognizing rights, or creating corporate entities, boroughs, universities, trading companies, utilities. It is privilege, immunity, publicly conceded right. The Great Charter *(Magna Charta)* is a glorious instance of the concept in the history of men who speak English. I have been following, where it led me, the article under the word *Charter* in the *Oxford English Dictionary on Historical Principles*. But surely the great Dictionary is mistaken when under meaning 3.2 *figurative*. "Privileged, licensed," it quotes Shakespeare's *Henry the Fifth*, "When he speakes, The Ayre, a Charter'd Libertine, is still," and shortly after that, Blake, *Songs of Experience*, "Near where the charter'd Thames does flow." Surely the eminent Victorian person who compiled that entry was little given to the modern critical sin of looking for ironies in poetry. The force of that reiterated word in the first two lines of Blake's poem must have something to do with a tendency of the word, in the right context (and Blake's poem is that context), to mean nearly the opposite of those meanings of advantage listed in the Dictionary. For chartered privilege is a legalistic thing, which sounds less good when we call it vested interest, and which entails an inevitable obverse, that is, restriction or restraint. How indeed could the street or the river be chartered in any of the liberating senses listed in the Dictionary? It is the traffic on them or the right

What to Say about a Poem

to build houses along them that is chartered in the sense of being conceded—to somebody. And this inevitably means that for somebody else—probably for you and me—the privilege is the restriction. Thus the strange twisted aptness, the happy catachresis, of the wanderer's calling so mobile and natural a force as the river chartered at all. The fact is that this meaning of the word *chartered* is not listed in the *Oxford Dictionary*.

We began with the Dictionary, but we have had to go beyond it, to correct it in a specific point, and even to reverse its general drift. Examples of dictionary explanation of words in poems almost always turn out to be not quite pure.

To turn away from the attempt at such explanation, then —what opportunities do we find for simply *describing* this poem—and first, with regard to its immediate historical contexts? Perhaps some note on the chimney sweeper will be needed for our twentieth-century American pupils. We can look a little to one side and see Blake's angry poem *The Chimney Sweeper* in the *Songs of Experience:* "A little black thing among the snow, Crying 'weep!' 'weep!' in notes of woe!" We can look back and see the companion *Chimney Sweeper*, tenderly comical, poignant, in the *Songs of Innocence.* ". . . I said 'Hush, Tom! never mind it, for when your head's bare You know that the soot cannot spoil your white hair.'" An Act of Parliament of 1788 had attempted to prohibit the employment of chimney sweeps until they were eight years old. In winter they began work at 7 a.m., in summer at 5. Their heads were shaved to reduce the risk of their hair catching fire from pockets of smouldering soot. An essay on the eighteenth-century London practice of

Hateful Contraries

chimney-sweeping would of course be an explication, *in extenso*, of the third stanza of this poem. We could add notes too for this stanza on the wars and armies of the period, on the condition of the London churches (the blackening of Portland limestone outside—suppositions about the failure of the ministry inside, priestly symbols of oppression in other lyrics by Blake), or for the fourth stanza we could investigate harlots in eighteenth-century London. But I believe it is part of the power of this particular poem that it scarcely requires any very elaborate descriptive explications of this sort. "We can do pretty well with the poem," says one commentator, "in contexts of our own manufacture or out of our own experience."[2]

Another external point of reference, a part of Blake's immediate literary and religious tradition, has already been named—that is, when we alluded to the simple metrics and the innocent language of the eighteenth-century evangelical hymns. Blake's *Songs of Innocence and of Experience,* says one critic, are "almost a parody" of such popular earlier collections as the *Divine Songs Attempted in Easy Language for the Use of Children* by the nonconformist minister and logician Isaac Watts.[3] Blake knew that collection well. And thus, a certain *Song* entitled *Praise for Mercies Spiritual and Temporal.*

> Whene'er I take my walks abroad,
>   How many poor I see;
> What shall I render to my God
>   For all his gifts to me.
>
> .   .   .   .
>
> How many children in the street,
>   Half naked I behold!

What to Say about a Poem

While I am cloth'd from head to feet,
And cover'd from the cold.

The echoes of such socially innocent hymnology in the minds and ears of Blake and his generation make, as I have suggested, a part of the meaning of his vocabulary and rhythm, part of a historic London sounding board, against which we too can enjoy a more resonant reading of the bitterness and irony of the wanderer in the chartered streets.

But to turn back to the words of our poem and to inquire whether any *internal* features of it deserve descriptive notice: For one thing, I should want a class to notice how the simple hymn-like stanzas of this poem are fortified or specialized in a remarkable way by a kind of phonemic tune, or prominent and stark, almost harsh, succession of similar emphatic syllables. This tune is announced in the opening verb *wander,* then immediately picked up and reiterated, doubly and triply:—*chartered* street, *chartered* Thames, "And *mark* in every face . . . *Marks* of Weakness, *marks* of woe." The word *mark* indeed, the inner mental act, the outer graven sign, is the very motif of this marking repetition. It was more than a semantic or dictionary triumph when Blake revising his poem hit on the word *chartered*—rejecting the other quite different-sounding word which we need not mention, which appears in the Rossetti manuscript.

The student of the poem will easily pick out the modulations of the theme through the rest of the poem: the rhyme words *man* and *ban,* the emphatic syllable of *man*acles, the *black'*ning Church, the *hap*less sigh, the *Pa*lace *Walls* . . . *Har*lot, *Blasts,* and *Mar*riage. But what is the meaning of this phonetic pattern? A certain meaning, not in the sense necessarily of what Blake fully intended or would have confessed or defined if we had asked him, but in the sense of something which is actually conveyed if we will let it be conveyed, has been pretty much implied in the very description of the pattern. According to our temperaments and our experiences, and as our imagination is more auditory, eidetic, or kinesthetic, we will realize the force of this phonetic marking in images of insistently wandering, tramping feet, in a savage motion of the arms and head, in a bitter chanting, a dark repetition of indictments. Any one of these images, as I attempt to verbalize it, is perhaps excessive; no one is specifically necessary. But all of these and others are relevant.

We have said that the word *chartered* when applied to the street and even more when applied to the river is an anomaly. A close inspection of this poem will reveal a good many curiosities in its diction. Notice, for example, the word *cry,* which occurs three times in the course of stanzas two and three. Why do men cry in the streets of London? In addition to various random cries of confusion, hurry, and violence (which we are surely entitled to include in the meaning of the word), there is the more special and more continuous London street *cry,* the "proclamation," as the Dictionary has it, of wares or of services. If we had plenty of time for history we could read Addison's *Spectator* on "Street Cries." A more immediately critical interest is served when we notice that the steadily clamorous background of the London scene of charter and barter merges by a kind of metaphoric glide, in the next two lines, into a medley of other vocal sounds, "cries," in another sense, of fear, "voices," "bans"—that is to say, legal or official yells, proclamations, summonses, prohibitions, curses. Are the kinds of cries

What to Say about a Poem

really separate, or are all much the same? In the next line the infant cry of fear merges literally with the cry of service —"sweep, sweep," or "weep, weep," as we learn the pronunciation from Blake's two Chimney Sweeper songs. The whole poem proceeds not only by pregnant repetitions but by a series of extraordinary conjunctions and compressions, by a pervasive emergence of metaphoric intimation from the literal details of the Hogarthian scene. Consider, for instance, how to *appall* is to dismay or terrify, and etymologically perhaps to make *pale*. Doubtless the syntax says here in the first place that the unconsciously accusing cry of the infant sweep strikes dismay, even a kind of pallor, into these irrelevant, mouldering, and darkening fabrics. At the same time the syntax does not forbid a hint of the complementary sense that the walls throw back the infant cry in ineffectual and appalled echoes. The strange assault of pitiful sounds upon the very color of the walls, which is managed in these first two lines by verbal intimation, erupts in the next two beyond verbalism into the bold, surrealistically asserted vision of the *sigh* which attaches itself as blood to palace walls.

> But most thro' midnight streets I hear
> How the youthful Harlot's curse
> Blasts the new born Infant's tear,
> And blights with plagues the Marriage hearse.

The devotee of Blake may, by consulting the Rossetti manuscript, discover that the poet took extraordinary pains with this last stanza of the poem (which was an afterthought): he wrote it and rewrote it, deleting words and squeezing alternatives onto his already used-up page. Clearly

Hateful Contraries

he intended that a lot of meaning should inhere in this densely contrived stanza—the climax, the *most* appalling instance, of the assault of the city sounds upon the citadels, the institutions, the persons of the chartered privilege. The new role of the infant in this stanza, lying between the harlot and the major target of her curse, and the impatient energy, the crowding of sense, from the harlot and her curse, through the blight, the plague, to the ghastly paradox of that final union of words—the marriage hearse—perhaps we had better leave this to a paper by our students, rather than attempt to exhaust the meaning in class.

I have perhaps already said too much about this one short poem. Yet I have certainly not said all that might be said. Relentless criticism of a poem, the technique of the lemon-squeezer, is not to my mind an ideal pedagogic procedure. It is not even a possibility. A descriptive explication of a poem is both more and less than a multiple and exhaustive précis. Our aim I think should be to say certain selected, intelligible things about a poem, enough to establish the main lines of its technical achievement, of its symbolic shape. When we have done that much, we understand the poem—even if there are grace notes and overtones which have escaped our conscious notice.

VIII

LET ME BACK OFF then from the poem by William Blake and return once more, briefly, to my main argument. *Explanation, description,* and *explication*: we can recognize three phases of our interpretation of the poem, though they prove to be more closely entangled and merged with one another

What to Say about a Poem

than we might have realized at the beginning. But are they all? Is there not another activity which has been going on in our minds, almost inevitably, all this while? The activity of *appreciation*. All this time, while reading the poem so carefully, have we not also been liking it or disliking it? Admiring it or despising it? Presumably we have. And presumably we ought now to ask ourselves this further question: Is there any connection between the things we have managed so far to say about the poem and the kind of response we experience toward it? Our liking it or our disliking it? Are we inclined to try to explain why we like the poem? Do we know how to do this? More precisely: Would a statement of our liking for the poem, an act of praise or appreciation, be something different from (even though perhaps dependent upon) the things we have already been saying? Or has the appreciation already been sufficiently implied or entailed by what we have been saying?

At the first level, that of simple dictionary explanation, very little, we will probably say, has been implied. And very little, we will most likely say, in many of our motions at the second level, the simply descriptive. It is not a merit in a poem, or surely not much of a merit, that it should contain any given vocabulary, say of striking or unusual words, or even that it should have metaphors, or that it should have meter or any certain kind of meter, or rhymes, as any of these entities may be purely conceived.

But that—as we have been seeing—is to put these matters of simple explanation and simple description more simply and more abstractly than they are really susceptible of being put. We pass imperceptibly and quickly beyond these matters. We are inevitably and soon caught up in the demands

Hateful Contraries

of explication—the realization of the vastly more rich and interesting implicit kinds of meaning. We are engaged with features of a poem which—given always other features too of the whole context—do tend to assert themselves as reasons for our pleasure in the poem and our admiration for it. We begin to talk about patterns of meaning; we encounter structures or forms which are radiant or resonant with meaning. Patterns and structures involve coherence (unity, coherence, and emphasis), and coherence is an aspect of truth and significance. I do not think that our evaluative intimations will often, if ever, advance to the firmness and completeness of a demonstration. Perhaps it is hardly conceivable that they should. But our discourse upon the poem will almost inevitably be charged with implications of its value. It will be more difficult to keep out these intimations than to let them in. Critics who have announced the most resolute programs of neutrality have found this out. Take care of the weight, the color, the shape of the poem, be fair to the explanation and description, the indisputable parts of the formal explication—the appreciation will be there, and it will be difficult to avoid having expressed it.

Explicatory criticism (or explicatory evaluation) is an account of a poem which exhibits the relation between its form and its meaning. Only poems which are worth something are susceptible of this kind of account. It is something like a definition of poetry to say that whereas rhetoric—in the sense of mere persuasion or sophistic—is a kind of discourse the power of which diminishes in proportion as the artifice of it is understood or seen through—poetry, on the other hand, is a kind of discourse the power of which—or the satisfaction which we derive from it—is actually increased

What to Say about a Poem

by an increase in our understanding of the artifice. In poetry the artifice is art. This comes close I think to the center of the aesthetic fact.

IX

ONE OF THE ATTEMPTS at a standard of poetic value most often reiterated in past ages has been the doctrinal—the explicitly didactic. The aim of poetry, says the ancient Roman poet, is double, both to give pleasure and to teach some useful doctrine. You might get by with only one or the other, but it is much sounder to do both. Or, the aim of poetry is to teach some doctrine—and to do this convincingly and persuasively, by means of vividness and pleasure—as in effect the Elizabethan courtier and the eighteenth-century essayist would say. But in what does the pleasure consist? Why is the discourse pleasurable? Well, the aim of poetry is really to please us by means of or through the act of teaching us. The pleasure is a dramatized moral pleasure. Thus in effect some theories of drama in France during the seventeenth century. Or, the pleasure of poetry is a pleasure simply of tender and morally good feelings. Thus in effect the philosophers of the age of reason in England and France. And at length the date 1790 and Immanuel Kant's *Critique of Judgment:* which asserts that the end or effect of art is not teaching certainly, and not pleasure in anything like a simple sensuous way—rather it is something apart, a feeling, but precisely its own kind of feeling, the aesthetic. Art is autonomous—though related symbolically to the realm of moral values. Speaking from this nondidactic point of view, a critic ought to say, I should think, that the aesthetic merit

Hateful Contraries

of Blake's *London* does not come about because of the fact that London in that age witnessed evils which cried to Heaven for remedy, or because Blake was a Prophet Against Empire, or a Visionary Politician, or because at some time, perhaps a few years after he had writen the poem, he may have come to view it as one article or moment in the development of an esoteric philosophy of imagination, a Fearful Symmetry of Vision, expanded gradually in allegorical glimpses during several phases of his life into a quasi-religious revelation or privilege which in some sense, at moments, he believed in. Blake's *London* is an achievement in words, a contained expression, a victory which resulted from some hours, or days, of artistic struggle, recorded by his pen on a page of the Rossetti manuscript.

Between the time of Immanuel Kant, however, and our own, some complications in the purity of the aesthetic view have developed. Through the romantic period and after, the poetic mind advanced pretty steadily in its own autonomous way, toward a claim to be in itself the creator of higher values—to be perhaps the only creator. Today there is nothing that the literary theorist—at least in the British- and American-speaking world—will be more eager to repudiate than any hint of moral or religious didacticism, any least intimation that the poem is to measure its meaning or get its sanction from any kind of authority more abstract or more overtly legislative than itself. But on the other hand there has probably never been a generation of teachers of literature less willing to admit any lack of high seriousness, of implicit and embodied ethical content, even of normative vision in the object of their study. Despite our reiterated denials of didacticism, we live in an age, we help to make an

What to Say about a Poem

age, of momentous claims for poetry—claims the most momentous conceivable, as they advance more and more under the sanction of an absolutely creative and autonomous visionary imagination. The Visionary imagination perforce repudiates all but the tautological commitment to itself. And thus, especially when it assumes (as now it begins to do) the form of what is called the "Tragic Vision" (not "The Vision of Tragedy"), it is the newest version of the *Everlasting No*. Vision *per se* is the vision of itself. "Tragic Vision" is the nearly identical vision of "Absurdity." (War-weariness and war-horror, the developing mind and studies of a generation that came out of the second War and has been living in expectation of the third may go far to explain the phenomenon, but will not justify it.) Antidoctrine is of course no less a didactic energy than doctrine itself. It is the reverse of doctrine. No more than doctrine itself, can it be located or even approached by a discussion of the relation between poetic form and poetic meaning. Antidoctrine is actually asserted by the poems of several English romantic poets, and notably, it would appear, though it is difficult to be sure, by the "prophecies" of William Blake. The idea of it may be hence a part of these poems, though never their achieved result or expression. Any more than an acceptable statement of Christian doctrine is Milton's achieved expression in *Paradise Lost*, or a statement of Aristotelian ethics is the real business of Spenser's *Faerie Queene*. Today I believe no prizes are being given for even the best doctrinal interpretation of poems. (The homiletic or parabolic interpretation of Shakespeare, for example, has hard going with the reviewer.) On the other hand, if you are willing to take a hand in the exploitation of the neuroses, the misgivings,

Hateful Contraries

the anxieties, the infidelities of the age—if you have talents for the attitudes of Titanism, the graces needed by an impresario of the nuptials of Heaven and Hell, you are likely to find yourself in some sense rewarded. It is obvious I hope that I myself do not believe the reward will consist in the achievement of a valid account of the relation between poetic form and poetic meaning.

NOTES

INTRODUCTION

[1] "The Critical Intimidation," republished in *The Charted Mirror, Literary and Critical Essays* (London, 1960). See especially pp. 184-85.
[2] *The Pooh Perplex: A Freshman Casebook*, by Frederick C. Crews (New York, 1963), is a delayed undergraduate spoof.
[3] The author of the verse *Essay on Rime* (1945) had no real call to come to the "defence of ignorance." He knows the shape of some of his targets but mistakes their location (Karl Shapiro, *In Defense of Ignorance*, New York, 1960).

HORSES OF WRATH

[1] This sentence, as it appeared originally in *Essays in Criticism*, January, 1956, provoked a protest from J. C. Maxwell, which, along with the response which the editor kindly permitted me, may be seen in the issue for July, 1956 (VI, 358-61). See also my chapter on Croce in *Literary Criticism, A Short History* (New York, 1957), pp. 499-521.
[2] See further Roy Harvey Pearce, *The Continuity of American Poetry* (Princeton, 1961), "Foreword: Toward an 'Inside Narrative,'" and "Afterword: The Idea of Poetry and the Idea of Man."
[3] *The Limits of Literary Criticism* (Oxford, 1957), pp. 57-59.
[4] See Ronald S. Crane and others, *Critics and Criticism Ancient and Modern* (Chicago, 1952).
[5] Hyatt H. Waggoner, "The Current Revolt Against the New Criticism," *Criticism, A Quarterly for Literature and the Arts*, I (Summer, 1959), 222.
[6] See Harold Bloom, "Dialectic in *The Marriage of Heaven and Hell*," *PMLA*, LXXIII (December, 1958), 501-504; and Hazard Adams, *Blake and Yeats: The Contrary Vision* (Ithaca, 1955).
[7] Cp. Bernice Slote, *Keats and the Dramatic Principle* (Lincoln, 1958), chapter III, "Siege of Contraries," chapter IX, "*Lamia*: A Quarrel in the Streets."
[8] Elizabeth Lane Beardsley, "Moral Worth and Moral Credit." *Philosophical Review*, LXVI (July, 1957), 326.

Notes for Pages 51 to 58

TWO MEANINGS OF SYMBOLISM

¹ Cp. Charles Feidelson, Jr., *Symbolism and American Literature* (Chicago, 1953), pp. 53-55, 259-60. The phrase "produces and posits" is quoted from Ernst Cassirer, *Language and Myth*, trans. Susanne K. Langer (New York, 1946), pp. 6-10. Feidelson's second chapter, "The Symbolistic Imagination," pp. 44-76, is an admirable description of the expressionist pole in symbolist theory.

² Cp. *post* p. 69 the distinction made by theorists of "symbolic form" between "discursive" and "presentational" symbols. These two meanings plus my second main meaning of "symbol" above, the special word- or thing-symbol, correspond to the "Three Meanings of Symbolism" defined by Northrop Frye, "sign," "image," mythopoeic "archetype," in his "Three Meanings of Symbolism," *Yale French Studies*, No. 9 (Spring, 1952), pp. 11-19.

³ Cp. Rudolf Arnheim, "Artistic Symbols—Freudian and Otherwise," *Journal of Aesthetics and Art Criticism*, XII (September, 1953), 94.

⁴ Cp. Arnheim, p. 94.

⁵ See *Sartor Resartus*, Book III, chapter viii, on the "Volume of Nature."

⁶ *Collected Writings*, ed. David Masson, VIII, 18-20, 410-11 (an essay, referring to Novalis and entitled "Modern Superstition," 1840). See René Wellek, "De Quincey's Status in the History of Ideas," *Philological Quarterly*, XXIII (July, 1944), 255.

⁷ "Catholic Orientation in Contemporary French Literature," in *Spiritual Problems in Contemporary Literature*, ed. Stanley Romaine Hopper (New York, 1952), pp. 236-38. Though I follow the phrasing of Mr. Fowlie, I do not mean to impute any of the difficulties that seem to be involved here to him rather than to his sources.

⁸ Auerbach speaks of "the important difference which obtains between figurism and other similar forms of thinking such as allegorism or symbolism. In these patterns, at least one of the two elements combined is a pure sign, but in a figural relation both the signifying and the signified facts are real and concrete historical events" ("Typological Symbolism in Medieval Literature," *Yale French Studies*, No. 9 [Spring, 1952], p. 6). Cp. his *Mimesis*, trans. Willard R. Trask (Princeton, 1953), pp. 73, 195, 201.

⁹ See Charles S. Singleton, "Dante's Allegory," *Speculum*, XXV (January, 1950), 78-83; reprinted in his *Commedia, Elements of Structure* (Cambridge, Mass., 1954), pp. 84-98.

¹⁰ At the same time they represent a strong tendency toward the creation of a modern canon of symbolic meanings. "Wherever we have archetypal symbolism, we pass from the question, 'What does this symbol, sea or serpent or character, mean in this work of art,' to the question 'What does it mean in my imaginative comprehension of such things as a whole'"

Notes for Pages 58 to 69

(Northrop Frye, "Three Meanings of Symbolism," p. 18). And see especially the later work of Frye.

[11] Edward Williamson, "Symbolism and the New Philosophy," digest in *The MLA Sixty-Sixth Annual Meeting* (December, 1951), "Romance Section," p. 23.

[12] R. P. Warren, *Brother to Dragons* (New York, 1953), p. 6. Jefferson speaks.

[13] See D. W. Robertson, Jr., and Bernard F. Huppé, *Piers Plowman and Scriptural Tradition* (Princeton, 1951), e.g. pp. 5-6, 240, clear indications of how their learning gets in the way of poetic criticism; or H. Flanders Dunbar, *Symbolism in Medieval Thought* (New Haven, 1929), p. 459, the poem as "cryptographic code."

[14] "Every symbol should be understood at one and the same time in all of these significations" (Dunbar, p. 20). See Charles S. Singleton, pp. 78-83, for a sceptical reaction to such dogma.

[15] *Quaestiones Quodlibetales*, VII, q.6, a.16; cp. the answer to the second objection to this article.

[16] *Recuerdo*, in *A Few Figs From Thistles* (New York, 1928), p. 2.

[17] *The Poems of Emily Dickinson* (Boston, 1937), no. cxxiv, p. 56.

[18] *Titus Andronicus*, IV, i, 102-103. Saint Augustine (*Confessions*, X, 8, 14) discusses memory as the "belly of the mind."

[19] *Vorlesungen Über Schöne Kunst und Literatur* (1884), I, 292. Delivered at Berlin in 1801.

[20] *Journals* (Boston, 1909-1914), VI, 18.

[21] Malcolm M. Ross, "History and Poetry, Decline of the Historical Concrete," *Thought*, XXVI (Autumn, 1951), 426-42; "Fixed Stars and Living Motion in Poetry," *Thought*, XXVII (Autumn, 1952), 381-99. Cp. his *Poetry and Dogma* (New Brunswick, 1954). Like these essays by Mr. Ross, Allen Tate's on Dante and Poe in *The Forlorn Demon* (Chicago, 1953) represent a reaction against the "angelism," the pure ideality, of symbolist poetics and an effort to return to something like a Dantesque historical and individual substantiveness.

[22] See *Enneads*, I, vi, 2; V, viii, 1.

[23] "The General principle of the inseparability of intuition and expression holds with special force for the aesthetic intuition. Here it means that form and content, or content and medium, are inseparable" (W. M. Urban, *Language and Reality* [London, 1939], p. 462). See Susanne K. Langer, *Philosophy in a New Key* (New York, Pelican Books, 1948), p. 229, on the distinction between discursive and presentational symbols; and Cassirer, *Language and Myth*, pp. 97-98, on "mere conceptual signs"; and Feidelson, p. 55: "The literary symbolist is inclined to consider poetry as peculiarly symbolic. . . ."

Notes for Pages 72 to 100

ARISTOTLE AND OEDIPUS OR ELSE

[1] Raymond Weil, *Revue des Études Anciennes*, LXI (January-June, 1959), 174-75; Thomas G. Rosenmeyer, *American Journal of Philology*, LXXX (July, 1959), 310-14; Frederick M. Combellack, *Classical Philology*, LIV (October, 1959), 261-65; G. M. Kirkwood, *Classical Journal*, LV (October, 1959), 36-39; D. W. Lucas, *Classical Review*, N.S. IX (December, 1959), 252-55; M. Joseph Costelloe, S.J., *Classical Bulletin*, XXXVI (March, 1960), 59-60; W. J. Verdenius, *Mnemosyne*, IV.xii (1960), 256-58; Thomas Gould, *Gnomon*, XXXIV (December, 1962), 641-49.

[2] See Jacob L. Moreno, *Psychoanalytic Treatment of Psychoses* (New York, 1945).

[3] Else, p. 383, n. 4. But on p. 3, Else is content enough to believe that Aristotle sets up *poiētikē* in a "special, colloquially given sense of 'poetic art.'"

[4] In *Ethics* VII.4, incontinence *(acrasia)* is described as *hamartia* fortified by vice *(kakia)*.

[5] *Poetics* XIV uses this same allusion to the lost *Cresphontes*.

[6] Simonides of Ceos (556-467) as preserved in Plato's *Protagoras*.

[7] "Recognition [in Chapter XVI]," says Else, "becomes more purely a structural or plot device" (p. 484). Yes, and thus it tells strongly against Else's theory.

THE CRITICISM OF COMEDY

[1] L. J. Potts, *Comedy* (London, 1949), pp. 10, 19-20.

[2] Cp. Jim Corbett, *Man-Eaters of Kumaon* (Oxford, 1946), pp. 97-98.

[3] See D. H. Monro, *Argument of Laughter* (Melbourne, 1951), especially pp. 214-19, 222-25, outlining the theories of Greig and Krishna Menon.

[4] Cp. A. O. Aldridge, "Shaftesbury and the Test of Truth," *PMLA*, LX (March, 1945), 129-56.

[5] "The Psychology of Humor," *American Journal of Psychology*, XVIII (October, 1907), 433-36.

[6] *The Basic Writings of Sigmund Freud*, trans. A. A. Brill (New York, 1938), p. 803.

[7] *Critique of Judgment*, Book II, par. 54; *The World as Will and Idea*, Book I, chapter xiii.

[8] Cp. Maynard Mack, Introduction to Fielding, *Joseph Andrews* (New York, Rinehart Editions, 1948), p. xiv.

[9] See *English Institute Essays 1948*, ed. D. A. Robertson, Jr. (New York, 1949).

[10] Søren Kierkegaard, *Concluding Unscientific Postscript*, trans. David F. Swenson (Princeton, 1944), p. 450.

Notes for Pages 101 to 121

[11] Joseph Jones, "Emerson and Bergson on the Comic," *Comparative Literature*, I (Winter, 1949), 63-71, quoting Emerson's *Complete Works* (Centenary Edition), VIII, 158-73. Proper quotations could of course be made to yield the opposite emphasis. The perception of the comic "appears to be an essential element in a fine character."

[12] *Laughter, An Essay on the Meaning of the Comic*, trans. Cloudsley Brereton and Fred Rothwell (New York, 1928), p. 200.

[13] For a fairly recent instance, see Sir Alan Herbert, upon attempting a presidential address to the English Association upon the topic of the "English Laugh," greeted with pursed lips by an anonymous *Times Literary Supplement* arbiter (August 11, 1950, p. 501). "The trouble arises when the teacher uses his pointer . . . the sample joke assumes the wistfulness of a waning autumn light."

[14] L. J. Potts, once more, in a translation of the Poetics (*Aristotle on the Art of Fiction*, Cambridge, 1953) which has the great merit of making Aristotle speak as if he knew what he meant—in a more or less continuous discourse.

THE CONCEPT OF METER

[1] Harold Whitehall, Seymour Chatman, Arnold Stein, John Crowe Ransom, "English Verse and What It Sounds Like," *Kenyon Review*, XVIII, 411-77.

[2] "Linguistics, Poetics, and Interpretation: The Phonemic Dimension," *Quarterly Journal of Speech*, XLIII (October, 1957), 254.

[3] The question is, of course, a psychological one, but the psychologists have not dealt much with it. A search of *Psychological Abstracts* for the last twenty years turns up (XXI [September, 1947], 387) one article (abstract 3211): Marguerite Durand, "Perception de durée dans les phrases rhythmées," *Journal de Psychologie Normale et Pathologique*, XXXIX (1946), 305-21. But Mlle. Durand apparently took isochronism for granted and had her passages (French and Czech) spoken to the beats of a metronome. Albert R. Chandler, *Beauty and Human Nature* (New York, 1934), pp. 244-56, gives a good account of some earlier investigations. Ada L. F. Snell, "An Objective Study of Syllabic Quantity in English Verse," *PMLA*, XXXIII (1918), 396-408; XXXIV (1919), 416-35, presents experimental evidence against the assumption that readers of English verse observe any kind of "equal time intervals."

[4] A kind of middle or double service is performed by traditional marks of prosodic scansion—which in part, in large part, call attention to objective features of linguistic structure, but to some extent also are used for "promoting" or "suppressing" (or indicating the promotion or suppression of) such features in favor of a certain pattern. This double character of

scansion marks has perhaps caused much of the difficulty in metrical theory.

⁵ We take this term from Leonard B. Meyer's excellent discussion of musical rhythm in *Emotion and Meaning in Music* (Chicago, 1956), pp. 102-103. Pulse is the division of time into "regularly recurring, equally accented beats." What Meyer calls "meter" in music depends on pulse; but in this respect it is different from meter in verse. What he calls "rhythm"—e.g., the difference between an iambic and an anapestic or trochaic pattern—can occur without pulse and meter, he holds, as in plain chant or *recitativo secco*.

⁶ *Practical Criticism* (New York, 1935), p. 232.

⁷ Elizabeth Wright, *Metaphor, Sound and Meaning in Bridges' "The Testament of Beauty"* (Philadelphia, 1951), p. 26, says that Bridges' lines are to be timed equally, with the help of pauses at the ends of the lines.

⁸ Yvor Winters, *The Function of Criticism* (Denver, 1957), pp. 79-100, 109-23, expresses a view of English meter in general and of Hopkins which we take to be substantially in accord with our own.

⁹ Alexander J. Ellis, "Remarks on Professor Mayor's Two Papers on Rhythm," *Transactions of the Philological Society 1875-1876* (Strasburg, 1877), p. 442, distinguished "nine degrees" of "force" or stress in English and likewise nine degrees of "length," "pitch," "weight," and "silence."

¹⁰ The problem of "rising" and "falling" meters is one which we are content to touch lightly. Temporal theorists, working on the analogy of the musical downbeat, tend of course to make all meters falling. George R. Stewart, Jr., a moderate timer, makes the following revelatory statement: "If a person comes upon a road and walks a few rods before arriving at the first milestone, he will have to pass five milestones, counting the first, before he has walked four measured miles; in other words, since the start and the finish must be shown, five markers are necessary to establish four units. In verse the stresses are the markers, and the feet are the units. Five stresses can mark off only four intervals, so that what we ordinarily call a five-foot line might be more properly described as a four-foot line with a little left over at beginning and end" (*The Technique of English Verse* [New York, 1930], p. 42). (For Mr. Stewart "rising" and "falling" are qualities of phrasing, not of meter, p. 37.) Suppose, however, that we are counting not "measured miles" but precisely milestones—not equal times but precisely stresses. And suppose that a man walks not a "few rods" but a full mile before reaching the first milestone. The first slack syllable of the iambic line is as much a mile as any other slack syllable. The line begins at the beginning of that syllable. The iambic line which starts with a strong and then *one* weak syllable is a more difficult matter. But many such lines, like the one from Shelley's "Skylark" which we discuss above, can be shown in one way or another to be in fact iambic. The shape of the phrases is likely to have much to do with it. Other lines of

Notes for Pages 133 to 163

this sort, such as some in Tennyson's *The Lady of Shalott,* may in fact be ambiguous—that is, they may be susceptible of being satisfactorily read either as iambic or as trochaic.

THE AUGUSTAN MODE

[1] F. R. Leavis, *Revaluation* (London, 1936), p. 83.
[2] William Empson, *Some Versions of Pastoral* (London, 1950), p. 224.
[3] James Sutherland, *A Preface to Eighteenth Century Poetry* (Oxford, 1950), p. 164.
[4] Review of Sutherland's *Preface, Times Literary Supplement,* November 6, 1948, p. 624.
[5] George Sherburn, "The Restoration and Eighteenth Century," *A Literary History of England,* ed. A. C. Baugh (New York, 1948), pp. 929, 932.
[6] "Mr. Pope in the Field," *Times Literary Supplement,* April 20, 1951, p. 245.
[7] Edwin B. Burgum, "The Neo-Classical Period in English Literature: A Psychological Definition," *Sewanee Review,* LIII (Spring, 1944), 248.
[8] R. H. Griffith, "The Progress Piece of the Eighteenth Century," *Texas Review,* V (April, 1920), 229.
[9] Cp. Richard C. Boys, *Sir Richard Blackmore and the Wits* (Ann Arbor, 1941).
[10] Maurice Johnson, *The Sin of Wit* (Syracuse, 1951), chapter III.
[11] W. H. Auden, "Alexander Pope," *Essays in Criticism,* I (July, 1951), 211; the same in *From Anne to Victoria: Essays by Various Hands,* ed. Bonamy Dobrée (London, 1937).
[12] Gilbert Highet, "'The Dunciad,'" *Modern Language Review,* XXXVI (July, 1941), 342.
[13] *Letters to his Son,* October 26, 1738, September 27, 1749.
[14] Warton, *Essay on the Writings and Genius of Pope,* Dedication (1756); Stockdale, *An Inquiry into the Nature and Genuine Laws of Poetry* (London, 1798), pp. 11-21.
[15] On the meaning of the phrase "selling bargains," see Harold Williams, ed., *Poems of Swift* (Oxford, 1937), II, 590.
[16] *Dehumanization of Art,* trans. Helene Weyl (Princeton, 1948), p. 35.
[17] A. O. Aldridge, "Shaftesbury and the Test of Truth," *PMLA,* LX (March, 1945), 129-56.
[18] Cp. L. I. Bredvold, "The Gloom of the Tory Satirists," *Pope and His Contemporaries, Essays Presented to George Sherburn* (Oxford, 1949), pp. 1-19.

Notes for Pages 184 to 208

Eliot's Comedy

¹ T. S. Eliot, *The Cocktail Party, A Comedy* (New York, 1950); *The Cocktail Party*, performed at the Henry Miller Theatre (New York) by the Sherek Players, directed by E. Martin Browne.

² William Barrett, *Partisan Review*, XVII (April, 1950), 354-59; Wolcott Gibbs, *New Yorker*, XXV (January 28, 1950), 47-48; Margaret Marshall, *Nation*, CLXX (January 28, 1950), 94-95; Brooks Atkinson, New York *Times*, January 29, 1950.

³ Henry Popkin, *Kenyon Review*, XII (Spring, 1950), 339.

⁴ Reading in the light of Eliot's *Idea of a Christian Society*, one reviewer has called them members of the "clerisy," charismatic personalities (George Miles, *Commonweal*, LII (May 5, 1950), 107.

Prufrock and Maud

¹ About the whole of *The Family Reunion* I find something hauntingly Tennysonian. The name of the dowager Amy and certain infelicitous family relationships tempt at least the jocular speculation that this is Eliot's version of *Locksley Hall Sixty Years After*.

² See Leonard Unger, "T. S. Eliot's Rose Garden," in his *T. S. Eliot: A Selected Critique* (New York, 1948), pp. 374-94.

³ Perhaps the title of this poem and its opening lines will come to mind as one reads another passage in *Maud* (I, x, 2): ". . . a lord, a captain, a padded shape, A bought commission, a waxen face."

⁴ "And my heart," he says, "is a handful of dust." For a student of Eliot the phrase may chime with an earlier description of the Hall which is Maud's ancestral home, glimmering "by a red rock" (I, iv, 2). I am not tempted to say that this coincidence does much to improve our reading of *The Waste Land*, I, 24-30.

Yet another passage in *Maud* suggests a grisly image in Part I of *The Waste Land*. "What will the old man say When he comes to the second corpse in the pit?" (II, v, 9) *That corpse you planted last year in your garden, has it begun to sprout?*

⁵ *North American Review*, LXXVII (July, 1853), 4. Another poem which might be cited in this context, one of Tennyson's which Eliot most admires, is *In Memoriam*. See the stanzas about the "long unlovely street" quoted in Eliot's essay of 1936 on Tennyson and that of 1942 (note 6).

⁶ "The Voice of His Time," *Listener*, XXVII (February 12, 1942), 211-12.

⁷ John C. Pope, "Prufrock and Raskolnikov," *American Literature*, XVII (November, 1945), 221. Eliot's subsequent advice to Professor Pope, that he had read *Crime and Punishment* during 1910 and 1911 in a French

Notes for Pages 208 to 234

translation and that *Prufrock* was completed in the summer of 1911 weakens the immediate "intentional" significance of the many striking parallels of phrasal music which Professor Pope demonstrates between *Prufrock* and the Garnett translation of the novel published in 1914 (*American Literature*, XVIII [January, 1947], 319-21).

[8] "In Memoriam," *Essays Ancient and Modern* (London, 1936), p. 182.

[9] "From Poe to Valéry," *Hudson Review*, II (Autumn, 1949), 341-42. Tennyson found it necessary to disclaim identity with the protagonist of *Maud* (Hallam Tennyson, *Memoir* [New York, 1898], I, 402, 408).

[10] Cp. Yvor Winters, *Primitivism and Decadence* (New York, 1937), chapter II.

[11] "I affirm that it is not natural to be what is called 'natural' any longer. We have no longer the mental attitude of those to whom a story was but a story, and all stories good" (Arthur Symons, *The Symbolist Movement in Literature* [New York, 1908], p. 134).

WHAT TO SAY ABOUT A POEM

[1] For information about this poem, I have consulted mainly, though not exclusively, Joseph H. Wicksteed, *Blake's Innocence and Experience* (London, 1928) and *Selected Poems of William Blake*, ed. F. W. Bateson (New York, 1957).

[2] David V. Erdman, "Blake; The Historical Approach," *English Institute Essays 1950* (New York, 1951), p. 200.

[3] Cp. Mark Schorer, *William Blake, The Politics of Vision* (New York, 1946), pp. 406-407.

INDEX

Abrams, Meyer, 15, 19, 108
Adams, Hazard, 245
Adams, J. Donald, xv
Addison, Joseph, 84, 162, 176, 236
Aeschylus, 11, 15, 77, 90
Aldridge, A. O., 162, 248
Alemoor (Andrew Pringle), Lord, 172
American Mercury, xvii, 6
Anstey, Christopher, 132
Aquinas, Thomas, St., 55-56, 62-63, 69
Aristotle, vii, 14, 19, 35, 39, 72-89, 96-98, 101, 106, 157, 159, 163, 175, 243, 248
Arnheim, Rudolf, 246
Arnold, Matthew, 5-6, 13, 18, 38, 206, 209
Arrowsmith, William, 103, 105-106
Atkinson, Brooks, 184, 198
Auchinleck (Alexander Boswell), Lord, 167-68, 177
Auden, W. H., 251
Auerbach, Erich, 57, 246
Augustine, St., 29, 247
Augustus, 224-25
Austen, Jane, 90

Babbitt, Irving, 6
Barber, C. L., 103
Barrett, William, 252
Bartlett, John, 65
Bateson, F. W., 10, 253
Baudelaire, Charles, 4, 65, 204

Beardsley, Elizabeth Lane, 27, 245
Beardsley, Monroe C., viii-ix
Bell, Clive, 29
Bellow, Saul, xv
Beowulf, 115, 130
Bergson, Henri, 97, 99, 101, 104, 106
Berkeley, George, 55
Blackmore, Richard, 153
Blackmur, R. P., 51
Blake, William, 16-17, 20-22, 25-26, 32, 132, 221, 223-24, 229-38, 242-43
Bloom, Harold, 245
Boehme, Jakob, 55
Boethius, 29
Bonaventure, St., 58
Boswell, James, 165-83
Boys, Richard C., 251
Bredvold, L. I., 251
Bridges, Robert, 126-27, 250
Brontë, Emily, 182
Brooks, Cleanth, ix
Browne, Sir Thomas, 19
Browning, Robert, 42, 209
Buddha, 15
Burgum, Edwin Berry, 11
Butcher, S. H., 74-75, 81-83, 87, 89
Byron, George Gordon, Lord, 223, 225

Caesar, Julius, 223
Canning, George, 119
Carlyle, Thomas, 5, 55, 151
Cassirer, Ernst, 15, 51, 246-47

Index

Chandler, Albert R., 249
Chatman, Seymour, 109-12, 115, 130, 139, 141
Chaucer, Geoffrey, 60-61, 114, 118, 127, 129, 139, 143-44, 176
Chesterfield, Philip Dormer Stanhope, Lord, 154-55
Chesterton, G. K., 196
Cibber, Colley, 184
Claudel, Paul, 56, 58, 71
Clough, Arthur Hugh, 206
Coalston (George Brown), Lord, 167
Coleridge, S. T., 4, 7, 22, 30, 55, 112, 130, 195
Combellack, Frederick M., 72
Congreve, William, 103
Conrad, Joseph, 186
Cook, Albert, 98
Cooper, Lane, 79
Corbett, Jim, 248
Cornford, Francis M., 15
Costelloe, M. Joseph, S.J., 72
Courthope, W. J., 9
Coward, Noel, 184
Crane, Ronald S., 245
Crews, Frederick C., 245
Croce, Benedetto, 4, 51, 68-69, 245
Cromwell, Oliver, 227

Daiches, David, xv
Dante, 28, 44-45, 47, 55, 57, 60-64, 71, 247
Dempster, George, 177
Dennis, John, 152, 158, 162
De Quincey, Thomas, 55
Dickinson, Emily, 65
Donne, John, 218
Dostoevski, Feodor, 26-27, 208
Doyle, A. Conan, 196
Draco, 82
Drummond of Hawthornden, William, 58
Dryden, John, 14, 63-64, 149-50, 153, 157, 164, 191-92, 224
Dunbar, H. Flanders, 247

Dunsany, Edward J. M. D. P., Lord, 136
Durand, Marguerite, 249

Eastman, Max, xvii, 91
Eliot, T. S., xiii, xvii-xviii, 7, 15-17, 22, 24, 30, 33, 45, 51, 67, 71, 103-106, 112, 130, 136, 144-45, 184-212, 252
Elliott, Robert C., 100
Ellis, Alexander J., 250
Else, Gerald F., vii, 72-89, 248
Emerson, Ralph Waldo, 55, 66, 101, 106, 249
Empson, William, 10-11, 44, 150, 153
English Institute Essays 1948, 248
Erdman, David V., 233
Erlich, Victor, 111
Etherege, George, 184
Euripides, 87, 103-105, 177
Everyman, 112, 129-30, 198

Faulkner, William, 16, 33
Feidelson, Charles, Jr., 51, 246-47
Fergusson, Francis, 14, 16
Fiedler, Leslie, xiv
Fielding, Henry, 96, 99, 163-64, 182
Fitzgerald, F. Scott, 188
Flaubert, Gustave, 13, 169
Ford, Ford Madox, 13
Foster, Richard, ix
Fowlie, Wallace, 56, 246
France, Anatole, xvii
Frazer, Sir James G., 15
Frere, John Hookham, 119
Freud, Sigmund, 6, 37, 84, 93, 96, 102, 104
Frost, Robert, 110-11, 116-17, 228-29
Fry, Roger, 29
Frye, Northrop, 17-20, 98, 109, 112-14, 122, 128-29, 246-47

Galileo, 68
Gardner, Helen, 12

Index

Garrick, David, 28
Garrod, H. W., xiv
Gatch, Katherine, 103
Gay, John, 150, 156
Gibbs, Wolcott, 252
Goethe, J. W. von, 76
Goldsmith, Oliver, 132, 172, 195
Gosse, Sir Edmund, xiv
Gosson, Stephen, 60
Gould, Thomas, 72-75
Gourmont, Remy de, 7
Gray, Thomas, 42-43, 113, 174
Greig, J. Y. T., 248
Griffith, R. H., 152

Harrison, Jane E., 15
Hazlitt, William, 18
Heffner, Ray L., 103
Hegel, G. W. F., 5-6, 46, 81, 103
Heine, Heinrich, 4
Heinsius, Daniel, 163
Hendren, Joseph W., viii
Herbert, Alan, 249
Herder, J. G., 15, 55
Hippocrates, 74
Hitchcock, Alfred, 84
Hobbes, Thomas, 91, 162
Hogarth, William, 237
Hollander, John, 117
Holloway, John, xiii-xiv
Homer, 28, 38, 79, 89, 150, 159
Hopkins, G. M., 45, 130, 250
Horace, 28, 106, 150, 156, 158-59, 161, 163, 224-25, 241
Housman, A. E., 120-21
Hulme, T. E., 7
Huppé, Bernard F., 247
Hurd, Richard, 8
Hutcheson, Francis, 29

Iamblichus, 195

James, Henry, 13-14
Jeffers, Robinson, 185
Jefferson, Thomas, 92

Jespersen, Otto, 130-31
Johnson, Samuel, 8, 28, 34, 91, 150, 164-65, 169-75, 177, 182-83
Jones, Joseph, 249
Jonson, Ben, 103-104, 163
Joyce, James, 16, 47, 60
Jung, Carl, 16, 106, 195

Kallen, H. M., 92
Kames (Henry Home), Lord, 167
Kant, Immanuel, 3-4, 29, 95, 241-42
Keats, John, 13, 22-23, 64, 128, 134
Kelly, Walt, 92
Kenyon Review, 108-109
Kierkegaard, Soren, 100, 248
Kipling, Rudyard, 120
Kirkwood, G. M., 72
Kline, L. W., 93
Knox, Bernard, 87-88, 103
Koestler, Arthur, 28, 95-96
Krieger, Murray, 24-25, 44, 243
Krishna Menon, V. K., 248

Lamb, Charles, 18
Langer, Susanne K., 15, 51, 247
Lanier, Sidney, 118
Lawrence, D. H., 132
Leavis, F. R., 251
Le Bossu, René, 14
Lévy-Bruhl, Lucien, 15
Lewis, C. S., 12
Locke, John, 152
Longfellow, Henry Wadsworth, 119
Longinus, 159
Lucas, D. W., 72
Lucas, F. L., 76
Lycambes, 100

Macaulay, Thomas Babington, Lord, 10
McDougall, William, 91
Mack, Maynard, 149-51, 248
McLuhan, Marshall, 33
Mallarmé, Stéphane, 4, 56, 211

Index

Mansfield, William Murray, Lord, 178
Marshall, Margaret, 252
Marvell, Andrew, 42, 135-36, 208-209, 224, 226-27
Marx, Karl, 5-6, 11, 38, 47-48
"Mary, Mary," 120
Mason, William, 174
Maxwell, J. C., 245
Melville, Herman, 16
Menander, 175
Meredith, George, 64, 97, 99-102, 104, 106, 122, 137
Meyer, Leonard B., 250
Miles, George, 252
Mill, J. S., 7
Millay, Edna St. Vincent, 64
Miller, Thomas, 167-68, 183
Milton, John, 16, 20, 42, 44-45, 47, 112, 114, 120, 124, 126, 128-29, 133-34, 142-44, 162, 218, 224-25, 243
Molière, 96, 99-100, 157-58
Monro, D. H., 248
Montgomerie, Margaret, 183
More, Paul Elmer, 6, 33
Moreno, Jacob L., 248
Mudrick, Marvin, 103-104
Murray, Gilbert, 15

Nation, 184
Newman, John Henry, Cardinal, 45
New Yorker, 184
New York *Times*, 184; *Book Review*, xvi
Nietzsche, Friedrich, 6, 26
Norton, Dan S., 108
Novalis, 246

Omond, T. S., 118-19
Orme, Robert, 177
Ortega y Gasset, José, 160
Oxford English Dictionary, 232-33, 236

Paoli, Pasquale, 183
Partisan Review, 184
Peacock, Thomas Love, 164
Pearce, Roy Harvey, 11-12, 245
Penjon, Auguste, 93, 99
Perrine, Laurence, 108, 137
Piers Plowman, 61, 112, 115, 118, 130, 247
Pike, Kenneth L., 113, 127
Pindar, 150
Plato, 29-30, 33-34, 53, 65, 69, 72, 74-75, 77-78, 80, 82, 91-92, 99, 163
Plautus, 103-104
Plotinus, 31, 69
Poe, E. A., 4, 211
Pope, Alexander, 11, 28, 42, 96, 100, 114, 128-29, 131-32, 143, 149-51, 153-54, 157-62, 225
Pope, John C., 208, 252-53
Popkin, Henry, 188
Pottle, Frederick A., viii-ix
Potts, L. J., 90, 97, 249
Pound, Ezra, 7, 51
Prall, D. W., 138
Prior, Matthew, 149, 150
Pythagoras, 48

Quiller-Couch, A. T., xiv

Raleigh, Walter A., xiv
Ramus, Peter, 35, 60
Ransom, John Crowe, 108, 135, 140
Rapp, Albert, 93-94, 98
Reid, John, 166-68, 183
Reynolds, Joshua, 28
Richards, I. A., xiii, 6-7, 17, 22, 24, 30, 37, 123-25
Richelieu, 84
Richter, J. P. F. (Jean Paul), 97, 100
Robertson, D. W., Jr., 247
Rosenmeyer, Thomas G., 72
Ross, Malcolm M., 247
Rossetti, D. G., 231, 234, 237, 242

Index

Rousseau, J. J., 179
Rushton, Peters, 108
Ruskin, John, 59

Sainte-Beuve, C. A., 9, 18
Saintsbury, George, E. B., xiv, 118
Santayana, George, 6
Saturday Review, xvi
Scala, Can Grande della, 61
Scaliger, Julius Caesar, 159
Schelling, Friedrich, 3, 15, 30
Schiller, Friedrich, 3
Schlegel, A. W., 3, 66
Schlegel, Friedrich, 3, 16, 30, 100
Schopenhauer, Arthur, 95
Schorer, Mark, 234, 253
Schwartz, Elias, viii
Scott, Sir Walter, 168-69, 227, 229
Sears, Donald A., ix
Sewall, Richard B., 88, 243
Shaftesbury, Anthony Ashley Cooper, Lord, 92, 162
Shakespeare, William, 9, 16, 28, 60, 65, 103-105, 112-13, 120, 128-29, 132, 143, 145, 182, 187, 193-96, 207-208, 210-11, 223-26, 232, 243
Shapiro, Karl, xv, 118, 245
Shaw, G. B., 103-104, 195
Shelley, P. B., 5, 42, 133, 164, 196, 250
Sherburn, George, 151
Sheridan, Richard Brinsley, 103-104, 194-95
Sidney, Sir Philip, 60
Singleton, Charles S., 246-47
Sitwell, Dame Edith, 121
Slote, Bernice, 245
Smart, Christopher, 55, 224
Smart Set, xvii, 6
Smith, Alexander, 206
Smith, Henry Lee, 109-11, 114-15, 117, 130-31
Smith, T. V., 92
Snell, Ada L. F., 249

Snyder, Alice, 22
Socrates, 81, 219
Solon, 82
Sophocles, 77, 79, 85-89, 98
Sound and Poetry, English Institute Essays 1956, 109, 112-13
Spenser, Edmund, 44, 63-64, 111, 129-30, 243
Stein, Arnold, 108, 140
Sterne, Laurence, 9
Stevenson, R. L., 168
Stewart, George R., Jr., 250
Stockdale, Percival, 157
Strabo, 38
Sutherland, James, xiv, 151
Swedenborg, Emanuel, 55
Swift, Jonathan, 96, 99, 150, 155-56, 163
Symons, Arthur, 211, 253

Taine, Hippolyte, 9
Tate, Allen, 247
Temple, William J., 183
Tennyson, Alfred, Lord, 10, 45, 71, 114, 118, 127, 129, 143-44, 201-12, 251-53
Theophrastus, 157
Thrale, Hester Lynch, 34
Times Literary Supplement, xv-xvi, 151, 249
Tolstoy, Leo, Count, 5
Trager, George L., 109-11, 114-15, 117, 130-31
Tuve, Rosamond, 12
Twain, Mark, 19

Unger, Leonard, 252
Urban, W. M., 51, 247

Valéry, Paul, 211
Vanbrugh, Sir John, 184
Vaughan Williams, Ralph, 121
Verdenius, W. J., 72
Vida, Marco Girolamo, 159

Index

Virgil, 64, 149, 223
Voltaire, 179

Wagner, Richard, 4
Walton, William, 121
Warren, Austin, 149, 151
Warren, Robert Penn, 59
Warton, Joseph, 157
Warton, Thomas, 8
Watts, Isaac, 224, 234-35
Waugh, Evelyn, 186
Weil, Raymond, 72
Wellek, René, 246
Wesley, Samuel, 153
Wheelwright, Philip, 15

Whitehall, Harold, 109-10, 113-14, 120, 126-27
Whitman, Cedric H., 88-89
Whitman, Walt, 64, 142
Wicksteed, Joseph H., 253
Wilde, Oscar, 103, 195
Wilkes, John, 181
Williamson, Edward, 58, 247
Winters, Yvor, 33, 195, 250, 253
Wordsworth, William, 7, 128-29, 143
Wright, Elizabeth, 250
Wycherley, William, 103, 184

Yeats, W. B., 16, 20, 23, 134-35, 223
Zola, Emile, 5, 13

www.ingramcontent.com/pod-product-compliance
Lightning Source LLC
Chambersburg PA
CBHW022053160426
43198CB00008B/219